Thirteen Months at Manassas/Bull Run

Thirteen Months at Manassas/Bull Run

*The Two Battles
and the Confederate and
Union Occupations*

Don Johnson

Foreword by Richard A. Sauers

McFarland & Company, Inc., Publishers
Jefferson, North Carolina, and London

LIBRARY OF CONGRESS CATALOGUING-IN-PUBLICATION DATA

Johnson, Don (Don E.)
Thirteen months at Manassas/Bull Run : the two battles and the Confederate and Union occupations / Don Johnson ; foreword by Richard A. Sauers.
p. cm.
Includes bibliographical references and index.

ISBN 978-0-7864-7320-5
softcover : acid free paper ∞

1. Bull Run, 1st Battle of, Va., 1861. 2. Bull Run, 2nd Battle of, Va., 1862. I. Title.
E472.18.J69 2013   973.7'31—dc23   2013030958

BRITISH LIBRARY CATALOGUING DATA ARE AVAILABLE

© 2013 Don Johnson. All rights reserved

No part of this book may be reproduced or transmitted in any form or by any means, electronic or mechanical, including photocopying or recording, or by any information storage and retrieval system, without permission in writing from the publisher.

On the cover: top *The Battle of Bull Run*, July 21, 1861, Kurz & Allison, 1889; bottom *The Second Battle of Bull Run*, August, 29, 1862, Currier & Ives, New York, 1862 (both Library of Congress)

Manufactured in the United States of America

McFarland & Company, Inc., Publishers
Box 611, Jefferson, North Carolina 28640
www.mcfarlandpub.com

To my two sons, Robin and Jeff, and to all my
former colleagues in the National Park Service,
with love and gratitude.

Table of Contents

Foreword by Richard A. Sauers 1
Preface and Acknowledgments 3
Prologue 5

ONE. War Preparations 7
TWO. A Major Clash Draws Near 16
THREE. Sudley and Groveton Communities 22
FOUR. The Union Resolve 48
FIVE. July 21—First Battle of Manassas 60
SIX. Interval of Occupation 89
SEVEN. Prelude to Second Manassas 108
EIGHT. August 28, 29, 30—
        Second Battle of Manassas 127
NINE. The Aftermath of the Second Battle of
        Manassas and an Analysis 172

Chapter Notes 181
Bibliography 187
Index 191

Foreword
by Richard A. Sauers

Battles between armies do not occur in a vacuum. However, far too many "battle books" ignore the contemporary occupiers of the ground over which soldiers clashed and died. In American Civil War literature, Gettysburg has perhaps been the exception to this trend. Several articles and a couple of books delve into the ordeal suffered by the denizens of the Pennsylvania town that became the center of the Civil War's greatest battle.

Students of the war who have read about the engagements at Manassas, Virginia, are familiar with the Henry House, Brawner Farm, and Sudley Church. But these were only three structures in the hamlets of Sudley and Groveton. This area became the site of the war's first major engagement on July 21, 1861. Thirteen months later, a second, larger battle swept over the region.

In writing about these two epic battles, Don Johnson has included the story of the 103 families and 280 people who lived in this sixteen-square-mile area of rolling hills, creeks, and farm fields that surrounded Groveton and Sudley. Between the battles, the area was occupied by Confederate forces until March 1862. Burial details changed the landscape as they tried to erase the human cost after each battle.

Johnson has written a compelling work that provides enough information to satisfy military history buffs and yet elaborates on the lives and experiences of the Virginia civilians caught up in the war that came to their very doorsteps. We all know about Widow Henry and her horrible death when her home was wrecked during the battle. Johnson provides many more details, revealing that she was the widow of a surgeon who had served on the USS *Constellation*. We learn that the Brawner farm, where John Gibbon's western brigade earned a nickname, was called "Bachelor's Hall." Facts like these clothe the skeletons of civilians barely mentioned in previous books.

Johnson has crafted an eminently readable work that provides continuity to a "burned over" region in northern Virginia that saw two battles, forcing its residents to endure a brutal wartime experience that those who survived never forgot.

Richard A. Sauers is the author of more than two dozen books, including the *Advance the Colors! Pennsylvania Civil War Battle Flags* (two-volumes, 1987–1991), *Guide to Civil War Philadelphia* (2003), *Meade: Victor of Gettysburg* (2004), *America's Battlegrounds* (2005), and *William F. Bartlett: Biography of a Union Civil War General* (2009). He is executive director of the Western Museum of Mining and Industry, Colorado Springs, Colorado.

Preface and Acknowledgments

The Civil War is the thing that makes America different. It was our most tremendous experience, and it is not quite like anything that ever happened to anyone else.
— Bruce Catton

The most defining period in American history, the Civil War, ended nearly 150 years ago as of this writing. Since then thousands of books have been written about the war, a large number exploring strategy, tactics, and participants from commanding generals to the common soldier. For the historian seeking to accurately reconstruct events and attach appropriate significance to them, the quest is elusive. For various reasons, in cross-referencing source material written and recorded by the participants, inconsistencies and inaccuracies leave us with the question "What really happened?"

In writing *Thirteen Months at Manassas/Bull Run*, I set about the task of describing the national events that took place during secession, recounting the activities leading up to the first major battle of the Civil War while concentrating on the communities and families where this battle would occur. In all accounts, I have strived to accurately describe the significant events throughout the thirteen-month period that the Confederate and Union armies occupied the Manassas area, inclusive of the two major battles fought there.

Past authors who have written about the first major battle of the Civil War (referred to synonymously as the Battle of Bull Run and the Battle of Manassas) have largely failed to satisfy some fundamental questions surrounding the engagement, i.e., regarding the units present, who they were, where they were at what time, when events took place, and so on. The reader will find I have answered most of these serious questions; however, it must be stated that some uncertainties remain and will probably never be resolved.

This, however, is not so with the events that took place at Second Bull Run, also referred to as the Second Battle of Manassas. National Park Service Historian John Hennessy authored the definitive account, titled *Return to Bull Run*. His book is truly the epitome of written studies on Civil War battles and is used by the Park Service as the principal tactical study of the Second Battle of Manassas. In my book, where I have given my interpretation of battle events for the Second Battle of Manassas, the accounts I provide do not conflict with any of the factual accounts found in Hennessy's work.

In addition, interpretations given at most national battlefields provided by the National Park Service follow guidelines whereby accounts they tell must have had at least two eyewitnesses. In narrating the scenes and events provided in this book, this too was the goal I endeavored to achieve while evaluating the sources to conclude "what really happened."

This has been an in-depth undertaking, requiring thorough research of accounts encompassing not just two major battles but also the devastating effects on the families caught between two opposing armies during the fighting, and the deprivations inflicted upon them by the presence of two different occupying armies at different times, one friendly and one hostile.

Behind this work are other individuals who shared with me their knowledge, assistance, encouragement, and much-needed support; however, all errors or omissions are solely mine. To them I extend my deepest appreciation and gratitude. Friends old and new helped me in the completion of this book.

My good friend Troy D. Harman was generous in giving me his unfailing support. In addition, he read my final manuscript and provided helpful suggestions. Troy is a Civil War historian, and park ranger at the Gettysburg National Military Park and published author. His latest book is *Lee's Real Plan at Gettysburg*.

Ed Raus, historian and retiree from the National Park Service, served as the chief of interpretation at the Manassas National Battlefield for many years and was my Civil War mentor during the years I worked at Manassas. He is the author of several books, the latest titled *Banners South*. A Civil War authority, Ed read my final manuscript and provided valuable suggestions.

Robbie C. Smith, of the Colonial National Military Park, is a historian and authority on American history, excels in knowledge of Civil War battlefield tactics, and is a valued friend. She provided relentless research and editing skills in addition to offering astute criticism.

James Burgess of Manassas National Battlefield is a museum curator and an authority on Civil War weapons and artillery. Jim is an icon at Manassas. He has been at the battlefield for more than three decades, during which time he has uncovered numerous details regarding the first and second battles of Manassas. These contributions have clarified our understanding of the two significant engagements and have added to the collective body of knowledge about the Civil War. Over the many years I have worked with Jim, he has shared with me very helpful material on the two battles fought at Manassas and collections in the archives.

My son Robin, of Hudson, Wisconsin, with his skills with computers and scanning techniques, has helped me in ways too numerous to count. I am also indebted to him for reading the entire manuscript, correcting errors and offering his comments.

I am much indebted to my granddaughter, Jessica, an English major graduate of Southern Virginia University. She spent countless hours applying her editing skills to the manuscript's final draft.

Lastly, I am grateful to my granddaughter, Rachael, an accomplished illustrator. She created the many maps for the book.

Prologue

"...On to Richmond..."

By February 1860, the clamor in the South for secession was beginning to reach its pinnacle. Jefferson Davis, then a U.S. senator from the state of Mississippi and an opponent of secession, submitted seven resolutions to the Senate in an attempt to consolidate opinion regarding states' rights. The Senate debated these for the next three months to no conclusion. On November 6, 1860, Abraham Lincoln, the Republican presidential nominee, was elected the sixteenth president of the United States of America. His election to the presidency helped to ignite the furor that would eventually bring on the secession of the Southern states from the Union. On February 9, 1861, a constitutional convention at Montgomery, Alabama, named Davis provisional president of the Confederate States of America. He was inaugurated on February 18, 1861. Davis immediately appointed a Peace Commission to travel to Washington, D.C., for the purpose of resolving the Confederacy's differences with the Union. The Lincoln administration refused to meet with them.

Leadership and politics having failed to stave off the hand of Civil War, the nation turned in conflict against itself. Within the next few weeks, a total of eleven Southern states seceded from the Union. Richmond became the capital of the Confederacy, and "On to Richmond" became the cry of Northern journalists, politicians, and church ministries.

Davis appointed General Pierre G.T. Beauregard to command the Confederate troops in the vicinity of Charleston, South Carolina. He also approved the cabinet decision to force the removal of the Union troops at Fort Sumter, which took place on April 12, 1861.

With the firing on Fort Sumter, South Carolina, the war began. Three days later on April 15, President Abraham Lincoln issued a call for 75,000 to volunteer for ninety-day enlistments, and soon thousands of troops were converging into Washington.

Prior to the firing on Fort Sumter, the Confederate Congress authorized President Jefferson Davis to activate the state militias for six months. Davis called for 27,200 men, and the day after Lincoln issued his initial call for volunteers, he asked for an additional 32,000. From the onset of secession through May of 1861, the Federal Army's active duty corps lost 286 of its approximately 1,100 officers to the Confederate cause. Of these, 184 were graduates of West Point. In addition, 99 West Point graduates no longer on active duty joined the Confederate Army.

ONE
War Preparations

Military Significance of Manassas Junction

As Lincoln's military strategists mulled over their options, the strategic value of Manassas Junction was an obvious factor; it was the railroads that accorded the most advantageous route to Richmond. Rail led straight through Manassas Junction, south along the Orange and Alexandria Railroad to Gordonsville, and then on east via the Virginia Central Railroad to the Confederate capital.

Manassas came into being as a village with the completion of the Orange and Alexandria Railroad in the early 1850s. Although a few houses were built and a post office established, the development really began in 1851 when the Orange and Alexandria was linked with a new railroad terminating in the Shenandoah Valley. The new railroad, named Manassas Gap Railway, extended westward through the Blue Ridge Mountains at a place called Manassas's Gap, located about five miles east of Front Royal. Almost immediately the name of the junction became Manassas Gap Railway Junction.[1]

By 1861, the village of Manassas Junction, or Tudor Hall as the post office was named, consisted of three to four houses, a two-story boarding house, a tavern, and a small crude office building occupied by the Adams and Company Express. There was no regular depot, only a rough structure situated on the Orange and Alexandria railroad about a quarter of a mile from its junction with the Manassas Gap Railway. Two railway cars, closely connected and placed at right angles to each other, housed the telegraph operations. The cars' interiors were divided into sections that provided rooms for the operations and the storing of telegraph batteries, the receiving of baggage, and dining by day and lodging by night for the operators.[2] Within the three- or four-mile area surrounding the village, the population numbered no more than five or six hundred inhabitants.

The significance of Manassas Junction in no way escaped the Confederates, notably General Robert E. Lee, at that point serving as Commander in Chief of the Virginia Provisional Army. Newly resigned from the United States Army to defend his native state of Virginia, Lee was a West Point graduate in the class of 1829. During his four years at the academy, "his awards and honors have been equaled by few cadets before or since."[3] He not only attained a top academic record, graduating second in a class of 46, but he also holds the distinction of being one of a very few West Point graduates to have never received a demerit. Lee was highly regarded for his expertise as a military engineer and served with much distinction during his 32 years with the United States Army. His leadership and actions were instrumental in several American victories during the Mexican War (1846–1848), and from 1852 through 1855, he served as superintendent of West Point. On April 18, 1861, at the request of President Abraham Lincoln, Francis Preston Blair, Sr., editor of the *Washington Globe* and a Lincoln confidant, made an informal offer to Lee to accept an army field command. After much agonizing over his situation, on April 20, 1861, Lee wrote two letters of resignation. A formal letter to Secretary of War Simon Cameron simply stated,[4] "Sir, I have the honour to tender the resignation of my Commission as Colonel of the 1st Regt of Cavalry." The second letter was to his old friend and chief Lt. General Winfield Scott and read as follows[5]:

> Since my interview with you on the 18th inst., I have felt that I ought no longer retain my commission in the Army. I therefore tender my resignation, which I request you will recommend for acceptance. It would have been presented at once but for the struggle it has cost me to separate myself from a service to which I have devoted the best years of my life, and all the ability I possessed. During the whole of the time, more than a quarter of a century, I have experienced nothing but kindness from my superiors and a most cordial friendship from my comrades. To no one, General, have I been as much indebted as to yourself for uniform kindness and consideration, and it has always been my ardent desire to merit your approbation. I shall carry to the grave the most grateful recollections of your kind consideration, and your name and fame shall always be dear to me. Save in defense of my native State, I never desire again to draw my sword. Be pleased to accept my most earnest wishes for the continuance of your happiness and prosperity, and believe me,
>
> Most Truly yours,
> R E Lee

On April 22, Governor John Letcher of Virginia asked Lee to accept an appointment as commander in chief of the Virginia Provisional Army with the rank of Major General. Lee accepted and the next day he assumed command of the military and naval forces of Virginia.[6] Two days later, on April 25, Lee's resignation from the U.S. Army was accepted. Eleven days later, on May 6, 1861, Lee sent the following dispatch to Brigadier General Philip St. George Cocke, Commanding Potomac Department[7]: "You are desired to post at Manassas Gap Junction a force sufficient to defend that point against an attack likely to be made against it by troops from Washington. It will be necessary to give this point your personal attention."

Cocke, a West Point graduate and well-to-do Virginia and Mississippi plantation owner, was stationed at Culpeper with four companies of infantry and cavalry. Acting upon Lee's instructions, Cooke immediately wrote Adjutant-General Garnett from Culpeper Court-House[8]:

> I immediately ordered the Powhatan troop of cavalry to march from this place this morning, to join Capt. J.S. Green's company, now at Amissville, Rappahannock County, and to proceed together to Manassas Junction, where there are two (raw, undrilled, ununiformed and armed with altered musket) Irish companies, lately sent out from Alexandria, and which I had ordered to be held and drilled at Manassas Junction.... I have also ordered one section (two pieces) of Captain Kemper's artillery ... which I shall take along to the same

point. The Powhatan troop of cavalry and the section of artillery are absolutely all of the force at all available at this time and at this place.... We have no ammunition of any kind, except the limited supply sent forward to Alexandria. I shall gather in as fast as possible the armed companies that have not been mustered into the service throughout my department ... and concentrate them here at Manassas and Alexandria, as occasion may require.

From three to five thousand muskets or rifles should be immediately forwarded to this point for the use of their Command; thence to be drawn for arming companies, as mustered into services....

On May 9, Cocke was informed that Colonels John S. Preston and Samuel Garland, with eleven companies under their command, had been dispatched with three thousand flintlock muskets to Culpeper.[9] The next day Lee ordered these troops to Manassas Junction with instructions[10]: "That the troops may be prepared for field service, it is desirable that they be removed from the towns and placed in camp, where their instruction may be uninterrupted and rigid discipline established. Officers and men will sooner become familiar with the necessities of service and make their preparations accordingly. It is impossible at this time to furnish tents, but unoccupied buildings might possibly be obtained or temporary plank huts established...."

On May 14, Cocke was able to write Lee that he had succeeded in assembling a force of 918 men at Manassas.[11] The next day, Cocke markedly stated its military importance in a dispatch to Lee, he wrote,[12] "It is obvious, sir, with a strong *corps* d'armee at Manassas, and at least a division at Winchester, these two bodies being connected by a continuous railway through Manassas Gap, there should be kept at all times upon that road ample means of transportation. These two columns—one at Manassas and one at Winchester—could readily co-operate and concentrate upon the one point or the other...."

Confederate Congress Authorizes High Military Command

On May 16, the Confederate Congress authorized five officers as full generals in the Army of the Confederate States of America (A.C.S.A.), to hold the corresponding rank in the order named.[13] During the next three weeks that followed, these five general officers subsequently received the following assignments:

1. *Samuel Cooper.* The senior general officer became the adjutant and inspector general of the Confederate Army. He was born on June 12, 1798, and raised in Hackensack, New York; he was a West Point graduate (class of 1815). On March 17, 1861, he resigned his commission, at which time he offered his services to the Confederacy. At the time of his resignation, he was the adjutant and inspector general of the U.S. Army with the rank of colonel. He had served with much distinction; among his many notable accomplishments during his 46 years of U.S. military service, he wrote *Cooper's Tactics: The First Concise System of Instruction and Regulations for the Militia and Volunteers of the United States*, which later became a standard. Cooper was what could be described as

a distant brother-in-law to Lee, since he was married to a sister of Lee's sister-in-law.

2. *Albert Sidney Johnston.* As the second ranking general in the Southern army, he was given command of the Western Theater, Department No. 2, and immediate command of the Central Army of Kentucky. Born in Washington, Kentucky, in 1803, a West Point graduate (class of 1826), he served in the army for a number of years and saw action in the Black Hawk War before resigning in 1834. For the next 17 years, Johnston served with much distinction in many different military positions. In 1836 he went to Texas and enlisted as a private in the revolutionary army. Within a year he had become the senior brigadier general and chief commander. From 1838 to 1840, he served as secretary of war of the Republic of Texas. During the Mexican War, he commanded a regiment of Texas volunteers and fought at Monterrey. In 1849, he was reappointed to the U.S. Army and served on the Texas frontier, where, in 1855, he was given command of the 2nd Cavalry with rank of colonel. From 1856 to 1858, he was commander of the Department of Texas, and in 1857, he led the Utah expedition against the Mormons and was brevetted brigadier general for his services. From 1858 to 1860, he commanded the Department of Utah and subsequently the Department of the Pacific until he resigned his commission on May 3, 1861.

3. *Robert Edward Lee.* After the Army of Virginia's accession to the Confederacy, Robert E. Lee became an advisor to Jefferson Davis. Upon this, Davis recounted,[14] "On my arrival in Richmond (April 29, 1861), General R.E. Lee, as commander of the Army of Virginia, was found there, where he had established his headquarters. He possessed my unqualified confidence, both as a soldier and a patriot, and the command he had exercised over the Army of Virginia before her accession to the Confederacy, gave him that special knowledge which at the time was most needful."

4. *Joseph Eggleston Johnston.* The command of the Army of the Shenandoah, the force assigned to defend Harpers Ferry, was given to fifty-four-year-old General Joseph E. Johnston, a West Point graduate from Virginia (class of 1829) and classmate of General Robert E. Lee. He served with distinction in the Black Hawk War, the Seminole War, the Mexican War and the Utah Expedition. During the Mexican War he was brevetted and wounded several times. On June 28, 1860, he was appointed quartermaster general of the Army with the staff rank of brigadier general. Ten months later, on April 22, 1861, he resigned his commission to enter the Confederate service.

Johnston vehemently protested the seniority rankings of the four appointed full generals to Davis, contending he had been wronged. He believed he should have been selected the senior general instead of Samuel Cooper and wrote a lengthy scathing letter to Davis stating, "I now and here claim, that notwithstanding these nominations by the President and their confirmation by Congress, I still right-fully hold the rank of first general in these armies of the Southern Confederacy...."[15] The incident left a blemished relationship between president and general in which Johnston harbored animosity toward Davis throughout the war years and beyond.

5. *Pierre Gustave Tautant Beauregard.* The command of all the Confederate forces in northeastern Virginia, combined to form the Army of the Potomac, was given to forty-three-year-old General Pierre G.T. Beauregard. Beauregard was West Point trained (class of 1838), served with distinction in the Mexican War, brevetted twice for gallantry, and served on General Winfield Scott's staff. From January 23 to 28, 1861, he was appointed superintendent of the West Point Military Academy, but was relieved when the War Department learned of his Southern sympathies toward secession. The following month he resigned his commission, and on March 1, he was appointed brigadier general in the Provisional Army, C.S.A. Serving in this capacity, he was honored as the hero of Fort Sumter commanding the Confederate attack. Beauregard was not promoted to full general until the day after the First Battle of Manassas with date of rank July 21, 1861, a sour note of contention with him.

Harpers Ferry — Northernmost Point of the Confederacy

Just as both sides saw the strategic value of Manassas Junction, they also recognized that of Harpers Ferry, the gateway to northwestern Virginia. Harpers Ferry is situated at the confluence of the Potomac and Shenandoah Rivers in a large hollow formed by mountains on three sides with Maryland across the river from it. Like Manassas Junction, Harpers Ferry's proximity to two railroads emphasized its importance; the Baltimore and Ohio Railroad and the Chesapeake and Ohio Canal were major lifelines for Washington, the territories to the south, the valley, and the west.

Harpers Ferry was also the site of one of the largest armories in the South. In the wake of Virginia's Secession Convention held in Richmond, a group of secession activists met in that city to discuss a plan in which the state militia, under its commander Major General Kenton Harper, would attack the armory and capture the more than 20,000 arms inside. The meeting was called by Virginia's ex-governor Henry A. Wise; in attendance were Wise; "Nat" Tyler, editor of the *Richmond Enquirer*; Alfred M. Barbour, ex-civil superintendent of the "US Government works" at Harpers Ferry; "Militia Captains Turner Ashby, Richard Ashby of Fauquier county, Oliver R. Funsten of Clarke county (all commanders of volunteer companies of cavalry), John D. Imboden (Captain of Staunton Artillery), and Captain John A. Harman of Staunton." Imboden was given the task of presenting the plan to Governor John Letcher, which he did after arousing him from his bed. The governor approved the plan. The movement would commence the next day, April 17, providing that the Virginia Secession Convention voted to secede.[16]

In the meantime, Wise received a message from his son-in-law Doctor Garnett of Washington that a Massachusetts regiment of one thousand men had been ordered to Harpers Ferry. If the militia were to succeed in removing the weapons, they would have to move quickly and secretly. Twenty-four hours before the Virginia militia forces reached

Harpers Ferry, knowledge of their plans was leaked, and word reached the forty-four-man Union garrison, under the command of Lieutenant Roger Jones, that the armory was going to be attacked. Knowing that reinforcements would not arrive in time and that he would not be able to hold on to the armory, Jones retreated, but not before setting fire to the structure. Although the Confederates were able to save most of the armory and five thousand muskets, more than ten thousand weapons were destroyed.[17] This action by the state of Virginia after it had seceded marks the first engagement of an organized warring faction and military movement in the Civil War.

On April 27, Thomas Jonathan Jackson was appointed a colonel by Virginia Governor John Letcher and sent to the Confederate post at Harpers Ferry to assume command, replacing 64-year-old Major General Kenton Harper of the Virginia militia.

Jackson was born at Clarksburg, [West] Virginia, on January 21, 1824. A West Point graduate (class of 1846), he served as an artillery officer in the Mexican War (1846–48) and later resigned his commission in 1851 to accept a teaching appointment at the Virginia Military Institute in Lexington, Virginia. Six days prior to Jackson's appointment to command a post at Harpers Ferry, he had been placed in charge of a VMI corps of cadets, sent to Richmond as drillmasters for new army recruits.

Jackson arrived in Harpers Ferry the day after his appointment. Lee's initial orders to Jackson directed him to muster new companies into service and to salvage and remove the arms manufacturing machinery from the armory. The order in part read[18]:

General Thomas Jonathan Jackson (1862). The last known photograph of Jackson. During a brief break in a series of battles in Northern Virginia in early 1862, Jackson was quartered at Winchester. While there, his good friend and medical director, Hunter McGuire, persuaded Jackson to sit for this photograph (courtesy of the Virginia Military Institute Archives).

> After mustering into the service of the state such Companies as may be accepted under your instructions, you will organize them into Regiments or Battalions, uniting as far as possible, Companies from the same section of the State. These will be placed under the senior Captains until field officers can be appointed by the Governor. It is desired that you expedite the transfer of the machinery to this place, ordered to the Richmond Armory, should it not have been done, and that you complete, as fast as possible, any gun or rifles partially contructed,

should it be safe and practicable. Your attention will be particularly directed to the safety of such arms, machinery, parts of arms, raw material and &c., that they be useful, to insure which they must be at once sent into the interior, if in your judgment necessary. If any artillery companies offer their services, or are mustered into the service of the State, and are without batteries, report the facts....

In addition to bringing several VMI cadets to serve as drillmasters, Jackson brought with him VMI teaching personnel to serve on his staff. Upon assuming command, his post strength was 2500 raw recruits. In the next few weeks, he trained and organized 4500 recruits into companies.

On April 27, 1861, Federal Secretary of War Simon Cameron created a new military department, called the Department of Pennsylvania, headquartered in Philadelphia under the command of Major General Robert Patterson.[19] The command consisted of U.S. regulars and militias from several Northern states, totaling about 18,000 troops.

May 10 would mark the beginning of a personal attachment and mutual admiration between two Confederate officers, both destined for future acclaim. Twenty-eight-year-old Lt. Colonel James Ewell Brown (J.E.B.) Stuart reported to Jackson for duty. Almost immediately a relationship of mutual respect, friendship, and understanding evolved between the two warriors. It has been said that Stuart was the only man in the Confederacy that could make Jackson laugh.

Stuart, a West Point graduate (class of 1854), was a master horseman and cavalry officer. In 1859, Stuart served as an aid to Colonel Robert E. Lee at Harpers Ferry in the capture of the insurgent John Brown. As many of the Federal officers from Southern states resigned their commissions to join their state militias and Confederate forces when their states seceded, so did Stuart when Virginia seceded. Jackson assigned the command of his cavalry to Stuart, except for a company of cavalry scouts that had been organized by Capt. Turner Ashby; these he assigned Ashby to command separately.

On May 23, General Joseph Johnston arrived to assume command from Jackson. Jackson was unaware of the change in command beforehand, and he received it with some consternation. For two days, Jackson refused to relinquish command until Johnston produced proper written orders. Johnston was not able to do so, but he did find in his possession correspondence signed by Lee that referred to Johnston as commanding officer at Harpers Ferry. Thereupon, Johnston assigned Jackson to take command of all the Virginia troops that he had organized.[20]

In May of 1861, a 26-year-old surgeon came upon the scene at Harpers Ferry at the time Jackson assumed command of the Army of Shenandoah. He was Dr. Hunter Holmes McGuire, M.D., who initially marched to Harpers Ferry as a private with Company F, Second Virginia Regiment. Soon after reaching Harpers Ferry, McGuire was commissioned by Governor Letcher as medical director of the Army of Shenandoah.

Years later, McGuire gave an interview to a newspaper reporter in which he said the following regarding his first meeting with Jackson: "When I reported to General Jackson for duty he looked at me a long time without speaking a word, and presently said, 'You can go back to your quarters and wait there until you hear from me.'" McGuire continued, "I went back to my quarters and didn't hear from him for a week, when one evening I was announced at dress-parade as medical director of the army. Some months afterwards, when I asked the General the cause of the delay, he said that I looked so young that he sent to Richmond to see if there wasn't some mistake." McGuire further explained, "Not long after this General Joe Johnston succeeded (then Colonel) Jackson in command of the army, and the latter was given command of all the Virginia forces at Harpers Ferry. Shortly after General Johnston took command I was relieved from duty by some regular old army surgeon. Jackson asked then that I should be assigned to his command."[21] As with Stuart and Jackson, this too was the beginning of a personal attachment and mutual admiration between two distinguished personages.

Dr. Hunter Homes McGuire, M.D. In May 1861, McGuire was assigned to Jackson's First brigade as medical director. Later, he became medical director of Jackson's 2nd Corps. During the next 35 years following the war, his many accomplishments included: founder and president of the Medical Society of Virginia, president of the American Surgical Association, and president of the American Medical Association. This photograph was taken in the early 1880s at time McGuire served on the faculty board at the Medical College of Virginia (later a part of Virginia Commonwealth University) (courtesy of Virginia Commonwealth University Special Collections).

Patterson's Federal force of 18,000 was camped in and around Hagerstown, Maryland, about 15 miles away from Harpers Ferry. Scott had been persistently urging Patterson to attack the Confederates at Harpers Ferry. Meanwhile, Johnston was adamantly pleading to Lee and Davis to be allowed to fall back to Winchester, declaring Harpers Ferry was indefensible. He believed that Winchester was key to the Shenandoah Valley since the town controlled all the major roads into the valley. He further reasoned that the one railroad to northern Virginia would be at his disposal. Finally, Johnston was given permission to abandon Harpers Ferry, and on June 15, after destroying bridges and military supplies which could not be taken with him, he departed for Winchester.[22]

Johnston's Army of the Shenandoah was now at 9,000 troops organized into four brigades[23]:

Jackson commanded the 1st Brigade of four Virginia regiments: the 2nd, 4th, 5th, and 27th, plus Col. William N. Pendleton's battery of 4 guns (Rockbridge Artillery). Later, on July 15, the 8-company-strong 33rd Virginia regiment was added to Jackson's brigade. Before long Jackson's brigade would become known throughout the

North and South as the "Stonewall Brigade," while at the same time Jackson would gain the soon-to-be famous sobriquet "Stonewall Jackson."

Colonel Francis Bartow of Georgia, a Yale graduate, a planter, and more recently, a congressman from the State of Georgia, commanded the 2nd Brigade of two regiments, comprising the 7th and 8th Georgia, plus Capt. E.G. Alburtis's battery of 4 guns (Wise Artillery).

Brigadier General Barnard E. Bee of South Carolina, a West Point graduate (class of 1845) commanded the 3rd Brigade of four regiments, comprising the 4th Alabama, 2nd and 11th Mississippi, and the 6th North Carolina, plus Capt. J. Imboden's battery of 4 guns (Staunton Artillery).

Brigadier General E.K. Smith was the initial commander of the 4th Brigade of three regiments, comprising the 10th Virginia, 1st Maryland, and 3rd Tennessee, plus Lt. R.F. Beckham's battery of 4 guns (Culpeper Artillery). Colonel Arnold Elzey of Maryland, a West Point graduate (class of 1837), took command on July 21 after Smith was wounded.

As Joe Johnston was redeploying from Harpers Ferry, Patterson was marching on Winchester; but when he learned that Johnston was already at Winchester, he withdrew to Martinsburg. Johnston took positions north of Winchester and prepared defenses along Bunker Hill.[24]

Two

A Major Clash Draws Near

A Spy for the Confederacy

While the Union and Confederate Armies were organizing, covert operations from inside Washington political and military circles were beginning. Rose O'Neale Greenhow, a grande dame of Washington society, had become a spy for the Confederacy. At 44 years of age, she was considered beautiful, vivacious, educated, compassionate, refined, and fearless, and she possessed a charismatic spirited manner of expression and conversation. Described as "a tall dark beauty, supple in her movements and full of grace," she used her Southern "feminine wiles" to charm military secrets out of high-ranking government officials, civilian and military.[1]

Born and raised on a plantation in Poolesville, Maryland, Maria Rosetta O'Neale and her two sisters were orphaned when she was a child. A few years later, when Rose was in her early teens, the three sisters left Rockville, Maryland, to live with their aunt, Mrs. H.V. Hill, who ran a fashionable Capitol Hill boarding house. In 1835, at the age of 18, she married Robert Greenhow, a State Department official. During the nearly three decades Rose lived in Washington, D.C., she became a leader in Washington society and came to know virtually everyone of importance, cultivating close friendships with such high-profile dignitaries as President James Buchanan, Daniel Webster, and Dolly Madison, as well as high-ranking military officers and many members of Congress. She was a devoted friend and follower of the celebrated senator from South Carolina and states' rights advocate, John C. Calhoun. She saw him as her mentor. In 1852, Rose became a widow soon after the birth of her fourth daughter, "Little Rose." Her strong sympathy for the Confederate cause and their right to secession was noted by those with similar views in Washington.[2]

For her covert activities, Rose had been recruited by suave ex–Union Army officer Thomas Jordan. When Jordan first made her acquaintance, he was a captain and assistant quartermaster in the U.S. Army; he was forty-two years of age and described as handsome and alert. A native of Virginia, a West Point graduate (class of 1840; he and William T. Sherman were classmates and roommates), he saw service both in the Seminole War and the Mexican War. Sometime prior to the secession of Virginia, Jordan had become acquainted with Rose at a dinner function held in her home. Later, he and Rose met socially on several occasions and talked at length of their Southern sympathies and what possibilities lay in the face of the mounting secession furor and the election of Lincoln.

Jordan was very busy in the intervening time between this visit and the next time he saw Rose again. The day after Virginia seceded he resigned his commission in the Union Army. Shortly thereafter he accepted a commission in the Confederate Army and was immediately appointed by General Robert E. Lee to the post of adjutant-general of the army assembled at Manassas Junction. A few days later Jordan received authorization from General Beauregard to organize a select group of Union citizenry for the purpose of obtaining and reporting every movement and plan of the Union army.

Within days after Virginia voted to ratify the Ordinance of Secession, Jordan met with Rose again. They discussed plans for instituting a covert operations network, including recruitments. All the informants would be persons who were either working in government departments or were otherwise in a position to obtain news of political or military importance. These informants would not be known to each other but would receive instructions from a central source and pass on the information they obtained to this same source. Greenhow would be the link between Jordan and this network. In addition, Greenhow's home, located at 398 16th Street, would be the center for this activity. Jordan was of the opinion that Greenhow's friendships with most of Washington's leading political and military figures gave her access to a great deal of information. To this she aptly stated: "The generals and politicos do seem incapable of holding their tongues." A cipher devised by Jordan was used in their communications.[3]

Rose O'Neale Greenhow. An outspoken proponent of Southern rights, 43-year-old Rose O'Neal Greenhow was a spy for the Confederate cause. She has been credited with being instrumental in the Confederates' success at the First Battle of Manassas. Arrested by Union authorities, she was sent to the Old Capitol Prison, accompanied by her youngest daughter, "little" Rose. While in prison, through clever ingenuity, she continued to send messages to the Confederate government, e.g., the fortifications for Washington City. Finally, not knowing what else to do, the Union government deported Rose to Virginia. This Mathew Brady photograph was taken during her time of incarceration at Old Capitol Prison (courtesy Library of Congress).

Confederate Congress Moves Its Seat of Government

On May 20, the Confederate Congress, then in session at Montgomery, Alabama, resolved that the seat of government of the Confederate States should be transferred to Richmond, and that the Congress should adjourn to meet there on July 20. It had become evident that Virginia would be the battleground of the coming struggle, and it was desirable, therefore, that the Confederate Government should have its headquarters in that state.

Union Forces Seize Alexandria and Invoke Martial Law

On May 21, Virginia voted to ratify the Ordinance of Secession. Three days later, at daybreak of May 24, columns of Union troops crossed the Potomac and seized Arlington Heights and the city of Alexandra south of the river. A Confederate battalion commanded by Colonel George H. Terrett and comprising about 500 troops was posted in the city there. In the early morning hours, Terrett was informed by his pickets that Union forces were crossing the Chain and Long bridges between Alexandria and Washington. At about 5:30 A.M., a Union officer approached from the waterfront bearing a flag of truce. He had landed from the steamer *Pawnee* with orders for the evacuation or surrender of the city. Terrett informed the truce bearer they would evacuate, and he was given until 9 A.M. to do so. Notwithstanding this agreement, at daybreak Union troops numbering more than 5,000, including infantry, cavalry, and artillery, swept through the streets in an effort to cut off and capture Terrett's force. A company of thirty-five men and horses of the Confederate cavalry were captured, but the main body of Confederates escaped and made their way south. About two miles outside of the city, they commandeered two trains and rode them to Manassas Junction, about twenty-seven miles west of Alexandria.[4] As the Union soldiers entered the city of Alexandria, two-thirds of the city's Virginia populace fled before them. Having captured the city, the invaders quickly invoked marital law on the townspeople.

One of the regiments in the vanguard of the Union columns was the colorful 11th New York Fire Zouaves, commanded by Colonel Elmer E. Ellsworth. The regiment, recruited by Ellsworth, was one of the first three-year regiments of the war. Less than a year before, Ellsworth had been a law student studying in the law office of Abraham Lincoln. The regiment took the name Zouave from a French-African corps and adopted their uniform, which consisted of a kepi, dark blue pants, a fireman's red shirt, and blue jacket with red trim.

Ellsworth's regiment had been encamped on the Potomac below the Eastern Branch, and was landed on the wharves of Alexandria under the guns of the *Pawnee*. As Ellsworth entered Alexandria at the head of a detachment from his regiment, he made his way to the Marshall House Hotel, known to be flying the "Stars and Bars" Confederate flag from its rooftop. Infuriated, Ellsworth stormed into the hotel followed by five of his Zouaves. Making his way up the hotel stairs, Ellsworth climbed out onto the roof and snatched the flag from its staff. The hotel proprietor, James Jackson, had been aroused from his sleep by a servant and told that "Lincoln men" were occupying his hotel. Armed with a double-barreled shotgun, he reached the turn in the stairway leading to the third floor, where he met Ellsworth descending the stairs with the flag wrapped around him, followed by the Zouaves. Zouave Private Francis E. Brownell, seeing Jackson with a shotgun, raised his musket, and both Jackson and Brownell fired almost simultaneously. Jackson was standing at the bottom of the stairway leading up to the third floor and was looking up the staircase. His shotgun blast struck Ellsworth in the heart; the load sent a piece of the flag into the heart, where it was later found. The ball from Brownell's musket struck Jackson between the eyes and passed out the back of his head. As Jackson went down, the other Zouaves rushed upon him, one stabbing him in the stomach with a Bowie knife, and another driving his bayonet through his body, pinning it to the floor.[5]

Sixteen years later, on January 26, 1877, Brownell was awarded the nation's highest award, the Medal of Honor, for his actions at the Marshall House Hotel.[6]

Manassas Defenses Undergo a Succession of Commanders

On May 22, Brig. Gen. Milledge L. Bonham arrived at Manassas Junction with a South Carolina brigade consisting of the 1st and 2nd South Carolina Infantry Regiments. The following day, by order of General Lee, Bonham assumed command of the Potomac Department from Cocke. Bonham had been an Indian fighter in the Seminole War, and was a Mexican War veteran and ex–United States congressman from South Carolina. Described as charming and handsome, sporting an immaculate trimmed mustache and chin beard, with gray hair flowing gracefully about his head, he had been the organizer of several South Carolina units. He was a lawyer and confidant of South Carolina Governor Francis Pickens and had been appointed brigadier general and commander of the Provisional Army of South Carolina.

That same day, Lee sent a dispatch to Bonham, stating the importance of Manassas Junction and emphasizing the need of entrenchments[7]: "The Manassas Junction is a very important point on your line, as it commands the communication with Harper's Ferry, and must be firmly held. Entrenchments at that point would add to its security, and, in connection with its defense, you must watch the approaches from either flank, particularly towards Occoquan."

On May 29, Lee inspected the Manassas Junction defenses and thereupon sent a quick dispatch to Adjutant-General Garnett that read[8]: "Number of troops, six thousand. Should be ten. Returned from Fairfax Court-House. All right."

Two days after having been "assigned to the command of the troops in the Alexandria line,"[9] General Beauregard wrote the following to President Davis[10]:

> I arrived here on the 1st [June] at 2 P.M. and immediately examined the site of this encampment and the place of its proposed defenses. The former is an open country, traversed by good roads in every direction without any strong natural features for the purpose of

Liberia (Beauregard's headquarters). On the eve of the Civil War, the Liberia plantation had grown into one of the largest and most successful in western Prince William County. During the initial occupation by the Confederates, many camps were established to house their troops; the grounds of Liberia were put to use for Camp Pickens. During the First Battle of Manassas and the interlude period of Confederate occupancy, Beauregard used the mansion as his headquarters. During the period of Union occupation, President Abraham Lincoln traveled to Liberia to confer with McDowell who was occupying the plantation mansion at that time (courtesy Library of Congress).

defense, and without running water nearer than three miles, except a few small springs at half that distance. The plans of the works are good, but too extensive to be finished in less than two or three weeks, and cannot be garrisoned with less than three to four thousand men. As this position can be turned in every direction by an enemy, for the purpose of destroying the railroads intended to be defended by it, it becomes a question whether these works could be held more than a few days when thus isolated.

I have reconnoitered closely several of the fords on Bull run and on Occoquan Run (about three miles from here), which offer strong natural features of defense; but they are so numerous and far apart that only a much larger force than I have been at my command (say not less than from ten to fifteen thousand men) could hope to defend them all against a well-organized enemy of about twenty thousand men, who could select his point of attack. I must therefore either be re-enforced at once, as I have not more than about six thousand effective men, or I must prepare to retire, on the approach of the enemy, in the direction of Richmond with the intention of arresting him whenever and wherever the opportunity shall present itself....

Liberia was a large, red brick, two-and-a-half story gabled-roof plantation home, dating back to 1825, which rested on an estate of 1,660 acres, and situated about one-half mile east of Manassas Junction village. It was the home of William James Weir, his wife Harriett and their two sons, Robert and Walter. It was the largest and most successful plantation in Prince William County; with a labor force of 90 slaves, they produced large fields of grain and raised horses, cattle, hogs, and a large herd of Merino sheep. Three days before the First Battle of Manassas, the two Weir sons joined the 49th Virginia Infantry Regiment. Robert joined Company A and Walter joined Company C. In early June, after Beauregard arrived to take command of the Confederate

Army, he found Camp Pickens laid out on the grounds of Liberia. Initially, Beauregard made his headquarters in tents set up on the grounds near the home, and although he did not use the home for his headquarters, his adjutant Col. Thomas Jordan did make use of the home for his office. William and Harriett remained at Liberia to operate the plantation. Soon after the battle, Beauregard moved his headquarters into the home.

> Nearly a year later [during the interlude of occupancy of Manassas], while McClellan with the main Union army was conducting his campaign on the Peninsula against Richmond, General McDowell, commanding the Union forces in northern Virginia covering Washington, stopped at Liberia on May 28 and 29, 1862, while moving forward toward the Shenandoah valley in an attempt to intercept Jackson near Strasburg. Jackson having escaped toward Harrisonburg, McDowell returned to Manassas and he and his staff made their headquarters at Liberia from June 10 until about the first of July [1862].[11]

Virginia Militia Transferred to National Army of the Confederacy

On June 8, Virginia Governor John Letcher issued a proclamation transferring all Virginia forces, ordnance, stores, etc., to the national army of the Confederacy.[12] The army's total strength amounted to 40,000 men and 115 pieces of artillery. Lee's role now became that of advisor to Jefferson Davis.

On June 23, Beauregard wrote to Secretary of War L.P. Walker: "Sir: I have the honor to inform the department that in consequence of the large re-enforcements I have lately received, I have divided my forces into six brigades...." Beauregard's six brigade commanders were: Colonel Milledge L. Bonham, Colonel Richard S. Ewell, Brigadier General David R. Jones, Colonel G.H. Terrett, Brigadier General Philip St. George Cocke, and Colonel Jubal Early. By this time Beauregard had stationed advance detachments at key points including Centreville, Fairfax Court-House, Germantown, the crossing of the old Braddock road with the Fairfax Court-House road, and Sangster's Cross-Roads. All these positions, he stated, "were in easy and short communication with each other and with these headquarters."[13]

As the month of June drew to a close, there was little of Manassas Junction that resembled the village of just two months earlier. Manassas had become a fortress covering a vast area of more than 50 square miles. The roads, the fields and the town were filled with thousands of soldiers. Around the Junction, massive fortifications had been erected running out in different directions from the station. Acres of trees had been felled to give free range to artillery, and at key positions in the field, men were constantly on guard. Camps had sprung up throughout the open countryside. From dawn to dusk troops were almost incessantly engaged in drill. Scouting parties, mounted and on foot, scoured the country daily. Soldiers on picket duty along the Bull Run watched nervously for the appearance of the enemy.[14] Aptly stated, this was the situation in Northern Virginia: "McDowell, at Alexandria with 35,000 men, and Patterson near Harpers Ferry, about 50 miles away, with 15,000, were opposed by Beauregard at Manassas with 22,000, and Johnston at Winchester with 11,000."[15]

THREE

Sudley and Groveton Communities

Almost all farmlands and families located in the sectors of Sudley and Groveton were tragically damaged by the military activities taking place throughout the area. Their geographical locations, the tide of battle, and fate determined which places and people would feature prominently in both the First and Second Battles of Manassas. These factors also determined those who would narrowly survive the first battle but be in the forefront of heavy fighting thirteen months later in the Second Battle of Manassas.

The two epic battles that took place over the fields and streams during the pinnacle of the fighting on July 21, 1861, and again on August 28, 29, and 30, 1862, encompassed an area of sixteen square miles surrounding the Groveton and Sudley areas. On the eve of the Civil War, the population of the Groveton/Sudley area was approximately 280 people, representative of 103 families; most were farmers. This chapter takes a look at some of those families soon to be caught up in the devastation when these two armies came together.

A Little Community Called Sudley

Tucked away in the northeast quadrant of Prince William County was a little community called Sudley. Although small, Sudley was the financial hub for the county.

Established at the confluence of Catharpin Run and Bull Run, the Sudley community began to take shape in the late eighteenth century with the construction of a grist mill on Catharpin Run in the 1770s. Less than a mile north of Sudley stood a great plantation house, Sudley Mansion, built by John Carter (son of Landon Carter Sr. and grandson of Robert "King" Carter) between 1760 and 1770. The mill and the community were given the name of Sudley after the Sudley Mansion. The Carters were the largest and wealthiest landowners in Prince William, Loudoun, and Fairfax Counties. This gave them social and economic influence throughout the tri-county area. Their property extended from the Woodland plantation in the northwest, to the Sudley Mansion plantation in the north, to the Pittsylvania plantation in the southeast. Each plantation, for the most part, rested along the Bull Run.

Further to the southeast, across the Fauquier and Alexandria Turnpike, lived descendants of the Carters: the Henrys on Spring Hill (Henry Hill), the Balls at Portici, and the Chinns on Chinn Ridge. By 1822, several families had moved into the area, prompting the building of the Sudley Methodist Episcopal Church on land donated by Landon Carter. The flourmill trade engaged heavily in export trade with England and interstate business with other Carter holdings in the Tidewater. The community soon flourished with the construction of a sawmill and the miller's house, as well as a general store established near the grist mill. Further improvements were made to the grist mill with the construction of a mill dam and headrace north on Catharpin Run. Catharpin Run was used as the water power source for both mills.

Roads had been cut through the wilderness to Sudley in order to facilitate travel to the mill, and by the 1820s, roads radiated from the mill to the Woodland and Sudley plantations, to the Stone House, and to the communities of Groveton and Haymarket. Farm roads were prevalent throughout the area, made by the passage of wagons to and from the individual farm fields, to neighboring farms, and to fords that crossed rivers and streams. All roads in the tri-county corridor led to the Sudley Mill. With the exception of the Fauquier and Alexandria Turnpike, the roads were no more than muddy ruts in winter and streaks of dust in summer. Although all were narrow, they were made passable by the respected practice that empty wagons gave way to loaded ones.

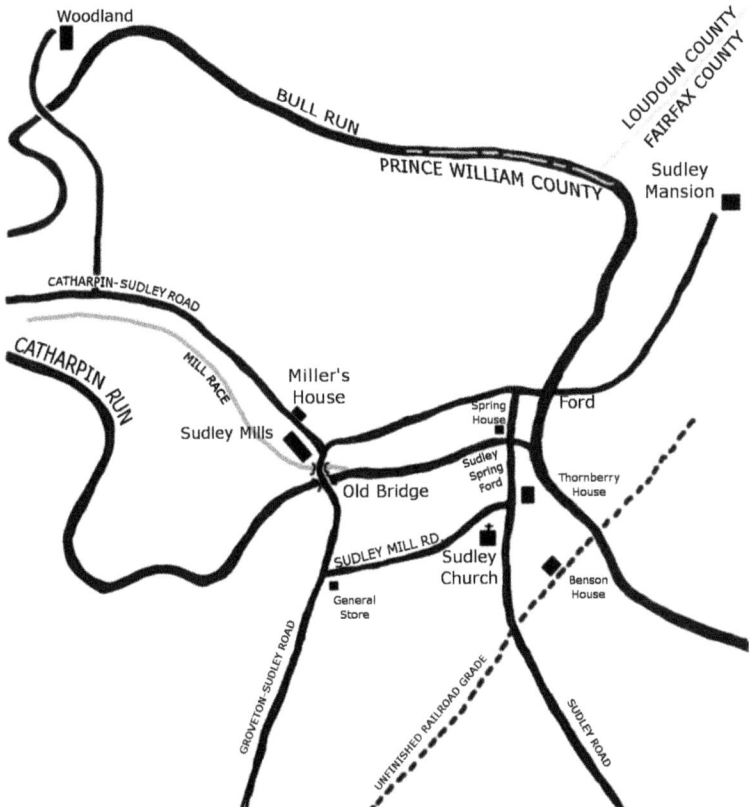

Sudley community — Sudley proper. Its thriving mill operations made Sudley the financial hub for Prince William county. All roads in the area led to Sudley. *Drawing by Rachael R. Johnson.*

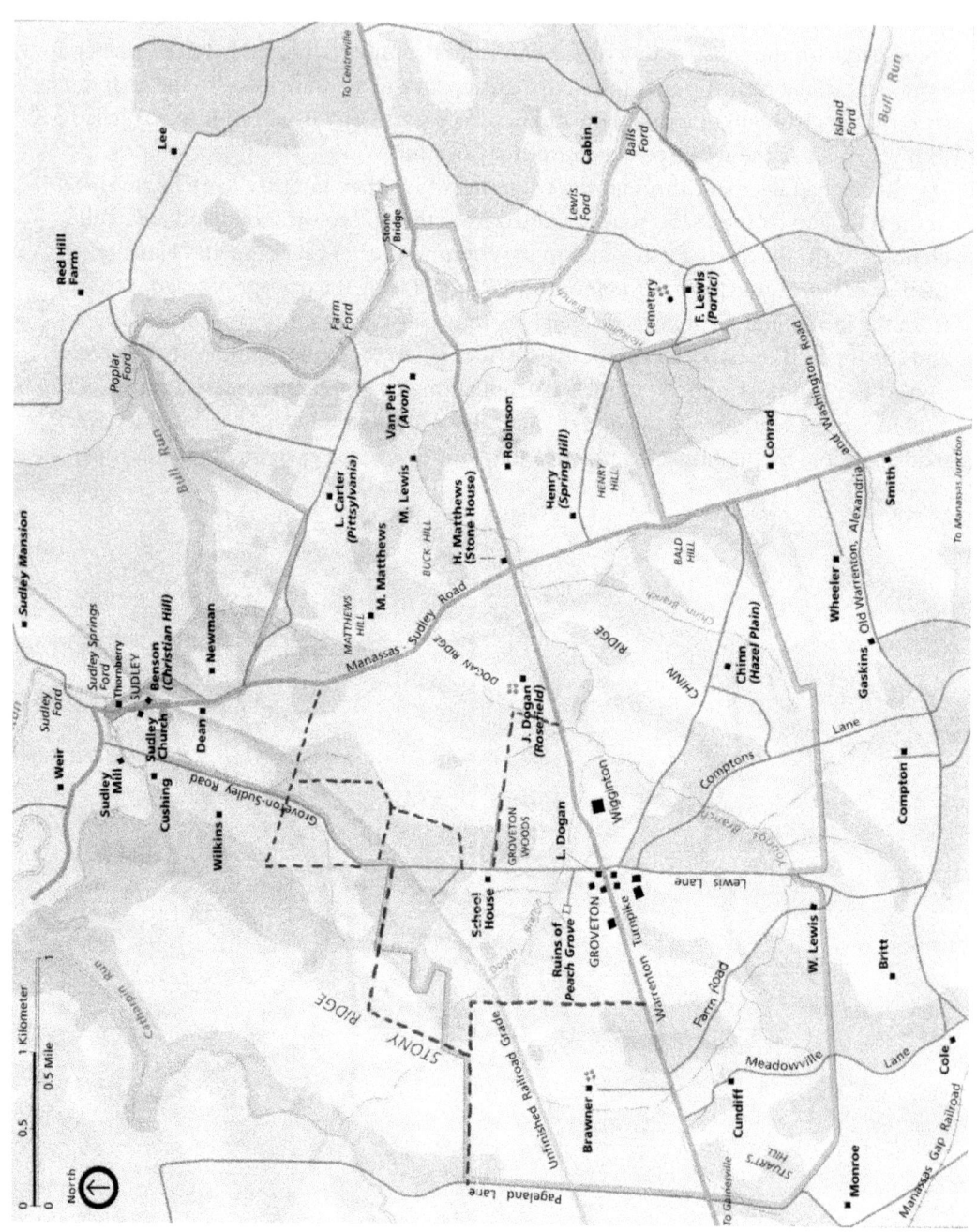

The Sudley Church and the Comptons

The Sudley Methodist Church was a red brick building of "simplicity" design, situated on a knoll above the confluence of Catharpin Run and Bull Run and to the southwest of Sudley Springs Ford. The pastor was 49-year-old Reverend Alexander H. Compton. On the ill-fated day of Sunday, July 21, the reverend was ill and bedridden at his farm called Greenville, located a little more than two miles southwest of Sudley along the old Warrenton-Washington Turnpike (modern-day Ball's Ford Road). The pastor's household consisted of his wife Felicia, age 48; their six children: Alexander, 21; Marianne, 16; James, 14; Anna, 12; Rose, 7; Felica, 4; and several slaves. One of their servant slaves, a young Negro woman named Lucy Griffith, was away and staying with the Henry family, having been hired out to assist in the care of Mrs. Judith Henry. The Henrys lived about one mile northeast of Greenville at a place soon to be made famous, Henry Spring Hill. Alexander, the Comptons' eldest son, was serving in the Confederate army in Company C of the 8th Virginia Infantry, and on that day his unit was being rushed to Manassas from Leesburg.[1]

Above: Sudley Methodist Church (March 1862). The heart of the Sudley-Groveton community, the church was a gruesome setting as Union medical personnel commandeered the church as a field hospital within moments of the first shots fired on Matthews Hill. Twice used as a hospital, it sustained heavy damage, especially during the First Battle of Manassas. Not seen in this Brady photograph was a large hole in the wall on the opposite side of the building, blasted by artillery.

Opposite: Sudley-Groveton sector. The fighting on July 21, 1861, and again on August 28, 29, and 30 in 1862, engulfed the hamlets of Sudley and Groveton and the surrounding area for sixteen square miles. (Courtesy MNB Visitor Brochure. Geographic details and landmarks added by Rachael R. Johnson).

This particular Sunday morning began like most other July days with the bright sun shinning and increasingly getting hotter, turning the air uncomfortably humid and warm. By 9 A.M., the inhabitants of the Sudley area, dressed in their best finery, had begun making their way over the dirt roads and farm trails to their house of worship. Before they could all gather inside, they were suddenly confronted by endless columns of marching soldiers approaching the Sudley Spring Ford from the north.

Within a time span of less than 2 hours, the Sudley Church was transformed completely, becoming the setting of many horrors after being commandeered for use as a makeshift Union hospital.

The Thornberrys

In the northeast quadrant of the intersection of Sudley Road and Sudley Mill Road (modern-day Featherbed Lane) lived the John Thornberry family. The Thornberry family consisted of 37-year-old John, his 34-year-old wife Martha, and their three sons (Samuel, age 13; Joseph, age 8; and John, 16 months) and two daughters (Laura, age 6; and Annette, age 3). Also living in the house with the family were two female slaves in their mid–to upper teens. Below the home, along the side of Sudley Road and near the community crossroads, John Thornberry operated a wheelwright shop. In addition to

Moderday photograph of restored Thornberry home (2010). Front view looking east. The lean-to on right side of house was added in 1870 for use as a post office and was not a part of the original dwelling in 1861 (photograph by Jessica Johnson).

fixing wagons at his wheelwright shop, he was an undertaker, a carpenter, and a blacksmith. Mr. Thornberry was also active in the Sudley Methodist Church Sunday school. On the day of the battle, no one was home. At that time, although he was in the area, John Thornberry was with Company A, 49th Virginia Infantry Regiment. In his absence, John's brother-in-law William Wilkins took Mrs. Thornberry and the children and two slave girls to his farm located southwest along Groveton Sudley Road (also part of modern Featherbed Lane) for safety.[2]

Two days before the battle began at Blackburn's Ford on the Bull Run, it was known that McDowell's army was on the march and approaching the Manassas area. It was at this time that Col. Cocke had ordered the 49th Virginia Infantry Regiment, under the command of sixty-four-year-old Colonel William "Extra Billy" Smith, to the Sudley Mills area to encamp and await Colonel Eppa Hunton and his 8th Virginia Infantry Regiment soon to be arriving from Leesburg. Arriving late in the afternoon, Smith's three-company regiment camped in and around the Sudley church. A bit of background:

> As a young man, Smith studied law and after being admitted to the bar, he established a law practice in Culpeper, Virginia. In 1831, he established a line of United States mail and passenger post coaches through Virginia, the Carolinas, and Georgia. It was in this role that he received his nickname. Given a contract by the administration of President Andrew Jackson between Washington (D.C.) and Milledgeville, Georgia, Smith extended it with numerous spur routes, all generating extra fees. During an investigation of the Post Office department, Smith's extra fees were publicized and he became known as "Extra Billy" in both the North and the South.[3]

Later, Smith gained prominence as a member of the State Senate from 1836 to 1841 and again as Virginia's governor from 1846 to 1849. Still later, he served three consecutive Congressional terms from March 4, 1853, to March 3, 1861.

Smith and his newly formed regiment had only been camped at the Sudley Church a short time when Cocke sent orders for the 49th to move to a point on Bull Run near the Lewis house, and report to him. When the 49th Virginia moved out, John Thornberry went with them as a new recruit.

The Bensons of Christian Hill

On a rise known as Christian Hill, located about three hundred yards to the southeast of the Thornberrys,' stood the Benson family home. The Benson family consisted of 36-year-old Amos, his 23-year-old wife Margaret, and their 13-year-old orphaned niece, Mary. The home was small, accentuated by a nine-foot-wide chimney with a sit-in style fireplace.

A few yards east of the home lay the bed of the Unfinished Railroad that ran through their property. Exactly as the name implied, it was a railroad that was never finished. With the coming of the two railroads in 1851 to Manassas Junction, the Manassas Gap Railway Company became dissatisfied by the high shipping costs charged to them by the Orange and Alexandria Railroad Company for the transfer of freight between the two railway lines. The owners of the Manassas Gap Railroad decided to build a spur, bypassing Manassas Junction. Operating as an independent line, the spur was to extend from the vicinity of Gainesville through Sudley Mill, Germantown, down the slopes of the Accotink, and around Annandale to Cameron and Jones Point at Alexandria. Work began in 1855, but in 1858 the railway ran into financial problems, and the backers of the spur pulled out. The grading had been completed, but the trusses, rail ties and rails were never laid.

The Bensons were devout members of the Sudley Methodist Church. The things they experienced on this tragic day and the actions on their part would become widely known 25 years later throughout the North and South. The Bensons were destined to play a vital role in the history of this small community and its church.

The Carters of Pittsylvania

Located three-quarters of a mile to the northeast of the Stone House and one-half mile east of the Sudley road lay the plantation of Pittsylvania. At one time Pittsylvania was a spectacular sight, graced by a beautiful mansion and several outbuildings with connecting walkways, formal gardens, herb gardens, a bowling green, and 145 slaves. The property was built between 1760 and 1770 by Landon Carter, the grandson of Robert "King" Carter, and was situated on a 2,823-acre tract. As the property passed from father to son, poor financial management beginning with Landon's son Wormeley had reduced the land to 1,927 acres. The Carter family slowly lost the influence and wealth it once held, and by the war's beginning, all but two of the plantation's outbuildings had fallen into ruins. The exterior of the mansion became so deteriorated that it was referred to as the "brown house" by the locals. The rich wallpaper brought from England, "some of the oldest and handsomest made," hung down in strips on the walls of the once magnificent interior.[4] Living at Pittsylvania at the time were a brother and four sisters, including 31-year-old Edwin Carter; Emily Carter, 66; Sarah J. Carter, 36; Virginia Carter, 21; and a widowed aunt, Ann H. (Carter) Edwards, 91. A few days prior to the battle, as it became evident a clash between the two great armies was forthcoming, Edwin, realizing that the fight was coming to them, decided to take his entire household, including their twelve faithful slaves, almost all female, to Gainesville to stay with friends for safety.

The Stone House and the Matthews

While the Fauquier and Alexandria Turnpike was being constructed through the Carter domains after the turn of the nineteenth century, Wormley Carter, or more likely his son, Thomas Otway Carter, descended from Landon Carter of Pittsylvania, constructed the Stone House sometime between 1814 and 1829 (the exact date is not known) for use as an "ordinary" by travelers along the new turnpike. The turnpike was a toll road with six tollgates along the route, at intervals of about five miles. The Stone House, located on the northeast corner of the intersection of the Sudley Road and the turnpike, stood directly across from a tollgate located on the southeast corner of the intersection. In 1850, Henry and Jane Matthews acquired the Stone House plus 137 acres of farm land surrounding the dwelling. In addition to farming the land, they continued to operate the Stone House as an inn and tavern serving the needs of travelers

The Stone House (March 1862). The Stone House was owned and operated by Henry and Jane Matthews as an "ordinary" for travelers along the turnpike. During the First Battle of Manassas, it was commandeered by the Union for use as a medical aid station. The picture, a Mathew Brady taken in March 1862, reveals some of the damage it sustained during the First Battle of Manassas. Thirteen months later, it once again found itself in the vortex of battle and came under heavy fire (courtesy Library of Congress).

and teamsters transporting products back and forth from Alexandria and Warrenton. Wheat from the farms of surrounding counties was carried in Conestoga wagons to the mill. The wagoners stayed at the Stone House tavern until the grinding was completed, thus providing much of the tavern's trade. On the eve of the battle, 51-year-old Henry and his 47-year-old wife Jane packed a wagon with what belongings they could gather and drove away to Gainesville to stay with friends.

By midday of July 21, 1861, the Stone House had become a focal point of the battle that raged around it. As the Union forces gained control of the crossroads, the Stone House was commandeered for use as a medical aid station or hospital.

The Matthews of Matthews Hill

One-half mile north of the Stone House lived 43-year-old twin brothers Martin and Edgar Matthews (no relation to Henry and Jane Matthews). Their farm home, situated on top of Matthews Hill, named after their family, was where the two armies first met as the battle started. In addition to the twin brothers, another brother, Carson, 45, and a sister or possibly Carson's wife Jane, 46, also resided therein. The foursome did

Martin and Edgar Matthews' farm and home (March 1862). The home was destroyed by fire sometime in 1900 (courtesy Library of Congress).

not stick around to witness the carnage that would be taking place on their land. Before the armies collided, the Matthews left to stay with friends to wait out the fate of their home and farm land in safety.

The Van Pelts of Avon

A mile to the northeast of the Stone House lived the Abraham Van Pelt family. The Van Pelt family consisted of 71-year-old Abraham, his wife Jeminia, 69, and their three children, a son and two daughters. Abraham Van Pelt found himself much an outcast in the community because of his outspoken disapproval of the Southern cause and secession. This sentiment did not prevail throughout the Van Pelt household, and sometime prior to the full escalation of hostilities, Abraham moved back to his home state of New Jersey, abandoning family, farm and holdings. Later his wife and one daughter, reacting to rumors and fear of being arrested, went north. Elizabeth, the Van Pelts' 36-year-old spinster daughter, did not leave with the other Van Pelts. She stayed in a log tenement on their neighbors' farm, Pittsylvania. During the battle, the home was used as a hospital, and Elizabeth assisted in the care of the wounded brought there. The home and farm known as Avon saw much activity during the next thirteen months.

In 1871, Elizabeth submitted a claim to the Southern Claims Commission against the United States for losses sustained by the Van Pelt home and farm during the war.[5] The decree authorizing the right to file a claim for damages stipulated that the filer had to show he or she was loyal to the Union during the war. Elizabeth's sister and mother

Sketch of the Van Pelt farm and home (Avon). First used as Colonel Nathan Evans's headquarters and later as a Confederate field hospital. The hill where the home and outbuildings stood played a prominent role as a signal station for Colonel Evans in the opening phase of the First Battle of Manassas. The home was destroyed by fire in 1915 (courtesy MNB Files).

were judged loyal to the Confederates; her brother, who was a scout for Union General Marsena Patrick at Second Battle of Manassas, wrote in support of her claim. However, the supporting evidence that was dominant in winning her claim was a letter from Confederate Colonel John Mosby stating that her father, Abraham Van Pelt, was "a notorious union man" and that Mosby had "an order from General Stuart for his arrest."

The Henry Farm and the Judith Henry Family

On a plateau near the intersection of the Sudley road and the Fauquier and Alexandria Turnpike rested the Henry farm, encompassing 137 acres and known as Spring Hill Farm. The Henry farmhouse was situated approximately 400 yards south of the turnpike and 200 yards east of the Sudley Road in the southeast quadrant of the intersection.

In the one and one-half story cottage lived 84-year-old Judith Carter Henry, her 53-year-old daughter Ellen Phoebe Morris Henry, and a young maid named Lucy Griffith who helped care for Mrs. Henry. Mrs. Henry was infirmed by age and bedridden. The Henrys and the Reverend Alexander H. Compton family were close friends, and Lucy Griffith was one of the Comptons' slaves.

At one time, the Spring Hill land was a part of the extensive Carter holdings and had been sold to a man named King who built the cottage in 1812. Later the farm was acquired by Landon Carter Jr. as a home for his sister Betsy Carter. In accordance with surviving English customs of the day, she had been left nothing of her father's land; she lived with her brother, who, as the eldest son, inherited Pittsylvania after their father's death. Betsy Carter remained a spinster and lived out her life with a few slaves she had inherited. Upon her death in the early 1820s she left her property to her sister, Judith Carter Henry.

Judith Henry was the daughter of Landon Carter Sr. of Pittsylvania and the widow of Dr. Isaac Henry. Dr. Henry had been a surgeon on board the frigate *Constellation* under Commodore Truxtun from 1798 to 1800. The Henrys were living near Philadelphia at the time Mrs. Henry inherited Spring Hill Farm. They took possession of Spring Hill in 1825, and four years later, Dr. Henry died there of pneumonia. He was buried in the Carter family cemetery on the Pittsylvania plantation. They had seven children, only four of whom reached the age of maturity: Ellen, John, Hugh Fauntleroy and Landon. Landon served in the Seminole War in Florida and died there of yellow fever. Only John, the eldest, married. He lived in Loudoun County with his family. Hugh lived in Alexandria, where he established a school for boys and tutored special pupils, providing the main support for his mother and sister.

The Henrys did not work the farm land, instead renting out small portions to other farmers. Near the Henry house were fruit trees, and to the south, Mrs. Henry had a small fenced field of sweet corn and a garden.

Ruins of the Henry home (March 1862). Photograph was taken during the interlude period of Union occupation. The original Henry house was a one and one-half story home made uninhabitable after being shelled by Ricketts's artillery that mortally wounded the family matriarch Judith Henry. Not long after the battle, only the foundation and part of the chimney of the Henry home remained. Confederate troops used boards from the house to build shelters and for firewood. The present house, a two-story, gable-end, vernacular dwelling, was constructed in 1870, partially overlapping the original house site; later, expansions were made that added another room to each floor, including a cellar. By the 1890s, the Henry family was charging visitors for tours of the battlefield. The house was bought by the Sons of Confederate Veterans in 1922 for use as a visitors' center. In 1940, the Henry House was donated to the National Park Service to become part of Manassas National Battlefield (courtesy Library of Congress).

On the day of battle, John had ridden out from Loudoun to spend the day, as he often did. When Mrs. Henry's other son Hugh learned of the Union army's movements toward Manassas Junction, he tried to get out of Alexandria to come to his mother, but was unable get through the heavy military activity on the roads. He didn't arrive until Tuesday, two days after the battle, when he learned the fate of the Henry home, his siblings, and his mother. Mrs. Henry had been killed during the battle and was buried the next day.

Robinson House and Family

On the same plateau where the Henrys resided, half mile east of the Henrys and 300 yards south of the turnpike, stood the James Robinson family home. The Robinson family consisted of 58-year-old James, his wife Susan, 56, and their four daughters. James was a free black man, born at Pittsylvania to a slave. According to family history, his father was Landon Carter. It is unknown if James was born free or given his freedom by the Carter family. James married a slave named Susan Gaskins and later bought her out of slavery with money he had saved over a long period of time while working at the Warrenton Springs Hotel. The Robinsons had a total of six children. He was only able to buy the freedom of four.

The Robinson farm home (March 25, 1862). Dating back to 1849, the Robinson house was destroyed in July 1993 by an unknown arsonist (courtesy Library of Congress).

James, affectionately known in the community as "Gentleman Jim," bought 170 acres of the Spring Hill property in 1840 from a man named John Lee. By 1849, James had erected a one and one-half story log cabin, which the Robinson family then occupied. By 1860, James Robinson had become the third largest property holder among free Negroes in Prince William County.

The Robinson house and farm lands would become one of the centers of wartime activities and was a site of some of the fiercest fighting during the first battle. During the Second Battle of Manassas, the Robinson family cared for some of the Union wounded. On the night of August 29, 1862, as battle raged along the Fauquier and Alexandria Turnpike, John Bouvier, a staff officer for General Marsena R. Patrick, was severely wounded with a gunshot through the lungs. The incident occurred as McDowell's forces were breaking off from a fight with the Confederate forces of John Bell Hood: "Riding back with his staff toward the Dogan house, Patrick had reached a dry ditch when he received a challenge from an unknown column of troops in the road. When Patrick identified his brigade the reply shot back, 'Surrender or we fire.' Patrick's group bolted for safety up the rise toward the house. A sharp volley followed, wounding two of Patrick's staff — one being Lt. John V. Bouvier...."[6] Initially, Bouvier was taken to the Dogan House and on the evening of the next day, as Pope's army retreated over the Stone Bridge, Bouvier was taken to a Negro cabin where he was treated by Jeb Stuart's surgeon, Talcott Eliason. Later, after being pardoned and sent to Washington, he was treated at a private home. Bouvier was not able to return to duty until November 1863.[7] In all probability, the Negro cabin where he was left was the Robinson family home.

Lt. John V. Bouvier was destined to live and become the great-grandfather of future First Lady Jacqueline Lee Bouvier Kennedy, wife of President John F. Kennedy.

The Dogans of Rosefield

Located one-fourth mile west of the Sudley Road along the Fauquier and Alexandria Turnpike in the northwest quadrant of the intersection, stood the John D. Dogan family home, known as Rosefield. The Dogan family consisted of 57-year-old John, his wife Ann, 51, and their young daughter Mary, 19. John Dogan was a prosperous farmer, having bought the Rosefield house with 166 acres in 1847. In time his estate expanded to 416 acres. John was a brother-in-law to the widow Lucinda Dogan, whose home and property joined further to the west. All of the battle damage to her property resulted from the Second Battle of Manassas.

The Dogans of Rosefield were in the forefront of heavy fighting on July 21, 1861, and as it became clear that Rosefield was going to be in harm's way, they left their home for safety, returning the next day. However, as was the case with so many other families and farms of this community, the destructiveness of war did not end here for Rosefield. Thirteen months later, the home was destroyed by fire, torched by Sigel's troops on August 30, 1862, during Union retreat at close of the 2nd Battle of Manassas.

The site of John Dogan's family home, Rosefield. The original home was destroyed by fire, torched by Sigel's troops on August 30, 1862, during a Union retreat at the close of the 2nd Battle of Manassas. The present home pictured above, built on the same foundations, is used by the NPS for office space (photograph by the author).

The Lewises of Portici

Located one-half of a mile to the southeast of the Henrys' farm home and 650 yards southwest of Lewis Ford Bull Run crossing, lay the plantation of Portici, a large brick-gabled mansion situated on a steep hill facing the west. The original 762-acre property was part of the vast land holdings of Robert "King" Carter. In 1732, Carter's grandson, Robert "Councilor" Carter, inherited the Lower Bull Run Track, which included the property that would later to be identified as the Portici estate. In 1788, Robert Carter's daughter, Elizabeth Landon Carter (second great-granddaughter of Robert "King" Carter) married Spencer Ball, and in 1812, the Balls acquired the estate from Elizabeth's brother, George Carter. In time, the Portici estate was passed down in succession, first from Spencer Ball to his spouse Elizabeth Carter Ball, and then to her son Alfred Ball. In 1853, the plantation home and 147 acres, including several slaves, passed to Alfred's sister, Fannie Tasker Ball Lewis, and then to her son Frank Lewis. Between 1855 and 1857, Frank Lewis reacquired portions of the original tract, enlarging the Portici estate to 528 acres.

In July 1861, as the grandeur of its past faded, Portici began its descent into the ravages of war. The enjoyment of lively activities and the gaiety of frequent guests and parties at Portici in decades gone by were lost in the chaos of the present as Frank, 39, and his wife Fannie, 30, saw and felt the horrors of war sweep across their home and property over the next thirteen months.

On July 18, Fannie was in bed about to deliver their fourth child when the cannon fire became incessant. Frank had been given a position in the Confederates' local supply department and was away from home at the time. As the sound of battle from Blackburn's Ford became increasingly louder, fear of being caught up in the impending action around Portici was cause for concern. Two of the Lewises' slaves, 41-

The Portici Mansion (March 1862), home of Frank and Fannie Lewis. It was put to use as Confederate General Joseph Johnston's headquarters during the First Battle of Manassas and subsequently became a field hospital. It was destroyed during the Second Battle of Manassas, reportedly by Union soldiers of Pope's retreating army (courtesy Library of Congress)

year-old farm hand William Beckley and one female servant became concerned for Fannie and for their own safety. The two, half-carrying Fannie, led her outside to a nearby gully, and while the woman comforted her, the man cut and gathered branches to lay her on. There she gave birth to a son she named John Beauregard Lewis; the middle name, Beauregard, was in honor of General Beauregard, the Confederate commander.

Following the baby's birth, a team of horses was hitched to a wagon, and Fannie, the newborn baby, Fannie's other three children, and the two slaves traveled out of harm's way to the home of Fannie's father, a farm known as Snow Hill located approximately 4 miles north of the community of Sudley. Over the next three days, savage battles raged across the fields and home of Portici.

On July 21, Portici was used by General Joseph Johnston for his headquarters while he ordered reinforcements from the Confederate defenses along the Bull Run into battle against McDowell's forces then on Henry Hill. In addition, during this time, the massive plantation home was used as a field hospital. Later it received much attention in a diary kept by Fanny Ricketts, wife of Union artillery officer Captain James Ricketts. Ricketts was seriously wounded, taken prisoner, and moved to Portici. Fanny obtained permission from General Beauregard to stay with her husband, and she cared for him in addition to assisting in the care of many other wounded. A copy of the Fanny Ricketts Diary is on file at Manassas National Battlefield Library.

Thirteen months later, during the Second Battle of Manassas, over the fields of Portici below the mansion, a cavalry battle took place. At that time, it was the largest cavalry battle ever to take place on the North American continent.

The Portici mansion was destroyed during the close of Second Battle of Manassas. However, accounts vary as to how this came about. One account states that as Pope's army retreated to Washington, Portici was one of the four exquisite homes within the Sudley Community to be put to the torch by his beaten army. Another account states that it was sometime later that Union soldiers set it afire during the time they occupied the area.

Hazel Plain Plantation (Chinn Family Home)

Chinn Ridge, named for Hazel Plain plantation owner Benjamin Chinn, is located in the southwest quadrant of the Sudley Road and the Fauquier and Alexandria

Ruins of the Chinn family home (Hazel Plain Plantation). View looking northeast, rear of home. Today, only the foundation walls and the bases of four massive chimneys remain of what was once one of the most spacious residences on the Manassas battlefields. Reputedly built in the late eighteenth century, the house derived its name from Benjamin T. Chinn, who purchased the property in 1853. Used as a field hospital during the First and Second Battles of Manassas, it stood until 1950 when the NPS decided to dismantle it. Note the well in left corner of image: The Chinns returned after the battle only to find they could not use the well, as it was filled with amputated arms and legs (courtesy Library of Congress).

Turnpike intersection. The Chinn family consisted of 53-year-old Benjamin, his wife Edmonia, age 33, and their two daughters, Courtenay and Sallie, ages 21 and 20 respectively. Benjamin Chinn was one of the most prosperous farmers in the county.

Chinn Ridge ran almost north and south for about a mile and rested between two branches of water in deep ravines about 3,500 feet apart, Young's Branch to the west and Chinn Branch to the east. The plantation home was situated on the ridge plateau approximately one-half mile west of the Sudley Road and approximately one-half mile south of the turnpike. The home faced mostly to the north in the southern sector of the plateau. In the immediate vicinity of the house were several outbuildings that included an unattached kitchen located to the east of the home, plus a few slave quarters. About 200 yards northeast of the house was a former wagon house; at the time of the two battles it was being used for a chicken coop and woodshed.

In the afternoon of July 21, 1861, the Union army under the command of General Irving McDowell made their last futile advance against the Confederate forces of General P.G.T. Beauregard as they charged across the fields of Benjamin Chinn's plantation at the First Battle of Manassas. Thirteen months later, on the afternoon of August 30, 1862, the Chinn Plantation home and farm lands were caught up again in some of the most horrific fighting of the Second Battle of Manassas as Confederate forces of Longstreet's wing made their famous sweep across "Chinn Ridge" (the battle fought on Chinn Ridge on August 30, 1862, is referred to in Official Records as "Manassas Plains"). The spacious home was used as a hospital during both of the Battles of Manassas. It is not known where the Chinn family members were or what they did during the two battles.

A Little Hamlet Called Groveton

Located along the main east-west corridor through Prince Williams County and just two miles southwest of Sudley proper sits the adjoining hamlet of Groveton at the strategic junction of the Fauquier and Alexandria Turnpike and the Groveton-Sudley Road. Groveton consisted of approximately seven structures. Three of them were situated on the southwest corner of the Turnpike and Groveton-Sudley Road intersection. There was a blacksmith shop (operated by Andrew Redman, a former slave of William Lewis, late father of Lucinda Dogan), and two houses. One of the houses served as the residence of Andrew Redman, located a short distance south of the blacksmith shop, while the other house, located a short distance to the east of Redman, was occupied by 52-year-old Samuel Haislip, a tenant farmer and hired hand of the Dogans. On the northwest corner of the intersection were four structures: a wheelwright shop (rented by F. Thornberry) approximately 100 feet west of the intersection; further to the west, a house serving as a residence, store and tavern (owned by Mary Jane Dogan, stepdaughter to widow Lucinda Dogan); while even further to the west was a barn. The Groveton House, home of Lucinda Dogan, was located slightly north of the wheelwright shop, next to the Sudley-Groveton Road.[8]

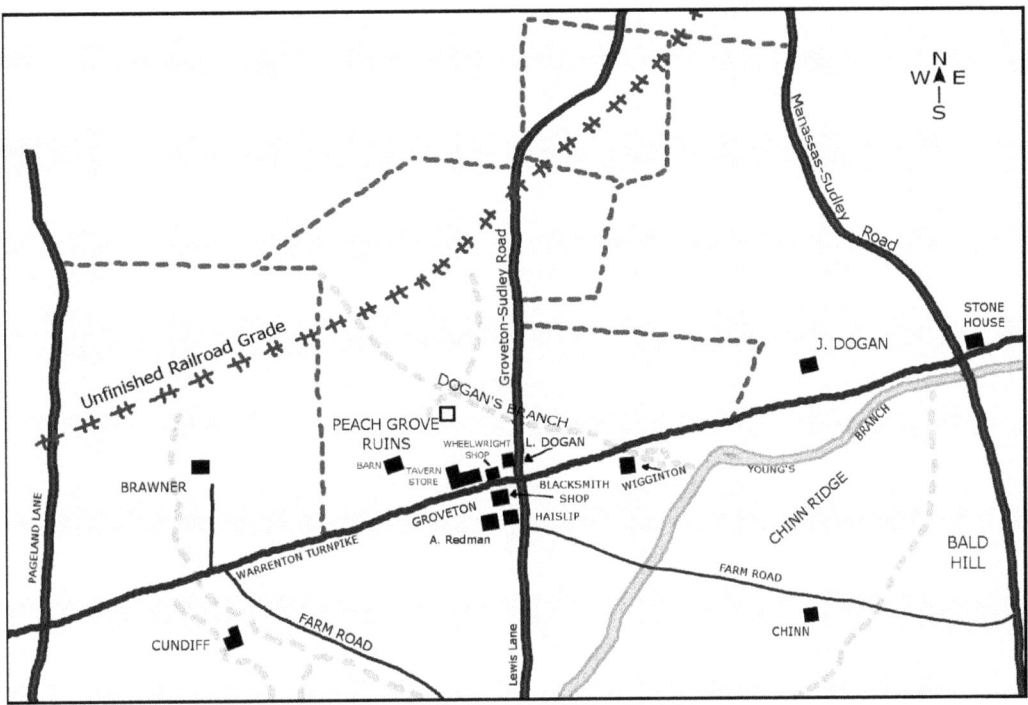

Groveton community — Groveton proper. Drawing by Rachael R. Johnson.

Situated about 300 yards east of the intersection, on the south side of the Fauquier and Alexandria Turnpike, was the Wigginton House. It was occupied by three ladies: 54-year-old Lucy Wigginton; her sister, 49-year-old Susan Wigginton; and their 21-year-old niece, Ann E. Wigginton. The Wigginton House was part of a small tract of 47 acres on Young's Branch reserved in fee simple for Lucinda Dogan's 9-year-old daughter Medora. The Wiggintons rented the house.[9] By end of July 21, the two sisters had played a compassionate role in serving the surviving Henry family with human kindness and comfort.

The Peach Grove Estate and Widow Lucinda Dogan Family

The house where Lucinda Lewis Dogan lived on the eve of the Civil War was in stark contrast to the home she was living in one year earlier. Widowed by the death of her husband William Henry Dogan in 1854, Lucinda Dogan had been living in their plantation home of Peach Grove, located approximately a quarter mile west of the intersection and north of the Turnpike. In 1860, the plantation's stone house was destroyed by fire.[10]

William Henry Dogan was married twice. His first wife, Jane A. Dawson, died approximately one year after their marriage, after giving birth to a daughter, Mary

Jane Dogan. Lucinda, his second wife, bore him eight children over the next ten years. After the tragic fire, Lucinda and her children moved into a 13' × 19' log house located at the northwest quadrant of the Groveton intersection. Typically used as quarters for slaves, farm help, or an overseer, it was made from large oak logs hewn and put together using a notched cornering pattern with the ends slightly extending. Lucinda enlarged their living quarters by moving a wood frame outbuilding from the site of the burned-out home and adding it to the right (north) side of the cabin.[11]

William Henry Dogan's Peach Grove estate had a total area of 710 acres. Although he had provided for his seven surviving children disproportionately in acreage, the total assessed value of the property left to each of the children was about equal. Lucinda was given the larger share, the main tract of Peach Grove, with buildings and 170 acres. William L.B. Wheeler, brother-in-law of Lucinda Dogan and guardian of the children, had the management of their estates. Lucinda ran the farm, a portion of which she rented from the children's estates, establishing about 400 acres surrounded by rail fences and divided into 8 fields. The combined Peach Grove estate properties

Groveton House — the home of Lucinda Dogan. Front view looking west — circa 1949, after the property was added to Manassas National Battlefield holdings. One of three remaining original structures on the battlefield (courtesy MNB Files).

and lands, including all the structures in the hamlet of Groveton, extended north beyond the unfinished railroad grade. In 1854, the commissioners of the Manassas Gap Railroad purchased a strip of land from William H. Dogan which ran through the Dogan property.[12] It was a part of the Unfinished Railroad that served as ready-made breastworks for Jackson's infantry. This easement, 4,245 feet long and eighty feet wide, was the site of some of the bloodiest fighting that took place in the Civil War.

Lucinda had a brother and three sisters. Her brother, Benjamin Franklin ("Frank") Lewis, was a bachelor and a representative in the state legislature for Prince William. Her sister's names were Mary, Bettie, and Addie. Mary remained single but Bettie married John Thomas Leachman, owner of Folly Castle, and Addie married William L.B. Wheeler, owner of Willow Green.

Groveton House — home of Lucinda Dogan. Modern day view (2010), looking west from Groveton-Sudley Road (photograph by Jessica Johnson).

By July 1861, the family living in the Groveton house consisted of 43-year-old Lucinda and her four daughters and two sons. The children's names were Ann, Kate, William, John, Medora, and Jenny, ages 17, 16, 14, 11, 9, and 7 respectively.

The mid–morning hours of Sunday, July 21, 1861, found Lucinda Dogan's family and other residents from around the Groveton community standing at the top of a hill 400 yards east of the Dogan home, drawn there by the thunderous roar of artillery and incessant rattle of musketry fire. Off in the distance to the east, they could see smoke above the trees by the Stone Bridge, and off toward Sudley they could see clouds of dust hovering over the woods. They were witnessing the opening phase of the first major battle of the Civil War. At the same time, seven miles to the east, on a hillside on the western sloops of Centreville, the approximately 200 civilians accompanying the Union army on the march from Washington saw the same thing.

Although the first battle did not extend to the Groveton community, during the intervening months between the first and second battles of Manassas, families living in the area experienced the inhumanity that takes place when two invading armies occupy the same area at different times, including the taking and destruction of property. It was also during this time that Lucinda lost her two oldest daughters, Ann and Kate, to typhoid fever. When warring armies again clashed thirteen months later for the Second Battle of Manassas, the Lucinda Dogan family and her farmlands were once more caught in the vortex of the calamity spreading across the area.

On August 28, 1862, General Jackson's wing of the Confederate forces was present on part of Lucinda Dogan's farmland. Captain W.W. Blackford, an engineer on General Stuart's staff, had been informed by a fellow cavalryman where some buttermilk could be had at a farmhouse a half a mile away. Blackford visited the farmhouse and obtained the buttermilk, returning to Jackson's bivouac site with a filled canteen to share with Jackson and staff. In later years, he gave the following account of the incident[13]:

> Finding General Jackson there [I] gave him some which he enjoyed very much, he said, and thanked me most cordially, for he was now in the best of humor since receiving the dispatch from General Lee. [Word from Lee was that Longstreet's wing was at Thoroughfare Gap.] Old Stonewall had taken a long, deep draught and there was not much left, but this I handed round to the other officers present. Just as the last drop was drained General Ewell rode up and asked what I had, and when I told him buttermilk, with sparkling eyes he said, "For God's sake, give me some," I shook the canteen and told him I was very sorry it was all gone, but if he would send his orderly with me I would show him where he could get some more and fill his canteen for him, a proposal he joyfully accepted. As I started with the orderly, three or four others joined the party and off we trotted. Upon coming in sight of the farmhouse, I discovered five horses hitched in front, which I found by a glance through my field glasses belonged to the enemy, as shown by their equipment.

Blackford and his party charged in and captured four of the five Union soldiers. In addition to the buttermilk, Blackford swept up hot corn cakes, butter, eggs and fried ham into his haversack.

As he and his party were leaving with the four captives and horses, they were fired on by flankers sent out by Hatch in advance of their forward columns, leading King's division marching east on the Warrenton turnpike. Blackford described what happened next: "General Ewell enjoyed the hot corn cakes and buttermilk immensely and had a hearty laugh at my report of the capture. 'Trust a cavalryman for foraging,' said he. Half an hour after this he lost his leg on almost the very spot we were then standing upon." Blackford continued, "Soon after reporting to General Jackson my capture of prisoners and the presence of infantry in large force, which information I had gotten from the prisoners, the head of their column appeared coming down the turnpike, with a heavy line of flankers out and everything in compact order. Jackson rode out to examine the approaching foe."[14]

Although Blackford didn't identify the farmhouse by name, from the description and setting that Blackford provided, it is most likely that he went to the farmhouse of Lucinda Dogan. In the vicinity of the turnpike, the only two farmhouses belonged to John Brawner and Lucinda Dogan. At this time, King's division would have been swarming over Pageland Lane and the turnpike intersection and eastward. They would have been easily seen by Blackford if they were at the Brawner farmhouse. There was a story in local folklore that General Ewell had a meal at Lucinda Dogan's farmhouse. From the account given by Blackford, it would appear that Ewell had a meal not *at* Lucinda's home, but *from* her home.

Sometime during the next day, in the aftermath of the Battle of Brawner Farm, a Confederate officer on horseback approached Lucinda. He came to warn her to "take your family away from the farm," as "there will be fighting here this day." As Lucinda and her children made their way to Folly Castle to be with her sister Bettie, a Union artillery battery with support went into battery opposite her home.[15]

The Leachmans of Brownsville (Folly Castle)

At the Groveton intersections, the Groveton-Sudley Road runs north, but as it continues south from the intersection, its name changes to Lewis Lane. The site where the John (Thomas) Leachman family lived, known as Brownsville but affectionately called Folly Castle,[11] is located approximately one mile south of the Turnpike on Lewis Lane. The family consisted of 39-year-old Thomas, his 37-year-old wife Betty (sister to Lucinda Dogan), two sons, John and Charles, ages 7 and 5 respectively, and two daughters, Edith and Mary, ages 4 and 2 respectively. In addition, 45-year-old farm hand John A. Cooper lived there. During the Second Battle of Manassas, the family remained at home, huddled in the cellar, except for Thomas, who was away, guiding for General Robert E. Lee.[16] He also is reported to have assisted Brig. General Fitzhugh Lee as a guide.

Folly Castle — the John (Thomas) Leachman home, in a painting by French artist Louis Kowalsky as a gift to the Leachman family in appreciation for their kindness they had shown him and his family. In 1885, Kowalsky along with his wife and two-year-old son spent six months at Folly Castle making battlefield sketches for Theophile Poilpot's cyclorama creation of the Second Battle of Bull Run. Folly Castle was destroyed by fire in the spring of 1900 (courtesy of descendant great-great-grandson Thomas Leachman).

The Brawners of Bachelor's Hall

Situated about an equal distance east of Pageland Lane and north of the Fauquier and Alexandria Turnpike was the home of the John C. Brawner family. The family consisted of 58-year- old John Brawner, his 51-year-old wife Jane, their five children named Mary, Sarah, James, Cornelia, and Charles, ages 31, 28, 27, 24, and 20 respectively. John Brawner was a tenant farmer who paid an annual fee of $150 and two-thirds of the harvest to use the farm (about 320 acres, owned by Augusta Douglas).

On the day of the Battle at Brawner Farm, the first day of the three-day Battle of Second Manassas, John became concerned for his family's safety after witnessing the military activity in his immediate surroundings. He packed up his family and placed them in a wagon, sending them to friends in Gainesville, about 5 miles to the west. John stayed behind to guard over their personal belongings, but late in the day, as the

Bachelor's Hall — the John Brawner farmhouse. View looking west-northwest. A photograph of the restored 1868 farmhouse in 2010, the year it was rebuilt. The original farmhouse, a two-story, four-room structure, was built about 1820; the house was caught in the crossfire of the battle on August 28, 1862, and suffered heavy damage. The present structure incorporates the original building and sits on part of the original foundation (photograph by Jessica Johnson).

situation became more dangerous, he left to join his family in Gainesville. Three days later, he returned to find their home severely damaged. Their furniture and personal effects were destroyed and all their farm animals dead, including a pet horse of Mr. Brawner. The Brawners' oldest son, James F. Brawner, was not home during the First and Second Battles of Manassas. On May 13, 1861, he enlisted in Co. B, 8th Virginia Infantry Regiment. During the First Battle of Manassas, James was fighting with Col. Eppa Hunton's 8th Virginia Regiment on Henry Hill. The Brawners' other son, Charles Brawner, was not home during the Second Battle of Manassas. On March 13, 1862, he enlisted in Co. B, 4th Virginia Cavalry. During the Second Battle of Manassas, Charles was fighting with B. Gen. Fitzhugh Lee's 4th Virginia Cavalry and subsequently fought in the area of his family's farm.

Meadowville: The John Cundiff Home

About a quarter of a mile south of the Fauquier and Alexandria Turnpike and almost directly south of the Brawner home lived 50-year-old John Cundiff. John had no family and lived alone except for a 21-year-old farmhand named Levi Payne. The

Meadowville — John Y. Cundiff home. This drawing of the Cundiff home by the author is his concept of the home after investigating archeological studies made of the home site. Today, only the foundation depressions and chimney bases are all that remain. This drawing is featured on the wayside located near the site.

farm had a total of 521 acres, of which 440 acres were actual farm land. Meadowville was used by Union Brigadier General Rufus King's division of Major General Irvin McDowell's Third Corps, Army of Virginia, as a hospital during and after the fight at Brawner Farm on the evening of August 28, 1862, the first day's fight of the three-day Battle of Second Manassas. It is not known where John Cundiff and his farmhand were or what they did during these turbulent hours. After the Second Battle of Manassas, Meadowville, having been riddled with shot, was uninhabitable. John moved to Gainesville to live with his 53-year-old widowed sister, Mary C. Gain.[17]

The Monroes

On a rise located along the east side of Pageland Lane about one-half mile south of the Fauquier and Alexandria Turnpike and Pageland Lane intersection rested the farm home of the William W. Monroe family. The Monroe family consisted of 45-year-old William, his wife Mary C., 46, and their seven children: three daughters, Susan M., age 19, Catherine, age 17, and Ann R., age 8; four sons, John P., age 15, William F., age 13, George L., age 10 and James H., age 2. The acreage of the farm is unknown; however, based on 1860 census records it would have been considered modest as its real estate value was at $3,250 and his personal estate was valued at $2,000.

Information about the family during the Civil War came to light in 1915 when a book titled *Battleground Adventures* was published which contained an interview with a subject described as the "Farmers Daughter." Although not identified by name, from the information contained therein, more than likely the lady being interviewed was Susan Monroe. The family home was uniquely situated on the threshold of activities of the two battles of Manassas. Less than a quarter of a mile south of their home was the Manassas Gap Railroad that ran east and west. Building up to the First Battle of Manassas, the family was able to watch trains that were running day and night carrying Confederate soldiers and supplies to Manassas. In addition, they witnessed from afar the explosion of artillery shells; after the battle, Mr. Monroe traversed the battlefield carrying water and blackberry wine made by Mrs. Monroe, giving aid to the wounded soldiers. During the interlude of the two battles when Union soldiers occupied the area, they suffered indignities at the hands of the soldiers, who stole their farm animals and personal possessions. In the frequent times the soldiers came around, Susan would wear a special hooped dress with hidden pockets to hide silverware and like items. The chickens which provided them eggs were hidden under the house. During the three-day battle of the Second Battle of Manassas and for days in the aftermath, thousands of soldiers traversed about their home and across their farm lands. General Lee made his headquarters on Monroe Hill, located north of the Monroe farm home. Monroe Hill was later renamed Stuart Hill. Susan also provided an eyewitness account of the funerals and mass burials that took place in the aftermath.[18]

Four

The Union Resolve

The Union Mobilizes Armies for War

General in chief of the U.S. Army was Brevet Lieutenant General Winfield Scott, hero of the war with Mexico. Born in Virginia in 1786, Scott entered the Army in 1808 during the presidency of Thomas Jefferson. He rose to prominence in the War of 1812 because of his exploits on the Niagara frontier. In 1841, he rose to rank of general. His brilliant campaign from Vera Cruz to Mexico City in 1847 further enhanced his position as the foremost American soldier of the age. In 1852, he was an unsuccessful candidate for the presidency. Now, nearly seventy-five years old, Scott was in poor physical health, extremely overweight, and physically incapable of riding a horse, so it was impossible for him to take to the field. Regardless, he still retained his mental faculties, and Lincoln looked to him to provide strategic military concepts.

To meet the immediate needs of war's mobilization, Scott chose two generals as field commanders for two new armies being freshly organized. He appointed sixty-nine-year-old Brevet Brigadier General Robert Patterson to command the 18,000 troops opposing Johnston's Confederate forces in the Shenandoah Valley. Patterson had served with the militia in the War of 1812 and had been Scott's second-in-command in Mexico during the Mexican War.

On May 28, Scott reluctantly bowed to political pressure from Treasury Secretary Salmon P. Chase and appointed forty-two-year-old Brevet Major General Irvin McDowell to command the Army of Northeastern Virginia. McDowell was a West Point graduate and had been commissioned in the artillery but spent most of his career as assistant adjutant general on Scott's staff. (McDowell and Beauregard were West Point classmates in the class of 1838. Out of the class of 45 cadets, Beauregard was ranked number two and McDowell's ranking was twenty-three.)

Of priority was McDowell's task to organize his command into five divisions:

1st Division: Commanded by Brigadier General Daniel Tyler, West Pointer and authority on artillery maneuvers. Tyler's division consisted of four brigades: 1st Brigade, under Colonel Erasmus D. Keyes, West Point graduate and instructor, Indian fighter, and specialist in coastal defense; 2nd Brigade, Brigadier General Robert C. Schenck, former

U.S. Congressman from Ohio, minister to Brazil and the United Kingdom; 3rd Brigade, Colonel William T. Sherman, West Pointer and Mexican War veteran; 4th Brigade, Colonel Isaac B. Richardson, West Pointer and Indian fighter, known as "Fighting Dick," a nickname he acquired during the Mexican War.

2nd Division: Commanded by Colonel David Hunter, West Pointer and Mexican War veteran. The division consisted of the 1st Brigade, led by Colonel David Porter, West Pointer and Mexican War veteran; 2nd Brigade, Colonel Ambrose E. Burnside, West Pointer, Mexican War veteran, and firearms manufacturer; distinguished also by his unusual growth of side whiskers, for which the term "sideburns" was coined.

3rd Division: Commanded by Colonel Samuel P. Heintzelman, West Pointer, Indian fighter and Mexican War veteran. The division consisted of 1st Brigade, led by Colonel William B. Franklin, West Point graduate, instructor and Mexican War veteran; 2nd Brigade, Colonel Orlando Bolivar Willcox, West Pointer, Indian fighter and Mexican War veteran; 3rd Brigade, Colonel Oliver O. Howard, West Point graduate, instructor and Indian fighter.

4th Division: Commanded by Brigadier General Theodore Runyon, native of New Jersey, Yale Law School graduate, admitted to the bar of New Jersey in 1846, honored with the degree of LL.D. by Rutgers College and Wesleyan University; commissioned brigadier general of militia 1857–1860, and in 1861 appointed brigadier general of New Jersey Volunteers. The division consisted of three New Jersey regiments (1st, 2nd, and 3rd New Jersey), one New York regiment (41st New York), and four New Jersey militias (1st, 2nd, 3rd, and 4th New Jersey Militia).

5th Division: Commanded by Colonel Dixon S. Miles, a West Point graduate. The division consisted of 1st Brigade, under Colonel Lewis Blenker, a German officer who had served with the Bavarian Legion; and 2nd Brigade, under Colonel Thomas A. Davies, a West Pointer and Indian fighter.

Initially, McDowell's Army of Northeastern Virginia numbered about 20,000, but a constant flow of barely-trained regiments were arriving. As early as June 3, Scott was pushing McDowell to come up with a plan. Mc Dowell insisted he must have ample time for the troops to receive proper training, that they were "green." Scott conveyed McDowell's concerns to Lincoln, and Lincoln replied, "The Confederates are green too."[1]

McDowell Presents His Battle Plan

Finally, on June 29, after several preliminary plans constantly changed due to new reports of Confederate activity, and pushed by the impatience of Lincoln and his administration, McDowell presented his plan before Lincoln and his cabinet. Present at the meeting were Scott; Colonel Joseph K.F. Mansfield, commander of the Department of the District of Columbia; Brigadier General Montgomery C. Meigs, quartermaster general of the Army; Tyler; and Major General John C. Fremont. McDowell proposed to take 30,000 men, keeping another 10,000 in reserve, and advance upon Manassas via three routes. Tyler would lead the largest column, moving by way of Vienna. David Hunter would command the center column, advancing by way of the Little River turnpike, and Heintzelman would lead the left-flank column. Tyler's column would cut between Centreville and Fairfax Court House to join Hunter's column. Heintzelman's column would continue straight along the line of the Orange and Alexandria and join Tyler's and Heintzelman's columns at a point north of Bull Run. Runyon's Division would take a position seven miles east of Manassas to guard communications. McDowell was aware that Beauregard had fortified the major crossings across the Bull Run along a stretch of eight miles and protected by well-placed artillery batteries. He did not want to confront the Confederate forces at any of those crossings. Instead he proposed advancing around their right flank and cutting off Beauregard's rail connection with Richmond by moving on the bridge crossing over Broad Run at Bristoe, about five miles south of Manassas. He reasoned that, with the threat of Beauregard's communications and supply route being severed, he would withdraw back to the Rappahannock, thus affording the Union forces a better position to do battle.[2]

McDowell was quick to emphasize that the success of his plan was predicated upon Patterson's holding Johnston. Scott assured McDowell that Patterson would be successful. Lincoln then asked when the campaign would begin; Scott spoke up and said, "In one week." McDowell was dismayed and almost horrified, as it gave him very little time.

As July 8 arrived, the day Scott reported the campaign was to begin, it was apparent the Army of Northeastern Virginia was not ready, as it was still being organized. Two more given dates came and went and McDowell's army still was not ready. All efforts to delay the advance until such time as adequate training might provide him with an effective fighting force had proved in vain. Pressure for a forward movement was enhanced by the realization that the term of enlistment was quickly expiring for a large number of the troops. The situation demanded action or the loss of their services.

Meanwhile, on July 9, Beauregard sent the following dispatch to President Davis[3]: "Enemy's force increasing, and advancing daily this side of the Potomac. He will soon attack with very superior numbers. No time should be lost in re-enforcing me here with at least ten thousand men—volunteers or militia...."

Confederate Clandestine Activities Unfold

The first results of Rose Greenhow's spy activities were about to unfold. McDowell's closely guarded plans and activities were not safe from Rose's special talents for gathering secret information. Within days after McDowell had disclosed his plans to Lincoln and Scott, Rose sent one of her newly acquired "agents" to Beauregard with a message alerting him of the Union plans. Betty Duval was a daughter of one of Rose's neighbors. Later she was described by General Bonham as "a beautiful young lady, a brunette with sparkling black eyes, perfect features, glossy black hair, a fine person of medium height."[4] Rose had helped Betty disguise herself as a country girl and had hired a farmer with a market cart to drive her across the Potomac at the Chain Bridge to Virginia and the home of friends, where she spent the night. Early the next morning, the young ladies of the house furnished Betty with a riding dress and a horse, and from there she rode fast and furious by back roads to the Confederate picket line at Fairfax

Court House. Upon being challenged, she shouted, "Quickly, take me to your commander, I have an important message for General Beauregard."

"General Bonham is our commander here, ma'am," answered one of the pickets. "I'll take you to him."

As Betty Duval was brought into Bonham's office, he was startled when he looked up and saw the young girl with the pretty face. Before he could speak, she immediately spoke out, "I am the bearer of a very important dispatch for General Beauregard."

Bonham quickly responded, "Yes, yes, I will have it safely taken to him at once." He quickly added, "I have seen you before ... yes, I recollect now, I once saw you in the gallery of the House of Representatives at Washington, last December it was."

"Yes," Betty responded, "I was there and I remember seeing you too, but you were Congressman Bonham then." With that said, she took out a tucking comb and let fall what Bonham later described as "the longest and most beautiful roll of hair I have ever seen on a human head." Betty then took from the back of her head, where it was safely tied, a small package not larger than a silver half-dollar. Rose had sewed up the packet in black silk, which she said "contained the important information."[5]

The small packet was taken by one of Bonham's staff, galloping his horse all the way to Beauregard's headquarters. Jordan, now a colonel on Beauregard's staff, delicately opened and decrypted the message. The message read, "McDowell has certainly been ordered to advance on the sixteenth." Beauregard telegraphed Davis and Cooper of this latest news and reiterated his critical need for Johnston to reinforce him. Davis responded to Beauregard that they needed further confirmation of McDowell's movements before he could order Johnston out of the valley. To this end, Jordan sent one of his new operatives, a man by the name of G. Donellan, into Washington to gather more information from Rose.

Two days after Rose had sent Betty Duval to Beauregard with her initial encrypted message of McDowell's date for advance, she sent Miss Duval a second time, repeating her same movements in reaching Beauregard as before. Rose's second encrypted message was information of the plan that McDowell had presented to Lincoln and Scott at their meeting of June 29. Beauregard not only knew the date of McDowell's planned advance, but also his plans to advance around the Confederate's right flank, cutting off Beauregard's communications and supplies and thus culminating in a final battle along the Rappahannock.

At one time, Donellan had been employed as a clerk with the Department of the Interior and was no stranger to Rose. Donellan arrived at the Greenhows' home on July 16 and presented a note from Jordan that simply stated, *"Trust the bearer."* Donellan departed Washington by buggy about noon of the same day with an encrypted note from Rose concealed on his person. After eluding and outwitting Union guards and making his way through the heavy military activity in the streets of Washington, Donellan successfully crossed the Potomac. When clear of Federal forces and at a prearranged place, he switched to a swift horse, and that same day, July 16, arrived at Liberia about 8 o'clock in the evening. After removing the message hidden in the heel of one of his boots, Donellan presented the message to Jordan. Jordan quickly deciphered it. It stated that McDowell with 55,000 troops "would positively commence this day to advance from Arlington Heights and Alexandria on to Manassas, via Fairfax Court House and Centreville."[6]

Federal Army Advances on Manassas

No longer able to ward off the prodding from the president and the press, on July 16, McDowell set the Federal army in motion. With excitement and high expectations, the army took to the road 35,000 strong and accompanied by many of Washington's elite in fine carriages. Splendidly dressed in new uniforms with regimental and national colors gaily displayed, the army advanced. The first day, the army reached Annandale, having covered only six miles. Oppressive heat, dust, thirst, heavy equipment and lack of discipline caused the raw recruits to straggle badly. Willfully they fell out along the way to drink from every stream and well they passed or to pick blackberries. In addition, looting and the destruction of property abounded as many carried off almost anything they could get their hands on.

The next day, marching four abreast with bands playing and flags waving, Hunter's division triumphantly entered Fairfax Court House. The excitement heightened as they encountered some of Beauregard's outpost scrambling away before them and leaving behind large quantities of forage and camp supplies.

From Fairfax Court House, the Union army slowly advanced toward Centreville, sending engineers and details with axes ahead to clear the roads of felled trees and uncover "masked artillery batteries."

Davis Responds to Beauregard's Plea

The collapse of his outposts, the lack of any word that Johnston was coming to his assistance, and the belief he was out numbered 2 to 1 only added to Beauregard's anxiety. On July 17, Beauregard sent a tempered-frustrated message to Richmond by telegraph that read[7]: "The enemy has assailed my outposts in heavy force, I have fallen back on the Bull Run, and will make a stand at Mitchell's Ford. If his force is overwhelming, I shall retire to the Rappahannock railroad Bridge, saving my command for defense there, and future operations. Please inform Johnston of this, via Staunton, and also Holmes. Send forward any reinforcements at the earliest possible instant and to every possible means...."

In the face of this crisis, Davis acted quickly and sent the following dispatch, dated July 17, 1861, to Johnston in Winchester[8]: "General Beauregard is attacked.

Colonel Wade Hampton. Founder, commander, and financer of the 600 strong Hampton's Legion (courtesy Library of Congress).

To strike the enemy a decisive blow a junction of all your effective force will be needed. If practicable, make the movement, sending your sick and baggage to Culpeper Courthouse either by railroad or by Warrenton. In all the arrangements exercise your discretion." In addition, Davis advised Beauregard he had ordered Brig. Gen. Theophilus Holmes's reserve brigade (consisting of the 1st Arkansas and 2nd Tennessee Infantry Regiments and the Purcell Artillery of 6 guns) up from Fredericksburg, and had dispatched Colonel Wade Hampton's six-company legion, McRae's regiment, and two battalions of Mississippi and Alabama troops under orders.[9]

The Hampton Legion was recruited and organized by Wade Hampton, a South Carolinian plantation owner. He recruited 600 men and organized them into six companies of infantry, four companies of cavalry, and one artillery battery, and personally financed their clothing, equipment, and weapons.

Hampton grew up in one of the wealthiest families in the South. Described as a large and agile man, six feet tall with broad shoulders, he had an active outdoor life as an exquisite horseman and avid hunter. Traditional stories claim he hunted bear with only a knife and credit him with killing as many as 80 bears; it was said he could lift his bear kills of 400 pounds onto the back of a pack horse, all by himself. He graduated from South Carolina University with a law degree but never pursued a law practice. Instead, he devoted himself to state politics and the management of his vast property holdings that included plantations in South Carolina and Mississippi. In 1852, he was elected to the South Carolina General Assembly and later to the State Senate, where he served from 1858 to 1861.

Hampton opposed secession, but he was loyal to his home state when war came, enlisting as a private in the South Carolina Militia. South Carolina governor Pickens was adamant that he accept a colonel's commission and encouraged him to organize a military unit. Although 42 years old at the time and with little or no military experience, Hampton was a natural cavalryman, since he was brave, audacious, and a superb horseman.

A General's Frustrations

As late as July 18, an exchange of messages between Scott and Patterson seemingly put concerns to rest which Scott and the president shared: would Patterson be successful in preventing Johnson from joining forces with Beauregard at Manassas? Scott had not heard from Patterson, and on July 18, 1861, sent him a steaming message that read[10]: "I have certainly been expecting you to beat the enemy. If not, to hear that you have felt him strongly, or, at least, had occupied him by threats and demonstrations. You have been at least his equal, and I suppose, superior in numbers. Has he not stolen a march and sent reinforcements toward Manassas Junction? A week is enough to win victories."

However, Patterson's response was not a true representation of the military actions developing in the valley. In a turnaround answer to Scott on that same date, he stated[11]: "Telegram of to-day received. The enemy has stolen no march upon me. I have kept him actively employed, and by threats and reconnaissance's in force caused him to be reinforced. I have accomplished in this respect more than the General-in-Chief asked, or could well be expected, in face of an enemy far superior in numbers, with no line of communication to protect."

Preparatory to the advance upon Manassas, McDowell had been assured by Scott that he would not have to face a combined Confederate force since Patterson would contain Johnston. Fast-moving events already set in motion fully justified Scott's earlier doubts about Patterson and his concern for the success of McDowell's invading force.

Beauregard Realigns His Defenses

On July 17, Beauregard had ordered all his forces back across the Bull Run. Bull Run is a small stream that begins near the village of Aldie, located 35 miles northeast of Sudley. It meanders about amid fields and roads until it empties into the Occoquan. It runs between Centreville and Manassas, about 3 miles from each place. By July 18, all six of Beauregard's brigades were entrenched at or near seven crossing points, having taken up positions at six fords and a bridge, with a portion of these forces in reserve within supporting distance. The combined strength of Beauregard's forces, totaling about 18,000, lay along an eight-mile stretch of Bull Run. He had skillfully realigned his defensive positions from east to west as follows[12]:

Union Mills Ford, near the railroad: Second Brigade, consisting of three regiments of infantry, four twelve-pounder howitzers, and three companies of cavalry; commanded by Colonel Richard S. Ewell. Ewell was a Mexican War veteran and Indian fighter.

McLean's Ford: Third Brigade, consisting of three regiments, two brass six-pounder cannon, and one company of cavalry; commanded by Brigadier General David R. Jones. Jones was a West Point graduate, Indian fighter and a Mexican War veteran.

Blackburn's Ford: Fourth Brigade, consisting of three regiments, and two six-pounder cannon; commanded by Brigadier General James Longstreet. Longstreet was a West Point graduate, Indian fighter, and Mexican War veteran.

Mitchell's Ford, in the center: First Brigade, consisting of four regiments, two batteries of artillery, and six companies of cavalry: commanded by Brigadier General Milledge L. Bonham.

Ball's and Lewis's Fords, three miles farther west and near Stone Bridge: Fifth Brigade, consisting of three regiments, one artillery battery, and one company of cavalry; commanded by Colonel Philip St. George Cocke.

Stone Bridge: Seventh Brigade, consisting of one regiment and a battalion of infantry, four six-pounder cannon, and two companies of cavalry; commanded by Colonel Nathan G. "Shanks" Evans.

The main road out of Centreville to Manassas crossed at Mitchell's Ford, where Beauregard had entrenched a portion of his forces under Bonham. About a half mile downstream, Longstreet covered Blackburn's Ford, where another road led to Manassas. With this the approximate center, the Confederate line stretched eight miles from Ewell's position at Union Mills to the right of Evans at the Stone bridge.

During the morning hours of July 18, Beauregard had transferred his headquarters from Liberia to a point about one mile southwest of Mitchell Ford, the McLean House.

History of the McLean House (Yorkshire Plantation)

Unfortunately, there are no known images of the Wilmer McLean Home. Dating back to circa 1809, Yorkshire was a large 2½ story house situated on 1200 acres of farm land located about 1⅛ mile south-southeast of Blackburn's Ford and 600 yards west-northwest of McLean's Ford. Virginia Beverly Hooe Mason, a wealthy widow with two young daughters, was sole owner of the estate. In 1853, one day prior to her wedding to the much-in-debt Wilmer McLean, Virginia signed a marriage contract that placed all her holdings in trust for her sole separate and exclusive use, and freeing her absolutely from all liability for the debts present and future of said Wilmer McLean.

In the mid–morning hours of July 18, 1861, the McLeans were visited by an aide to General Beauregard, who announced he was serving notice that the house would become the general's temporary headquarters. It is believed they went to stay at the A.S. Grigsby farm adjacent to the McLean property on the north side of Bull Run. Mrs. McLean's second daughter, Ocie Mason, was an outgoing teenager and an excellent equestrienne. In the early morning hours of July 21, she was out riding dangerously between the lines on the day of the great battle and came across Union soldiers constructing a barricade near their artillery position. Brazenly she shouted out, "Why are you obstructing our roads?"—and then quickly turned her horse and galloped off to report what she saw to General Ewell at Union Mills.

The Battle of Bull Run at Blackburn's Ford began about noon on July 18, and while a meal was being prepared for General Beauregard and his staff, an artillery duel had begun between opposing batteries. A Union shell overshooting its target crashed into the chimney of the kitchen dwelling and exploded in an iron skillet of stew, causing heavy damage. A second shell hit the main house. A large barn built by the McLeans in 1857 featured prominently during the First Battle of Manassas and the days after. It was used as a hospital and as a holding facility for Union prisoners, notably the captured Congressman Alfred Ely. Ely was observing the battle near the Bull Run when he was caught up in the Union army's frantic retreat and taken prisoner. He was held overnight in the McLean barn prior to being sent off to Libby Prison in Richmond.

Shortly after the Battle of Manassas, Mrs. McLean packed up her four children, Maria Mason, age 17; Ocie Mason, age 16; John Wilmer Mclean, age 7; and Lucretia Virginia McLean, age 4, and left for Appomattox, Virginia. Wilmer remained in the Centerville-Manassas area until March of 1863 working for the Confederate quartermaster, buying supplies in Richmond then selling them at exorbitant prices to the army in Manassas. At war's end, Wilmer McLean became known as an individual upon whom fate had fallen with a strange twist: the war began with the chaos inside his house and kitchen and ended almost four years later with the surrender ceremony of Gen. Robert

E. Lee to Gen. Ulysses S. Grant in the parlor of his home at Appomattox, a remote village some 125 miles distant from Manassas.

July 18, Battle at Bull Run — Blackburn's Ford — Prelude to First Battle of Manassas

By noon of July 18, most of the main body of McDowell's army had reached its objective and was gathering along the heights of Centreville. In the late morning hours, Brigadier General Daniel Tyler, McDowell's lead division commander, had advanced on Centreville and seized the town.

McDowell's written orders to Tyler to take the town of Centreville had been explicit: "After advancing on the town, observe well the roads to Bull Run and to Warrenton. Do not bring on an engagement, but keep up the impression that we are moving on Manassas."[13]

About noon, with his 4th Brigade commander Isaac Richardson leading, Tyler advanced with skirmishers thrown out to "scour the thick woods" of the Bull Run bottom lands.[14] The northern bank of the stream rose with a steep slope at least fifty feet above the level of the water, leaving a narrow path in front of the ford of some twenty yards. The southern bank was almost a plain, elevated only about five or six feet above the water for several hundred yards.[15] After discovering a low opening near the stream, Richardson ordered up two howitzers to "blast the Confederates out and sweep all road approaches to Blackburn's Ford." Confederate artillery responded and a sharp artillery duel followed but quickly ended as Richardson's batteries were forced to withdraw.[16]

It was then that Richardson ordered up the 12th New York, which boldly advanced but immediately broke as they came under severe heavy fire from Longstreet's Virginians. Early's brigade moved rapidly up to aid in the repulse.

Reports of Tyler's zealous attack at Blackburn's Ford and forced withdrawal to Centreville spread rapidly throughout McDowell's command. It had a depressing effect on Union morale. McDowell was vocally critical of Tyler's actions that had exceeded his orders and brought on an early confrontation.

However, Tyler's action did reveal to McDowell that Beauregard had amassed his strength in the sector of Blackburn's Ford and further southeast along the Bull Run as far as Union Mills Ford and near the railroad. In addition, McDowell also determined that the terrain for a left flank movement around the Confederates' right was not suitable for moving his army en masse. Forced to come up with a new plan to defeat his awakening foe, McDowell began reconnoitering for ways to move around on Beauregard's left. He sent two of his engineers, Major John G. Barnard and Captain Alexander, to scout out the area. The engineers found a local citizen, Mathias C. Mitchell, who told them that he knew of some back trails and that he would lead them to a crossing over the Bull Run about three miles upstream from the Stone Bridge. McDowell spent the next two days developing his new tactical plan and bringing up supplies, all of which led to costly delays.[17]

Evans Begins Defensive Preparations at Confederates' Far Left Flank

Anticipating an attack in his sector, Evans, with his small command of some 1100, was busily engaged in strengthening his defenses at the Stone Bridge. The 37-year-old colonel was a West Point graduate and known for being a tough, irreverent fighter and a hard drinker. In the early morning hours of July 18, the sound of the axe and the crash of falling trees could be heard, as the Fourth South Carolina and Major Roberdeau Wheat's 1st Louisiana Tigers built roadblocks along the pike in the area of the Stone Bridge, close to where the Van Pelt house sat on the hill. Wheat's Special Battalion of Louisiana Volunteers was known initially as Wheat's Battalion, later as the Louisiana Tigers. They were a unique Confederate Unit recruited from the docks of New Orleans by Wheat and haughtily described as "lawless brigands." Company B was known as the "Tiger Rifles," commanded by Capt. Alexander White. Later they gave their name and character to the whole battalion. It was the only company in Wheat's Battalion that wore the Zouave uniform. They wore trousers of blue and white striped bed ticking, red jackets, and skullcaps with a long black tassel. The company was armed with Harpers Ferry short rifles, with saber Bowie knife bayonets. The rest of the battalion wore blue uniforms.

Stone Bridge (March 1862). Ruins of the Stone Bridge, looking west towards Evans's position in the area of the hill where the Van Pelt house sat. The barren appearance is the result of the trees' having been cut by Evans's forces for construction of makeshift roadblocks along the pike, west of Stone Bridge. The picture depicts the bridge after it was blown up by McDowell's retreating army (courtesy Library of Congress).

Johnston Eludes Patterson and Reinforces Beauregard

The tactical situation that allowed Johnston to elude Patterson began on July 16. Patterson moved on Johnston and occupied Bunker Hill, keeping him in check at Winchester, 9 miles to the south. Communication had been heavy between Scott and Patterson. Patterson had been informed that July 16 was the date set for McDowell to begin his march on Manassas, and Scott was pressing Patterson hard to suppress and keep Johnston from reinforcing Beauregard. Subsequently, Patterson's orders from Scott were[18] "to hold rebel forces in his front on the alert and to prevent it from re-enforcing Manassas Junction by means of threatening maneuvers and demonstrations...."

Patterson, confused and uncertain, reasoned that by now it would be too late for Johnston to reinforce Beauregard and that he had indeed fulfilled his orders from Scott to prevent Johnston from assisting Beauregard at Manassas. He made an ill-fated decision to fall back to Charlestown to be closer to Washington and his line of communications. Thirty-three miles now separated Johnston and Patterson. This latest movement by Patterson severed the close link of the two armies and accorded Johnston the opportunity to break away. Acting promptly upon Davis's telegram of July 17, Johnston made provisions for his 1700 sick to be cared for at Winchester, and began demonstrating against Patterson to cause him to believe he was being heavily attacked.

Jeb Stuart and his cavalry unit of 350 men were sent to Charlestown to seal off roads and communications from Patterson and to screen Johnston's movements by creating dust and confusion.

Having completed the details to begin his stealth march to Manassas, Johnston and his staff rode hard to Piedmont Station to organize the rail transportation needed to carry his army to Manassas. In military history annals, this is the first time rail transportation was used to transport troops into a battle.

While Patterson was wiring Scott about his successful defense of his position against overwhelming odds, Johnston was moving rapidly by forced marches and rail to reinforce Beauregard. The past few months had proved stressful and confusing for the old warrior, bringing about his forced retirement six days after the battle at Manassas.

Starting about noon on July 18, Jackson led the Confederate troops from Winchester and forded the Shenandoah River. At nightfall, they reached the village of Paris near Ashby Gap (where modern Route 50 crosses the Blue Ridge), where they spent a few hours resting and sleeping. At first light the next day, they marched south, passing near Edmonds and on to Piedmont Station (modern-day Delaplane) where the road (modern day Route 17) and the railroad both crossed Goose Creek.[19]

Arriving at Piedmont on the line of the Manassas Gap, Jackson's brigade was the first force to entrain for Manassas. On July 19, Jackson detrained at Manassas Junction 2,500 strong,[20] having traveled twenty-three miles marching and thirty-four miles by train, a total distance of fifty-seven miles in twenty-five hours.

At sunrise the next morning, the 7th and 8th Georgia of Bartow's brigade arrived, more of Johnston's reinforcements, numbering 1,400 men. About noon, Johnston himself arrived accompanied by Bee with the 4th Alabama, the 2nd Mississippi and two companies of the 11th Mississippi.[21]

Shortly after Johnston's arrival, the two commanders met and the first order of business was the subject of command. Prior to Johnston's departure from the Shenandoah Valley, he anticipated a possible confrontation with Beauregard concerning who would command when the two armies merged. He wired Davis on the subject. Davis's reply was awaiting Johnston when he detrained in Manassas and it alluded to the fact that Johnston was a full general, Beauregard was a brigadier general, and therefore Johnston was in command.[22] Johnston then issued a general order dated July 20, 1861, that read: "By direction of the President of the Confederate States Genl. Joseph E. Johnston assumes command of the Army of the Potomac."

From the time Johnston's command began detraining at Manassas Junction in the late hours of July 19, the Confederate camp became a scene of feverish activity. As Johnston's reinforcements moved up to position in the line, Beauregard and Johnston conferred on plans for an offensive. Having prior knowledge of McDowell's initial plans, Beauregard was not aware that instead of advancing around the Confederate right, he would be advancing on the Confederate far left flank. At 4:30 A.M. on July 21, Beauregard completed his battle plan and dispatched it to Johnston who quickly approved it.[23] In essence, the strategy of Beauregard's plan was to turn McDowell's left flank and cut off the expected retreat of McDowell's forces to Washington.

Five

July 21 — First Battle of Manassas

The First Shot

Sunday, July 21, dawned with a blood red sky. A typical early morning Virginia summer day began with the drone of the locust and the listless stirring of the trees gave early promise that the day would be hot. Dust lay thick upon the brush and the uniforms of the men. From a fitful sleep, broken frequently by the oft repeated distant railway whistle at the Junction, the Confederate camps began to stir. Since 4:30 A.M., muffled voices of command and the sounds of cannon wheels on the Fauquier and Alexandria turnpike drifted across the hills. The sounds carried an ominous import to the Sudley community and surrounding areas.[1]

Shortly after sunrise, a sharp-ringing thunderous report shattered the early morning quiet. The shot was fired from a 30-pounder Parrott rifle nicknamed "Long Tom." The gun was attached to the battery of Captain J. Howard Carlisle, the commander of Company E, 2nd U.S. Artillery, and was under the direction of Lieutenant Peter C. Hains of the U.S. Artillery Corps. Hains placed the massive gun in battery on the high ground, east of Bull Run and in the middle of the Fauquier and Alexandria Turnpike. The shell exploded west of the Stone Bridge in the area of Evans's position. Smoke shrouded the ponderous gun as the recoil pushed it back six feet from its firing position. With this shot, the first major battle of the Civil War was on. Hains's artillerymen quickly moved into action and the 30-pounder belched fire twice more. From their vantage point, the artillerymen could see crowds of Confederates off in the distance beyond the Stone Bridge, in the adjacent woods.[2] There was no response from Evans's artillery: not only were all his guns outranged, but Evans wanted his guns to remain silent so as to create a ploy.

McDowell Puts His New Plan in Motion

Since 2:30 that morning, McDowell had been putting into action his new plan for a three-pronged attack. Tyler's initial role was to make a feinting thrust at the Stone Bridge, while Richardson demonstrated at Blackburn's Ford. The two diversions would be for the purpose of screening the main flanking columns of the divisions of Hunter and Heintzelman while they advanced upon the Confederate left by way of Sudley Ford. Miles's division was to protect the rear at Centreville while Runyon's division covered the road to Washington.³ The success of his plan would be predicated on two essentials: rapid execution and the element of surprise.

Delays plagued the movement from the start. Initially there was a long wait to permit Keyes's brigade of Tyler's division to move up from the rear, then a further delay was caused by Hains's big 30-pounder Parrott blocking the road.⁴ At 2½ tons, the gun required ten horses to pull it.

Shortly after Hains fired his 30-pounder Parrott on the Confederates' left flank, per McDowell's plan, Richardson's guns opened at Blackburn's Ford. A short distance to the west of Cub Run Bridge, McDowell's main column made a right turn off the Fauquier and Alexandria Turnpike and followed a narrow trail-like road to Sudley Ford. From the start, McDowell's march had been plagued with delays, and it was not until 9:30 A.M. that they reached the ford. Here the men stopped to drink and fill canteens from Bull Run. Despite delays causing McDowell's advance to be more than two and a half hours behind schedule, they confidently felt that success would still be theirs.⁵

Johnston and Beauregard Await the Confederate Attack

While McDowell was putting his new plan in motion, the Confederate commanders were busy trying to launch Beauregard's plan to turn McDowell's left flank. About 8:30 A.M., Beauregard and Johnston rode to the top of a hill near Mitchell's Ford to watch and await the opening phase. Beauregard's plans called for his center and right to advance and vigorously attack the Federal left flank and rear at Centreville, while his left under Cocke and Evans would sustain a possible Federal attack in the quarter of the Stone Bridge. The center was likewise to advance and engage the enemy in front, and directions were given for the reserves, "when without orders," to move toward the sound of the heaviest firing. Beauregard's forces to the right of Mitchell's Ford were to advance via the Bull Run crossing at that point; Bonham would advance from Mitchell's Ford, Longstreet from Blackburn's Ford, D.R. Jones from McLean's Ford, and Ewell from Union Mills by the Centreville road. Ewell, since he had the longest march, was to begin the movement, and each brigade was to be followed by its reserve.⁶

Earlier, Beauregard had received reports that enemy forces were advancing from Centreville on the Fauquier and Alexandria Turnpike and were deploying a force in front of Evans. Upon receiving dispatches of enemy movements from his observation signal officer at Signal Hill, coupled with the sounds of scattering musketry fire on his left, Beauregard ordered Jackson's brigade "to the support of General Bonham, afterwards to support General Cocke, and finally to take such position as would enable him to reinforce either Bonham or Cocke as circumstances might require."⁷ In addition, he sent the brigades of Bee and Bartow, under the overall command of Bee, to bolster the support on his left.

Meanwhile, in rear of Mitchell's Ford, Beauregard and Johnston had been impatiently waiting for the sound of conflict to open in the quarter of Centreville. Shortly,

General D.R. Jones reported that while he had long been ready for the movement upon Centreville per Beauregard's orders, General Ewell had not come up to form on his right, though he had sent him a copy of his own orders at 7 A.M. and again at 8 o'clock, which recited that Ewell had already been ordered to begin the movement. Beauregard immediately dispatched orders to Ewell to advance. Ewell swiftly acknowledged receipt of this last message from Beauregard while also advising him he had received no prior orders to advance.

By 10:15 A.M., the firing on the Confederate left had begun to increase in intensity, indicating a severe attack. Seeing that his plans had gone awry, Beauregard realized a change in tactics was desperately needed to respond to events unfolding on his left. Beauregard's original plan involved a flanking attack on the Federal left, but the early movements of McDowell in the execution of his new plan, the delayed arrival of Johnston's reinforcements and miscarriages in the dispatching of Beauregard's orders, combined to prevent its execution.[8] From its concept, it was a poorly near-executed plan. After deciding to abandon his plan altogether, Beauregard then ordered Ewell, Jones, and Longstreet to make strong demonstrations all along their front on the other side of Bull Run so as to detain the enemy. Of paramount importance, they needed to hurry up all available reinforcements, including the reserves, to the left and fight the battle there. Beauregard discussed his views with Johnston, who agreed with him. He then ordered Holmes's reserve brigade with 6 guns, Colonel Jubal Early's Brigade consisting of three regiments, and the Washington Artillery of 5 guns plus two regiments of Bonham's brigade, to move swiftly to the left and support Cocke and Evans.[9]

About noon, after concluding their instructions to their commanders along the Bull Run, Johnston and Beauregard rode hard to the sound of battle, the point of conflict.

Morning Phase — The Opening Clash — Matthews Hill

From Signal Hill, a high observation point to the east of Manassas Junction, the Confederate signal officer, Capt. Edward P. Alexander, had been scanning the horizon to the north to detect a possible flanking attack. Prior to the secession of states, Capt. Alexander had been a signal officer in the Federal army. While serving in that capacity, he was instrumental in developing the wig-wag signaling system of communication. Like so many other Federal officers from Southern states, Alexander resigned his commission to join the Confederacy when Virginia seceded. In so doing, Alexander brought with him the wig-wag signaling system and implemented its functions for the Confederacy.

With field glass in hand, he was examining the area in the vicinity of Sudley Ford when, at about 8:45 A.M., his attention was drawn to the glint of the morning sun on a "brass field piece." A closer look revealed the glitter of bayonets and musket barrels. Quickly, he signaled to Evans at the Stone Bridge (Avon Hill), via the signal station at McLean's Ford, "Look out for your left; you are turned."[10] This message, which was to play such an important part in the tactical development of the battle, represents the first use under combat conditions of the wig-wag signaling system in modern warfare.

After signaling to Evans, Alexander wrote a note to Beauregard which he hurried off by courier. The note read as follows: "I see a column crossing Bull Run about 2 miles above Stone Bridge. Head of it is in woods on this side; tail of it in woods on other side. About a quarter of a mile length of column visible in the opening. Artillery forms part of it." The message caught Beauregard's immediate attention and he reacted by sending Jackson, Bee, and Bartow to reinforce his left.

From about 8 A.M., it had become increasingly apparent to Evans that Tyler's action in his front was simply a deceptive action made to disguise what was really intended. Now warned by Alexander of the approach of the flanking columns, Evans quickly conferred with Wheat. They reached a daring decision to slow the Union army's advance. After sending a courier to Cocke to advise him of his next movements, Evans left four companies consisting of a force of about 200, plus two pieces of artillery to guard the bridge, and with his remaining 900 rushed northwestward to an area near Pittsylvania. From there, Evans separated his command and led the 4th South Carolina southwestward and took up a position along a swell on the north side of Buck Hill that separates a knoll at the foot of Matthews Hill. A section of Capt. H.G. Latham's battery of 6-pounder smoothbores, commanded by Lt. Clark Leftwich, was placed on the left near the Sudley Road and supported by the 4th South Carolina. A second section of Latham's battery, commanded by Lt. George S. Davidson, was in battery just north of the turnpike, about a mile west of the Stone Bridge. Evans's keen actions foiled McDowell's plan for Tyler to keep the Confederates' left occupied while Hunter and Heintzelman could begin their crossings at the fords. In addition, by not responding in kind to Hains's artillery fire and Tyler's infantry movements about the Stone Bridge, Evans denied Tyler the knowledge that the Confederates' true strength in his front was only four companies of infantry. An indecisive Tyler did not attempt to force the passage of the Stone Bridge.

Meanwhile, Wheat led his Louisiana battalion west across the fields into position approximately 300 yards above and to the right of the 4th South Carolina. Skirmishers of the 4th South Carolina that were out in front saw the distinct uniforms of the Louisiana Tigers and in the excitement, mistaking them for the enemy, started firing on them. In outrage, the Louisianans turned and fired back at the Carolinians. Very quickly, the mistaken identity was sorted out, but not before two Louisiana Tigers were casualties.

Evans's initial line generally ran in a southwest-northeast direction. A grove of trees on Evans's right flank afforded some cover, while fences and shrubbery along the Sudley road helped to screen the left.[11]

While McDowell's forces were filling canteens and drinking water from Bull Run at Sudley Ford, scouts returned from a reconnaissance of the area and reported seeing Confederate columns in their front moving north. McDowell now knew his army had been discovered and any element of surprise was lost. Realizing the urgency of his predicament, he hurriedly began moving his forces across the Bull Run and Catharpin Run via Sudley Ford and Sudley Spring Ford and through the small community of Sudley.

The residents of Sudley and the farm families in the surrounding areas were well aware that a battle was imminent but did not know exactly when or where it would be taking place. This was Sunday, and many of the families that resided in the area were devout Christians and regular churchgoers. However, this particular Sunday, all were aware of the military activity taking place throughout the countryside. Despite the dangers, they elected to make their way to their house of worship. Regular church services would not be held on this day, and it would be some time before they would be held again.

As the scene unfolded before them, the church congregation stood about the church grounds in small groups. Fear and anxiety shrouded the small mass of onlookers as they witnessed McDowell's main body leave Sudley Spring Ford. They watched as it moved south below Thornberry's Wheelwright Shop and continued south, passing in front of the Sudley Methodist Church. The weary troops passed by in a slouchy marching manner, a combination of quick-stepping and fast-rushing as officers on horseback pushed them on. No longer did their uniforms appear fresh and brightly colored as they had four days earlier, for now they were sweaty and grimy. Knowing they were going into battle, the naïve young troopers maintained a false semblance of jubilation and excitement despite the weight of their pack rolls slung on their backs, carelessly resting their muskets on their shoulders. Their canteens and other accoutrements rattled and clanged loudly as they marched.

Many among the congregation had mixed feelings about their allegiance. In the past, there had been some who had vehemently spoke out as Unionists, while most held the sentiments of their state. As McDowell's army continued to march by, some showed signs of fear, while a few brandished fists at the invaders. The gravity of the situation shortly became a reality and they quickly left the area to seek refuge for their families. Little did they know at the time that upon their return, nothing would ever be the same.

Leaving the Sudley community and moving south down the Sudley Road, Col. David Hunter pushed his division, consisting of Col. Ambrose Burnside's brigade of four regiments plus artillery, the three regiments and a battalion of Col. Andrew Porter's brigade with artillery that followed, and three brigades of Samuel P. Heintzelman's Division. Leading Burnside's brigade of mostly New Englanders was the 2nd Rhode Island, ten companies strong, followed by the 2nd New Hampshire, the 71st New York, and the 1st Rhode Island. Five companies of the 2nd Rhode Island were sent out as skirmishers.

As Burnside's brigade approached Matthews Hill, the 2nd Rhode Island commander, Col. Slocum, called in his 5 companies of skirmishers and began advancing with his complement of 10 companies.[12] The initial encounter came at about 10:15 A.M., when the 2nd Rhode Island crested Matthews Hill and Major Roberdeau Wheat's 1st Louisianans opened up. While advancing with his brigade, Slocum was shot from his horse when crossing over a fence. He was hit three times, and within a few moments, a shell from the Confederate battery on Buck Hill hit Slocum's second in command, Major Sullivan Balou, crushing one of his legs and killing his horse. Slocum's orderlies initially carried their fallen commander to the home of Martin and Edgar Matthews. There, they removed a door from inside the home on which they placed Slocum. He was then carried to the Sudley Church, which was being used by Union surgeons as a hospital. Balou was taken directly to the Sudley Church.

During this initial clash, Colonel David Hunter also became a casualty after being shot in the neck and cheek; he was the first high-ranking officer to be wounded in the first major battle of the Civil War. The change of command for Hunter's Division now fell upon his 1st Brigade commander, Colonel Andrew Porter.

The 2nd Rhode Island was hit hard by the initial deadly volley that left gaps throughout their ranks. Although stunned, they were able to close ranks and continued to advance, but Wheat's 1st Louisiana Tigers once again leveled a murderous volley of musketry, and the Rhode Islanders advanced no further. After hitting the 2nd Rhode Island, Wheat saw other Union forces moving in a southwesterly direction onto Dogan Ridge. Immediately, he led his Tigers across the Sudley road, placing them into line of battle and resting his right flank about 20 yards west of the Sudley road on Dogan Ridge and to the left of the 4th South Carolina.

Union commanders were anxiously trying to move their units into line of battle; Porter's brigade with Captain Charles Griffin's Battery D, 5th U.S. Artillery complement of four 10-pounder Parrotts plus two 12-pounder howitzers, and Captain James B. Ricketts' Battery, 1st U.S. Artillery complement of six 10-pounder Parrotts moved into position on Dogan Ridge. In the excitement and rush, Porter's and Burnside's brigades became intermingled; confusion was fierce.

Burnside was desperately trying to bring up the rest of his brigade while trying to untangle the confusion. The 2nd Rhode Island battery of six 14-pounder brass James rifles, led by Captain William H. Reynolds and accompanied by Rhode Island Governor William Sprague, was moving up behind the 2nd Rhode Island Infantry. Burnside yelled to Reynolds to "forward your artillery," and the artillery went into battery in front of the 2nd Rhode Island, on the southern crest of Matthews Hill.

Frantically deploying his brigade into line of battle, Burnside ordered the 71st New York and 2nd New Hampshire into the fight, but the confusion continued and their deployment was badly fumbled. Burnside then ordered the 1st Rhode Island into line of battle behind Reynolds's guns; almost in unison, the 2nd Rhode Island made a left flank movement and went into line of battle to the left of the 1st Rhode Island. From right to left, Burnside formed his brigade with the 1st Rhode Island on his right flank, followed by the 2nd Rhode Island, then the 71st New York with their two Dahlgren boat howitzers in their front, and finally the 2nd New Hampshire. He then rode hard to Porter and pleaded for him to let him have Major George Sykes's battalion of U.S. regular army infantry. Porter agreed, and Burnside sent the regulars to his far-left flank, next to the 2nd New Hampshire. From Heintzelman's division, Burnside got the 1st

Minnesota, sending them to his left flank, where they went into line of battle to the left of the U.S. Regulars.[13]

Meanwhile, at about 10 A.M., the two Confederate brigades under the command of Brigadier General Bernard Bee with Colonel Francis Bartow's brigade temporarily attached had arrived on Henry Hill. Bee selected the ground for Captain John D. Imboden's battery, and the two brigades were placed on either side of the battery. Immediately, Imboden's battery of four cannon prepared to go quickly into action in their strong position behind the northern crest of Henry Hill, north-northeast of the Henry house. Bee's first impulse was to hold Henry Hill from the forward crest, believing Evans would fall back toward him. At the time Imboden was unlimbering, Griffin's battery of six guns was simultaneously doing the same thing on Dogan Ridge.[14] Griffin was deployed west of the Sudley Road about midway between the road and the John Dogan farm house.

As the odds were fast building up against Evans, he was in desperate need of help. He sent a staff member riding hard to Henry Hill to ask Bee for reinforcements. Bee immediately complied, but first ordered Imboden's battery to hold fire until the 4th Alabama could cross in his front. He sent the 4th Alabama regiment, led by Colonel Jones, to cross the valley of Young's Branch and to take position in the woods near the right of Evans's line. Bee went forward with them. From the time they left the northern rim of Henry Hill and advanced up the slopes of Matthews Hill, they were under heavy fire from Union artillery pieces.[15]

Having seen his 4th Alabama into line of battle, Bee rode back to Henry Hill for the rest of his command, the 2nd Mississippi and two companies of the 11th Mississippi; he directed Bartow to hold his 7th Georgia in reserve and to move forward with his 8th Georgia. Bartow sent his 7th Georgia, led by Colonel Lucius J. Gartrell, to the right, and forward of the Robinson house, to be held in reserve near the turnpike.[16] As the units started advancing onto Buck Hill and the southern slopes of Matthews Hill, they too came under the heavy artillery fire. Bartow then placed his 8th Georgia to the right of the 4th Alabama. The Confederates' strength on Matthews Hill now was about 2400. Their line of battle was Evans's brigade on the Confederate left, Bee's brigade in the middle; positioned from left to right, the 11th Mississippi, the 2nd Mississippi and the 4th Alabama. Bartow's 8th went into line of battle to the right of the 4th Alabama.[17]

After the 4th Alabama redeployed, Imboden ordered his artillery pieces loaded with spherical case shot, with the fuse cut for 1,500 yards. Bee had hardly given the order for the 4th Alabama to move before the six James Rifles of Reynolds's Rhode Island battery opened with elongated cylindrical shells. The firing of both batteries now became very rapid. Imboden's batteries sustained their first injury when a shell passing between two of his guns exploded amongst the caissons. About this time, Reynolds's guns began to fire too low, striking below the crest ten to twenty yards in Imboden's front. The angle of the shells striking the crest was sufficient for the projectile to ricochet on over Imboden's position. After they had been engaged for perhaps a half hour, Griffin brought four of his battery's guns into position near the

John Dogan home, about 400 yards south and west of Reynolds's battery, and commenced a vigorous fire upon Imboden's position. Imboden observed, "It is no exaggeration to say that hundreds of shells from these five rifle-guns [Reynolds's battery] exploded in front of and around my battery on that day, but so deep in the ground that the fragments never came out. After the action the ground looked as though it had been rooted up by hogs."[18] Joining Imboden briefly on his right came two guns from Richardson's section of the Washington Artillery, but under the hot incoming Union artillery fire, they quickly limbered up and reported back to the artillery park at Portici.

To Burnside's right, across the Sudley road on Dogan Ridge, Colonel Andrew Porter of Hunter's Division was busily placing into line of battle his brigade consisting of the U.S. Marine Corps Battalion, 27th New York, 14th New York, and 8th New York, supported by Palmer's 2nd U.S. Cavalry, plus the artillery batteries of Griffin and Ricketts already in action. This was the force that Wheat saw going into position after his initial attack on Burnside's Rhode Islanders and had subsequently crossed over to his left to meet them.

With Wheat out in front leading his Louisianans, they charged. Some reports state that some of Wheat's Tigers threw down their rifles and charged with their Bowie knives only. Wheat received a wound that, except for his fortitude, would have been fatal. Wheat was hit in the torso just under and forward of the left armpit. The bullet passed through his lungs and exited the other side of his chest in an area almost identical to where it entered from the other side. He was carried off the field, and while being attended to by a surgeon, was told that his wound was fatal. Wheat simply answered, "I don't feel like dying." When the surgeon told him, "But there is no instant on record of recovery from such a wound," Wheat responded with, "Well, then, I will put my case on record."[19]

TYLER SENDS SCHENCK'S BRIGADE TO MAKE FLANK ATTACK BY WAY OF LEWIS FORD

While Evans's and Burnsides' forces were in the initial phase of the battle developing on Matthews Hill, Tyler ordered General Robert C. Schenck's brigade to cross over the Bull Run. Acting upon McDowell's battle plans that he was to force the passage of Bull Run by way of the Stone Bridge and attack the enemy in flank at the time when Hunter and Heintzelman would begin their attack on Matthews Hill, Tyler made a decision to attempt a different crossing. Upon being advised that Hunter's division was in contact with the enemy, Tyler sent General Robert C. Schenck to advance across the Bull Run at Lewis Ford, where Young's Branch empties into the Bull Run, about 800 yards below the Stone Bridge. At about 10:30 A.M., Schenck sent his 1st Ohio to test the ford defenses and the 2nd Ohio and 2nd New York to support them. The 1st Ohio spotted a Confederate artillery battery of four pieces positioned on a hill covering the ford and supported by four infantry regiments from Cocke's brigade. The battery of artillery was two sections of Captain H.G. Latham's

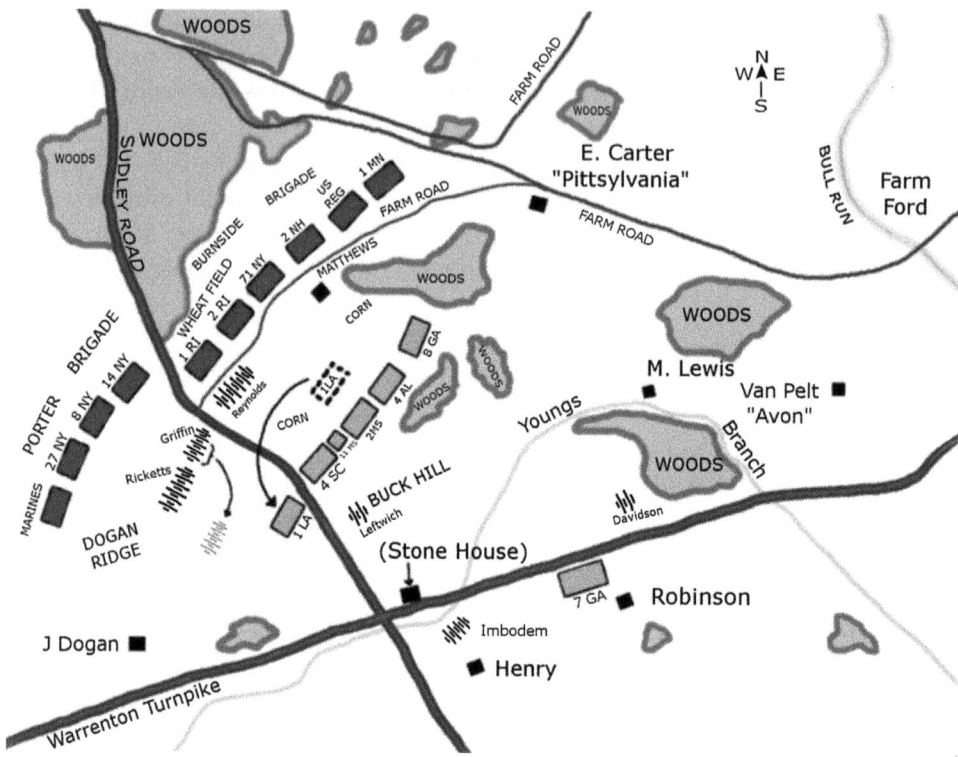

Opening Phase — Matthews Hill: Troop Positioning at Pinnacle of Engagement 11:15–11:30. Movement Times (A.M.): 9:30 — Evans's arrival; 10:00 — Burnsides' arrival; 10:15 — First shots fired; 10:45 — Bee, Bartow reinforcements arrive and engage; 11:30–12:30 Confederate retreat (drawing by Rachael R. Johnson).

Lynchburg artillery and a section of the Loudoun artillery commanded by Lieutenant Heaton.

The 1st Ohio advanced to within 350 yards, followed by the 2nd Ohio and the 2nd New York. Schenck called for artillery, but before it could be brought up, his forces had been detected by the Confederate artillerists; they immediately opened up with heavy shot and shell. Schenck withdrew after being driven back and did not attempt to cross the Bull Run again.[20]

CONFEDERATES OVERWHELMED AND BEGIN WITHDRAWAL FROM MATTHEWS HILL

Hardly had the reinforcements on the Confederate right arrived before they were hit by a heavy attack from Sykes's U.S. regulars and the 1st Minnesota. For the next hour, hard, heavy, and bloody fighting continued across the fields of Matthews Hill.

About 11:30 A.M., Evans, Bee, and Bartow were faced by Union forces that heavily overlapped their left and right flanks. They had no choice but to retreat. Casualties on both sides were heavy; Bee's 4th Alabama had lost all their field grade officers, leaving only its company commanders to command. Bartow's 8th Georgia had lost nearly 200 men out of an initial strength of 800. Exhausted and weary, they began to pull back.

As the Confederates retreated, the combined batteries of Griffin and Ricketts, totaling 9 rifled pieces and two howitzers, pounded Henry Hill. The sight of the retreat and the artillery bombardment excited the Union forces, and they were jubilant and energized with victory. General McDowell and his staff triumphantly rode among the brigades, wildly waving their hats and shouting, "They are running! Victory! Victory! The day is ours."[21] General McDowell had been ill for several days with a stomach ailment and rode in a buggy most of the time during the battle.

Soon after McDowell's arrival at the front, Burnside approached and asked permission to withdraw, stating that his brigade had borne the brunt of the battle, that it was out of ammunition, and he wanted to refit and fill cartridge boxes.[22] In the excitement, McDowell gave consent, and Burnside marched his brigade to the rear. Thereupon, they stacked arms and took no further part in the fight.

Midday Phase — Confederates Fall Back to Henry Hill

By noon, forward movements of the 21st New York and Sykes's U.S. regulars broke what stubborn resistance the Confederates had left. The broken detachments fell back in a demoralized retreat and took position near the rear of the Robinson House. As they were retreating, Clark Leftwitch withdrew his artillery section to Henry Hill and continued firing until he expended all his ammunition. Davidson had moved his section south across the turnpike onto Robinson's lane and fired canister at one hundred fifty yards. He too subsequently withdrew to the artillery park at Portici.[23]

As the Confederates began their retreat, a large portion of McDowell's force of 16,000 from his flank march had crossed the fords. At about 12:30 P.M., in response to orders sent to Tyler from McDowell, an additional force of about 2,000 under the commands of Colonels William T. Sherman and Erasmas D. Keyes (Tyler's Division) joined McDowell. They had successfully crossed the Bull Run at a farm ford that Sherman scouts had discovered 800 yards above the Stone Bridge.[24] They were accompanied by Tyler, who personally followed behind them. By this time, Heintzelman's division had reached the field to greatly increase the pressure on the Confederate line.

Tyler had received the orders from McDowell at 11 o'clock, but it was not until one hour later that Sherman and Keyes received them from Tyler. McDowell was still agitated with Tyler after the affair at Blackburn's Ford, and his action on that day. He had failed to force the passage of Bull Run at that point (Stone Bridge) and attack the enemy in flank as planned for when Hunter and Heintzelman made their attack on Matthews Hill. The bitterness between the two would continue throughout the rest of their lives. In a letter to Maj. Gen. James Fry in 1884, McDowell had this to say in reference to the 1st Battle of Manassas: "If there is anything clearer to me than anything else with reference to our operations in that campaign, it is that if we had

had another commander for our right we should have had a complete and brilliant success."[25]

HAMPTON COVERS CONFEDERATE WITHDRAWAL

Sometime in the early morning hours, Hampton's Legion arrived at Manassas Junction by train from Richmond. Due to heavy delays, the journey took more than 36 hours and the men had not eaten. After hurried meals were prepared and quickly consumed, Hampton led his 600 eager men on an exhausting three-mile march in quick-time, passing near Portici. There he encountered a scout who informed him, "The enemy has turned our left flank and are advancing." Guided by the sound of heavy fire, Hampton double-quick-timed his men to Henry Hill. He was without his artillery and cavalry since they were not able to accompany the rest of the Legion by rail and were still en route by way of overland roads from Richmond.

Upon reaching Henry Hill, Hampton found Imboden's battery heavily engaged in a duel with Griffin and Ricketts's guns. While Evans and Bee's forces were in retreat from Matthews Hill, Imboden was holding his position on Henry Hill to cover the retreat. Hampton quickly moved his legion in position to support Imboden. As he observed the broken Confederate units retreating onto Henry Hill, Hampton looked off to his right and in the distance he saw columns of Union infantry advancing toward the turnpike opposite the Robinson driveway. Even though he understood the gravity of the situation, and realized that he would be leaving Imboden unsupported, notwithstanding, he quickly moved to the Robinson house and took possession of the ground immediately around it. Within moments he came under heavy fire from Ricketts's battery on Dogan Ridge and promptly moved forward, forming his men near the turnpike cut north of the Robinson house.

KEYES ATTEMPTS FOOTHOLD ON
HENRY HILL NEAR ROBINSON HOUSE

While forming his men along the turnpike road, Hampton immediately came under heavy fire from forward columns of Keyes's brigade. After following Sherman across the Bull Run at a ford above the Stone Bridge, Keyes, accompanied by Tyler, formed his brigade on the Van Pelt property. Tyler made no attempt to contact McDowell and on his own volition, ordered Keyes to advance onto Henry Hill and take out an artillery battery that was firing on them. His four-regiment brigade comprised the 1st, 2nd, 3rd Connecticut Infantry and the 2nd Maine. Keyes sent his 2nd Maine and 3rd Connecticut to charge across the turnpike and up the northern slopes of Henry Hill below the Robinson house. They immediately met heavy musketry from Hampton's Legionnaires; however, Hampton was pushed back. By this time, Jackson's Brigade was just making its presence known on Henry Hill, and Colonel Harper's 5th Virginia had moved to assist Hampton. They both were pushed back about 100 yards southeastwardly to the rear of the Robinson house; however, very quickly, Hampton's Legion and the 5th Virginia rallied and Keyes's advance was arrested. Joined by the emergence of some of Bee's and Evans's gathering remnants, Keyes was forced to retreat back across the turnpike.[26]

Hampton describes his action moments after he had initially moved his Legionnaires into position near the turnpike[27]: "Here we were attacked by a column which came from the direction of the Headquarters of General Evans [Van Pelt House] almost on our right, and we were nearly surrounded, the enemy being on three sides of us, and Generals Bee and Evans having both advised me to fall back. I gave orders to this effect...."

Jackson Advances and Makes a Stand on the Southern Slopes of Henry Hill

Sometime after Jackson's brigade had taken position in support of Bonham and Cocke, he received a request from Colonel Cocke to guard Stone Bridge. While moving at Cocke's request, he was advised that General Bee was being "hard-pressed." Without hesitating, Jackson readied his men and in double-quick time rushed his brigade forward to the sound of battle. His brigade was composed of five Virginia regiments: the 2nd, commanded by Colonel J.W. Allen; the 4th, commanded by Colonel J.F. Preston; the 5th, commanded by Colonel K. Harper; the 27th, commanded by Lt. Colonel J. Echols; and the 33rd, commanded by Colonel A.C. Cummings. In addition, there was a section (two 6-pounder smoothbores) of Captain P.B. Stanard's Richmond battery (Thomas Artillery).

Emerging via a farm road that ran through some pine woods on the southern slopes of Henry Hill, Jackson encountered remnants of Evans's and Bee's broken commands recoiling before the Federal onslaught. It wasn't long until Bee approached at a hard gallop and "he and Jackson met face to face. The latter was cool and composed, but Bee was covered with dust and sweat, his sword in his hand and his horse foaming. 'General,' he said, 'they are beating us back!' 'Then, sir, we will give them the bayonet.'..."[28] This brief encounter ended with the understanding that Bee, covered by Jackson, would rally and re-form on the right and rear of Jackson's command.[29]

While the Confederate forces retreated from Matthews Hill, only Imboden's four cannons on the northwest crest of Henry Hill were still engaging the enemy. Imboden described the scene and his actions:

> For at least a half-hour after our forces were driven across Young's Branch no Confederate soldier was visible from our position near the Henry house. The Staunton Artillery, so far as we could see, was "alone in its glory." General Bee's order had been, "Stay here till you are ordered away." To my surprise, no order came, though, as I afterward learned, orders to withdraw had been sent three-quarters of an hour before through Major Howard of Bee's staff, who had fallen, desperately wounded on the way.[30]

While Imboden was stalwartly defending from his position on the crest of Henry Hill, Griffin's and Ricketts's batteries were ordered to redeploy about 300 yards further south on Dogan Ridge. That placed them about halfway between the Dogan house and Sudley Road.[31]

As the Confederates scrambled from Matthews Hill in retreat, Reynolds advanced his battery of James rifles about 500 yards forward onto Buck Hill. After positioning and unlimbering, Reynolds resumed firing onto the Confederates on the northern rim of Henry Hill.[32]

Nearing 1 P.M., from along Sudley Road and the turnpike below the Henry house, McDowell's infantry regiments were massing to charge and capture Imboden's battery. After being apprised of these developments and learning from his sergeants of "pieces" that his ammunition was almost entirely exhausted, Imboden took action to limber up and move out as quickly as possible. His battery had suffered a loss of over half his horses, leaving only two-horse teams to bear the burden of six-horse teams. While Imboden was driving his limbered battery away from its position, a shot from Ricketts's battery exploded under one of the gun carriages, dropping the cannon barrel to the ground. Making his way to the rear, Imboden came upon Jackson deploying his brigade.[33]

Unbeknownst to Imboden at this time, Bee had indeed sent orders earlier for his withdrawal. Upon meeting up with Jackson, he expressed at his anger Bee for what he then regarded as bad treatment in leaving him so long exposed to the threat of capture. He burst out, "Damn it, General, I had to give up my position for lack of support!" Almost immediately after he had spoken, Imboden realized that he had blundered, as it was a well-known fact that the use of profanity in the presence of Jackson was something one didn't do. However, as there was no time for admonishment, Jackson simply assured him, "I'll support your battery. Unlimber right here."[34]

Shortly thereafter, a lull ensued for one hour across the battlefield as McDowell began reforming his forces about the Stone House and in the valley of Young's Branch. During this time, as the battered, retreating regiments of Evans's, Bee's, and Bartow's commands were gathering in the open fields and woods south of the Robinsons' home, Hampton's battered legion and Colonel Gartrell's 7th Georgia were also reforming to the right and rear of Jackson.[35]

Jackson had discerned that his position on the southern slopes of Henry Hill was the most favorable place for meeting the enemy. In posting his brigade, he placed Imboden's guns and two 6-pounder smoothbores from Captain P.B. Stanard's battery (the Thomas Artillery) in front of his infantry. The 4th Virginia was formed in rear of the guns, the 27th Virginia partially to the right and behind the 4th, the 5th Virginia on the far right of the battery with the Robinson house in its front, the 2nd Virginia to the left of the batteries, and the 33rd Virginia on the left of the 2nd Virginia. The ground held by Jackson was "below the brim of the plateau, nearly east of the Henry house, and to the left of the hollow occupied by the remnants of Evans, Bee, Bartow and Hampton's commands."[36]

BEAUREGARD ASSUMES FIELD COMMAND

Meanwhile, at about 12:30, Beauregard and Johnston arrived upon the field and rode over to the right held by Bee's and Evans's commands. Beauregard describes the scene[37]:

Five. July 21— First Battle of Manassas

We found the commanders resolutely stemming the further flight of the routed forces, but vainly endeavoring to restore order, and our own efforts were as futile. Every segment of line we succeeded in forming was again dissolved while another was being formed; more than two thousand men were shouting each some suggestion to his neighbor, their voices mingling with the noise of the shells hurling through the trees overhead, and all word of command drowned in the confusion and uproar.

In assessing the situation, Beauregard believed he was better acquainted with the area than Johnston and the best-able field commander. He said as much to Johnston and suggested that he take the field command while Johnston saw to sending forth reinforcements as soon as possible. Johnston agreed and rode directly to the Lewis house to direct those movements from there.

Beauregard quickly began the formation of his battle line. Jackson's brigade staunchly held the center. The midday lull gave Jackson a chance to reinforce his artillery, and he sent for more cannons. Johnston, now at Portici directing reinforcements to Beauregard, ordered forward the batteries Jackson requested. As they arrived, Jackson selected their positions. After the guns were in position, the Rockbridge Artillery battery commander and chief of artillery for the Army of the Shenandoah, Col. William N. Pendleton, took charge.[38]

Jackson's Alignment of Artillery in His Front[39]

Center: The two guns of Stanard's Thomas Artillery were in battery with the Rockbridge Artillery, and their combined six guns were in the center of Jackson's line. The Rockbridge Artillery battery consisted of two of the Virginia Military Institute (VMI) cadet 6-pounders, a regular 6-pounder, and a 12-pounder howitzer. In place from left to right stood one gun of the Rockbridge Artillery, two guns of Stanard's, and then the three remaining guns of the Rockbridge Artillery. These six guns faced northwest and on a line diagonal to the pines. Their sector of fire was left and right of the Henry House. (Initially the four guns of Staunton's artillery (Imboden) were positioned in this line, but were only in place a short time. The battery was sent back to the artillery park at Portici, as they were out of ammunition following their defensive stand covering the Matthews Hill fight and retreat.)

Left: To the left of Stanard's and the Rockbridge Artillery were the five guns of Walton's Washington Artillery. The Washington Artillery faced due west at an angle to the pines. Their sector of fire was Ricketts's right section.

Right: To the right of Stanard's and the Rockbridge Artillery was Heaton's two-gun section of the Loudoun Artillery. Heaton's sector of fire was to the left of the Robinson house.

Far right flank: The last of the artillery to arrive was the Arburtis Battery of Wise Artillery commanded by 23-year-old Lieutenant John Pelham, placed on the high ground behind the 5th Virginia. In addition, one gun of the Rockbridge battery joined Pelham's four 6-pounders. Their sector of fire was to the right of the Robinson house.

The complement of artillery consisted of 13 guns in Jackson's immediate front and 5 guns (perpendicular to his front) on his right flank for a total of 18 guns.

After positioning his brigade, Jackson ordered his men to lie down. Imboden's Staunton Artillery was out of ammunition, and Jackson sent it back to the artillery park located near Portici. He then ordered Imboden to remain, instructing him to "go from battery to battery and see that the guns were properly aimed and the fuses cut to the right length."[40]

Afternoon Phase — McDowell Resumes the Offensive

GRIFFIN'S AND RICKETTS'S ARTILLERY ADVANCE ONTO HENRY HILL

About 1:30, Major Barry delivered McDowell's order to Captains Griffin and Ricketts: "Advance two batteries to an eminence about 800 yards in front of the line previously occupied by our artillery, and very near the position first occupied by the enemy's batteries" (the position on Henry Hill previously held by Imboden). Neither of the battery commanders liked the idea. Ricketts did not hesitate to obey the order and only asked Barry to "name the spot clearly to me," but Griffin expressed his objections to Barry no uncertain terms. In speaking before the Joint Congressional Committee on the Conduct of the War, Griffin testified:

> I hesitated about going there because I had no support.... Barry told me that the Fire Zouaves [11th New York] would support us ... that they were just ready to take the double-quick and follow us. I told him if such was the case, I wished he would permit them to go and get into position on the hill ... let the batteries come into position behind them, and then let them fall back. And I told him the better place for our battery was on a hill [Chinn Ridge] about 500 yards in the rear of the one to which we were ordered. He said that General McDowell's order was to go to the other hill ... and he also refused to let the Fire Zouaves go on the hill first and form into line. I told him they would not support us ... he said, "Yes, they will ... at any rate, it is General McDowell's order to go there." I said, "I will go ... but mark my words, they will not support us."[41]

Lieutenant Charles Hazlett of Griffin's battery led the 11-gun column off Dogan Ridge, through the intersection of Sudley Road and the Turnpike and across Young's Branch, where one of Ricketts's gun carriers broke a wheel. While Griffin's battery moved on, the broken wheel on Ricketts's gun was quickly replaced. However, immediately after crossing over Young's Branch, Hazlett turned left off Sudley Road and onto the Henry fields on the northwestern shoulder of Henry Hill. Believing that this was a mistake, both Griffin and Barry galloped forward and ordered the battery to countermarch to Sudley Road. They then moved south to the Henry farm entrance lane. This delay allowed Ricketts's battery to move into position on Henry Hill first. Ricketts unlimbered his battery in the field that included a part of Mrs. Henry's rail-fenced small corn field just south of the Henry House. As his six 10-pounder Parrott rifles took position, he came under fire from sharpshooters of Hampton's Legion in and around the Henry house. To counter this, Ricketts turned at least part of his battery on the house and fired.[42]

Inside the house was the Widow Mrs. Judith Henry, 84 years old and bedridden.

Also in the house were her spinster daughter Ellen, her eldest son John, who was visiting at the time, and Lucy Griffith, a hired slave house servant. Earlier that morning, the three attempted to move Mrs. Henry to safety using her featherbed mattress to carry her. After they got as far as Sudley Road, she became frightened and fretful and insisted they return to the "safety of her home." While Ricketts was moving his artillery into position outside the Henry home, Lucy took refuge under Mrs. Henry's bed, and Ellen crouched in the fireplace. One or two Confederate sharpshooters moved about inside and an undetermined number were outside. It is unknown where John was at the time. Ricketts testified that when he fired on the house, he "thoroughly riddled it." Mrs. Henry sustained five wounds from shrapnel, one nearly taking off her leg. She died later that evening, the first civilian to be killed in battle in the Civil War. Lucy sustained a serious arm wound and Ellen sustained permanent hearing loss as a result of concussion from the exploding shells.

The sharpshooters were driven out, and moments later, Griffin arrived with his battery and was moving his five pieces into place just north and east of the Henry house.

Ricketts's artillery was not deployed in the conventional battery formation. His six pieces were in battery in two three-gun sections, with a large gap separating the two sections, located on the summit of Henry Hill. Mrs. Henry's small cornfield was located south, near the home and surrounded by a rail fence. Ricketts's left section was deployed within the fenced area of the cornfield and his right section was south of the fence. McDowell's and Barry's chosen location for the guns proved to put his forces at a disadvantage. In this case, it was height and elevation versus distance. Of the eleven guns, nine were the rifled 10-pounder Parrotts, typically used for long-range shots. The combination of gun emplacements on the high brow of the hill to fire on targets at close range accentuated the elevation factor. The cannoneers could not get enough lower elevation and consequentially, for the most part, their shots went over their target and exploded in the trees.

Unfortunately, the decision made years ago to build the Manassas National Battlefield Museum and Visitor Center directly on the spot where the nucleus of the battle action took place deprives the visitor of a complete visual and imaginary concept of both the First and Second Battles of Manassas. Ricketts's right artillery section took in the total area where now sits the Visitor Center. In addition, the center of fighting involving the guns took place over this same area, including the Visitor Center Parking Lot.

Griffin's and Ricketts's Artillery Take Center Stage Against Jackson

As Griffin's and Ricketts's artillery were going into battery, Jackson was no more than 1,200 feet away, moving about his line on his horse, Little Sorrel, observing the action taking place around the Henry house. There were no infantry to be seen on the crest of the hill at that time. Sometime between 2:15 and 2:30, Jackson saw Griffin's and

Ricketts's guns going into battery. It was then that the combined six guns of Stanard's and the Rockbridge artillery went into action, which prompted a duel. At this range and elevation, the Confederate smoothbores had the advantage. Lieutenant Hazlett of Griffin's battery described the exchange: We were "in full relief on top of the hill," while the foe "were a little behind the crest of the hill. We presented a better mark for them than they did for us. It was a 'galling' fire. The duel continued unabated for half an hour."[43]

Jackson's chief of artillery Colonel Pendleton, dressed in an army uniform and wearing a civilian hat, was in the center of Jackson's line with his Rockbridge Artillery. Pendleton was also an Episcopalian minister. The Rockbridge battery had four guns that he named "Matthew, Mark, Luke and John" and described them as having "a powerful language." Before his first order to fire, he paused, bowed his head in solemn reverence and said, "O Lord ... have mercy on their soul." The figure of Pendleton at his guns and the result of his effective fire were very noticeable by his opponents on the battlefield. After the battle was over, one of the captured opposing gunners wanted to know, "Who was that devil in the center of the Confederate line?" One of his captors replied, "Oh, that was Saint P., for Pendleton."[44]

SHERMAN, PORTER, FRANKLIN AND WILLCOX ADVANCE

Since his victorious routing of the Confederates from Matthews Hill, McDowell had been desperately trying to organize his forces in preparation for making an organized attack onto Henry Hill. The brigades of Sherman, Porter, Franklin, and Willcox had been converging in the area surrounding the crossroads of Sudley Road and the Turnpike and became entangled, creating much confusion. Prior to the initial artillery duel on Henry Hill, Barry and Heintzelman set about bringing up supporting units for Griffin's and Ricketts's artillery batteries. After some delays they eventually obtained four: from Heintzelman's Division, they got Colonel W.C. Farnham's 11th New York (Fire Zouaves) of Colonel Willcox's brigade and the 1st Minnesota of Colonel Franklin's brigade; from Hunter's Division (Colonel Andrew Porter commanding), they got the U.S. Marine Corps Battalion of Colonel Porter's brigade and the 14th Brooklyn, also of Porter's brigade.

Heintzelman personally joined with Colonel Farnham of the 11th New York. They (the Fire Zouaves) were the first to move into place, taking position first to the rear of Ricketts's right section before moving to their right. Major J.G. Reynolds's Marine Battalion came up on the rear of Ricketts's left section. Colonel W.A. Gorman's 1st Minnesota eventually took position on the 11th New York's right. Colonel A.M. Wood's 14th New York (Brooklyn) was directed by Porter's chief of staff, Colonel Averell, to double-quick south down the Sudley Road into the woods, to the right and rear of Ricketts's right section. Averell recorded that he became increasingly concerned about the possibility of the enemy shielding themselves in the woods on the right flank of the guns.[45]

HEINTZELMAN LEADS UNION ATTACK AGAINST JACKSON

As the 11th New York moved into position, led by Heintzelman on horseback and accompanied by Colonel Farnham and Colonel Averell, they saw a line of infantry in their front, dressed in what Heintzelman later described as "citizens clothes" (non-uniform, civilian clothing). Heintzelman approached and said, "Hello! What men are these?" His question was answered by a few scattered shots: they were the 33rd Virginia of Jackson's brigade. Immediately realizing it was an enemy force, Heintzelman ordered the Zouaves to charge them. The Virginians were firing more furiously now. Colonel Farnham cried out to his regiment, "Down, every one of you!" The 1st Minnesota, which was on the Zouaves' right, fired one volley, and then they too fell to the ground. As the firefight raged, the Yankees fired a few more rounds, and then both the 11th New York and 1st Minnesota quickly retreated.[46]

While the combined assault of the 11th New York and 1st Minnesota had been developing, Reynolds's Marine Battalion was ordered to "afford the necessary support." As they moved to cover the 11th New York, the Marines met a galling fire from Jackson's charging forces and became almost paralyzed. They fired a few shots and then broke and ran down the hill to Sudley Road.[47]

"General, you are wounded"

The fight was intense at times; Jackson was moving over to near his left flank when Imboden approached. He stopped to ask Jackson permission to rejoin his battery that had retired to Artillery Park at Portici. Imboden described what took place next:

> The fight was just then hot enough to make him feel well. His eyes fairly blazed. He had a way of throwing up his left hand with the palm toward the person he was addressing. And as he told me to go, he made this gesture. The air was full of flying missiles, and as he spoke he jerked down his hand and I saw that blood was streaming from it. I exclaimed, "General, you are wounded." He replied, as he drew a handkerchief from his breast-pocket, and began to bind it up, "Only a scratch ... a mere scratch," and galloped away along his line....[48]

Stuart Launches a Cavalry Charge

While this initial clash was taking place on the Confederates left, Jackson sent orders to his cavalry officer, Colonel J.E.B. Stuart, instructing him to protect his flanks, particularly his left flank. The strength of Stuart's cavalry regiment was about 300 present for duty. In responding to Jackson's orders, Stuart divided his force and sent half with his second in command, Major Swan, to cover Jackson's right flank, leading the remainder to Jackson's left.[49]

As Heintzelman's two regiments fell back toward the rear, they scattered about along the Sudley Road. Lieutenant William W. Blackford, whom Stuart had appointed that day to be his adjutant, rode with Stuart and Stuart's two company commanders, Captains Welby Carter and J.B. Hogue. Blackford recorded their experiences in his book *War Years with Jeb Stuart*, and described in great specificity their actions of this day[50]: "Seeing a mass of men in the road, dressed in their gaily colored uniforms, Stuart waved his sword and ordered a charge, but instantly pulled up and called a halt." Turning to Blackford he said, "Blackford, are those our men or the enemy?" Blackford replied he could not tell, but he heard "that Beauregard had a regiment of Zouaves from New

Orleans," dressed like those men. Just then, however, "all doubt was removed by the appearance of their colors, emerging from the road ... the Stars and Stripes."

The charge resumed:

> I had not thought which of my weapons to draw until I started.... As the scarlet line appeared through the smoke, when within a couple of horse's lengths of them, I leaned down, with my carbine cocked, thumb on hammer and forefinger on trigger, and fixed my eye on a tall fellow I saw would be the one my course would place in the right position for the carbine, while the man next to him, in front of the horse, I would have to leave to Comet [Blackford's noble horse]. I then plunged the spurs into Comet's flanks and he evidently thought I wanted him to jump over this strange looking wall I was riding at, for he rose to make the leap; but he was too close and going too fast to rise higher than the breast of the man, and he struck him full on the chest, rolling him over and over under his hoofs and knocking him about 10 feet backwards, depriving him of all further interest in the subsequent proceedings, and knocking the rear rank man to one side. As Comet rose to make the leap, I leaned down from the saddle, rammed the muzzle of the carbine into the stomach of my man and pulled the trigger. I could not help feeling a little sorry for the fellow as he lifted his handsome face to mine while he tried to get his bayonet up to meet me; but he was too slow, for the carbine blew a hole as big as my arm clear through him.

Blackford also stated, "This regiment ... they say it was the Fire Zouaves ... was completely paralyzed by this charge, and though their actual loss in killed and wounded was not very great, their demoralization was complete."[51]

Stuart's cavalry charge, which struck both the 11th New York and the 1st Minnesota, caused disorientation within both regiments to the extent they were unable to rally. They retreated in disarray and did not fight as units the remainder of the afternoon.[52]

Meanwhile, the batteries of Griffin and Ricketts on Henry Hill "continued to suffer. Ricketts's battery was damaged by the first volley of Confederate fire, taking heavy losses in both men and horses. Griffin's battery also suffered from heavy artillery fire."

> In turn, the Confederates suffered little real damage, though the close-range Union artillery fire had a nervous affect on them. This fact made Colonel Arthur C. Cummings of the 33rd Virginia wary and concerned. He felt that his men could not stand the tension much longer and rode out a distance in front of the regiment to assess the situation. After a short time, Cummings saw Union guns moving along Sudley Road, and much to his surprise, they came into position in his front, not 250 yards away.[53]

BEAUREGARD SENDS REINFORCEMENTS TO BOLSTER JACKSON'S LEFT AND RIGHT FLANKS

After the initial infantry clash, a lull took place, lasting some 10 minutes. During this time, reinforcements from Cocke's and Bonham's brigades hurried up from fords lower down Bull Run. Upon their arrival, Beauregard quickly sent them into position to the right and left of Jackson.

One of these units was the 49th Virginia Volunteers, commanded by Colonel William (Extra Billy) Smith. Smith's 49th Virginia, consisting of just three companies, had only just organized three days before, but on the march from Lewis Ford onto Henry Hill, Smith had encountered one lost South Carolina company and two Missis-

Five. July 21— First Battle of Manassas 79

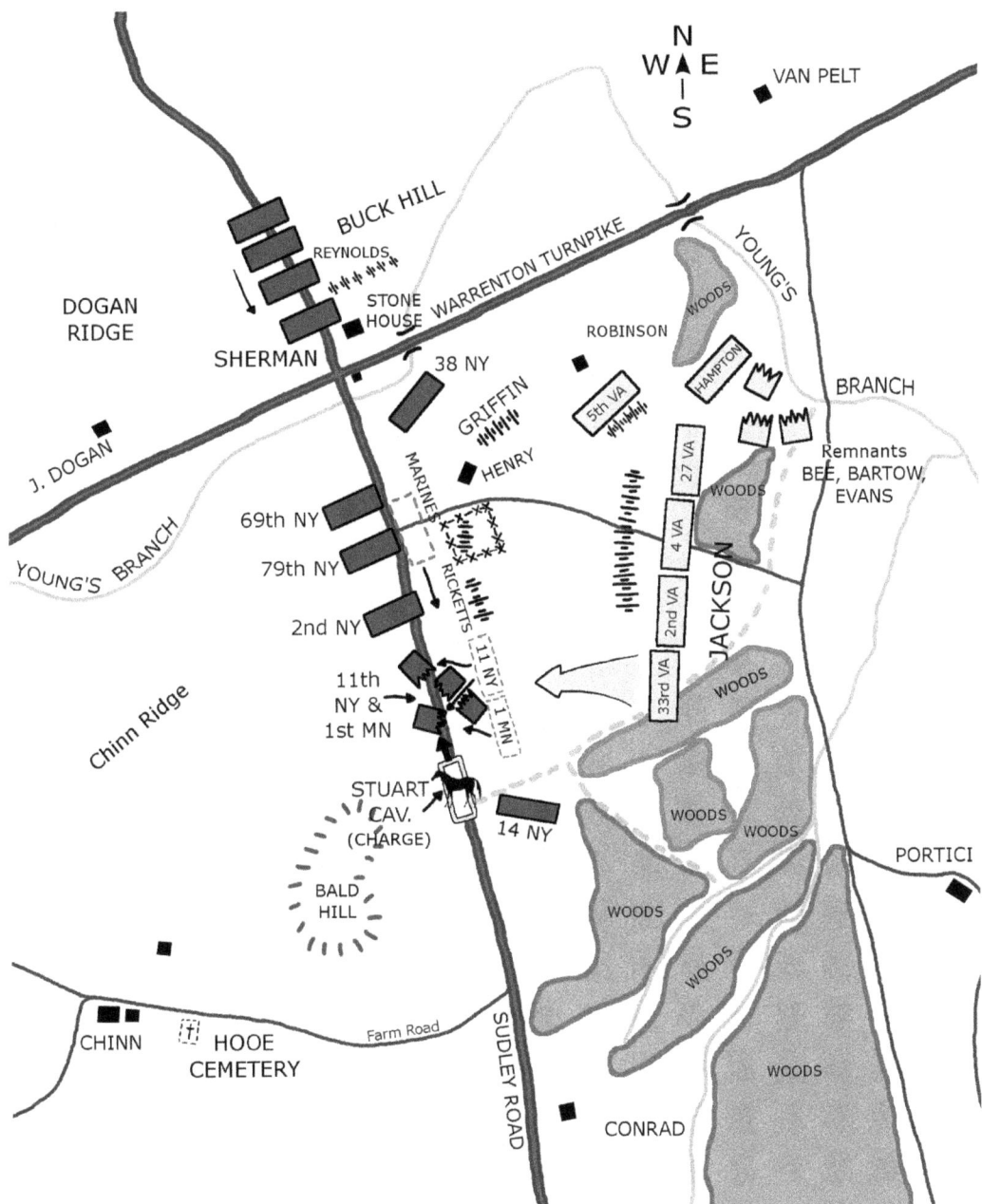

2:15–2:45 P.M.— Initial Infantry Clash on Henry Hill (drawing by Rachael R. Johnson).

sippi companies that were also lost. (Sometime after the war, Smith identified the three companies, one as the Confederate Guards and the other two from Mississippi. The Confederate Guards, part of the 4th South Carolina of Evans's Brigade, initially had been left to guard the Stone Bridge.) Smith directed them to fall in with his regiment, which they did, thus bringing his total strength to 450 men. After he found Beauregard near the Robinson house, he was promptly directed to take up a position to the left of the 33rd Virginia of Jackson's line "in the edge of the belt of pines bordering the southeastern rim of the plateau...."[54]

Beauregard then turned his attention to the right, held by the tired and battered commands of Bee and Evans. Hampton's badly mauled legion and seven companies of Hunton's 8th Virginia (the Prince William, Loudoun Regiment) were placed in their support.

Griffin Makes a Devastating Move

The Union guns that Cummings observed unlimbering in his front were two of Griffin's guns. Griffin, seeing that his battery was being worsted in its close and exposed position north of the Henry House, decided to move and gain an enfilading fire on the line of Confederate artillery. Leaving his three Parrotts with Lieutenant Hazlett, Griffin accompanied his two howitzers, taking them behind the Henry house and down onto the Sudley Road. From there, he moved south and then up again onto Henry Hill beyond the far right of Ricketts's battery. There, he unlimbered and fired two shots at Walton's Washington artillery along Jackson's line.

While Griffin was placing his guns into position, Smith's 49th Virginia was moving up on the 33rd Virginia's left. After firing the two shots, Griffin looked off to his right, and in the pine woods he saw what he was certain was Confederate infantry. Immediately, he ordered his guns turned and loaded with canister, but before he could give the order to fire, Major Barry galloped over from Ricketts's position and shouted to him, "Captain, don't fire there, those are your battery support!" Griffin was sure they were Confederates and argued with Barry, "They are Confederates, as certain as the world!" Barry insisted they were not.[55]

Griffin testified later as to what next took place: "The line of infantry got uncomfortably close," said Griffin, "so close that he ordered his guns limbered and moved." It was then the 49th Virginians came out of the woods and from a rail fence, leveled their pieces and fired a volley. That was the last of us." The volley tore through the section, knocking down horses and men, and what men were not killed or wounded, fled north down the Sudley Road.[56]

As soon as the 49th fired the volley decimating Griffin, Cummings's 33rd Virginia charged forward and captured the guns. However, Colonel A.W. Woods, 14th New York (Brooklyn) of Porter's Brigade, clad in their gaily colored Zouave uniforms with the highly distinguishable bright red trousers, came up the hill and out of the pine woods from the direction of Sudley Road. At the time, some men of the 33rd Virginia were struggling with the guns in an attempt to move them. The 14th New York rushed forward, drove the 33rd Virginia from Griffin's guns, and pushed on toward the Confederate line. Some of the 14th New York made it to within yards of the Confederate guns. Others had moved around the left of the Confederate line and sporadically fired upon the Virginians. The 33rd was in confusion and passed through the left of the 2nd Virginia while falling back, throwing part of that regiment into disarray as well.

While Griffin moved his two howitzers from around the Henry house, Lt. Hazlett limbered his three Parrotts and retired from that area.

Jackson Orders a Counterattack

"...YELL LIKE FURY..." — BIRTH OF THE REBEL YELL

The rest of Jackson's line, however, stood solidly, and when the Federals approached their line, Jackson ordered the 4th and the 27th Virginia to charge and drive them back. In preparing them for the charge, Jackson shouted out his instructions not to fire until they were within 30 yards of the enemy, and then while charging forward with the bayonet to "yell like fury."[57] This was the birth of the famous "Rebel Yell," which would be heard across nearly every battlefield for the next four years. Union veterans have described the yell as "bloodcurdling," saying that it "drew fear into them."

As the regiments moved forward, the 4th Virginia was thrown into some confusion, and two companies of the 27th Virginia rushed ahead to lead the charge. Leading the 27th was acting Captain Charles R. Norris. At the young age of 17, Norris was from the Virginia Military Institute class of 1864, and one of the VMI cadet drillmasters that Jackson had brought with him when he left VMI. In a display of maturity well beyond his years, Norris dashed across the fields of Henry Hill wielding a sword and shouting commands over the cries of the "Rebel Yell" from his followers. As the charge swept towards Ricketts's gun positions, the youthful warrior was felled by a Minié ball which struck him in the upper left torso, killing him instantly. On the left, Lieutenant Colonel Lackland of the 2nd Virginia was able to gather about 100 men of that regiment and join in the advance.

"YONDER STANDS JACKSON LIKE A STONE WALL..." — BIRTH OF THE MOST FAMOUS NICKNAME IN AMERICAN MILITARY HISTORY

While Jackson had been preparing the 4th, 27th, and 2nd Virginia Regiments for a countercharge, events were taking place behind his lines that would mark a historical high point of the Civil War.

By 2:30, Beauregard had mostly succeeded in reforming the confused Confederates of Bee's and Evans's commands that had retreated off Matthews Hill just two hours earlier. However, General Bee and his 4th Alabama were missing. The tired and used men of the 4th Alabama were recovering in the fields 400 yards behind the right of Jackson's line, lying in wait for someone to tell them what to do. The Alabamians had lost all their field grade officers on Matthews Hill, leaving only company-grade officers to lead. The command fell upon the shoulders of the ranking company commander, Capt. Goaldsby. Bee was not available at the time. He had been unable to locate any members of his brigade and was apparently scouring the battlefield looking for them. What happened next has been attested to by four eyewitnesses: Capt. Goaldsby, Regimental Chaplain Hudson, Lieutenant Robbins, and Private Robert

Coles, all members of the 4th Alabama. Bee had been separated from his command for quite some time, Jackson was hotly engaged, and Bee desperately wanted to get back into the battle. Coming upon the Alabamians at a gallop, Bee did not recognize them and shouted out, "What regiment is this?" An Alabamian quickly replied, "Why, General, don't you know your own men? This is what is left of the 4th Alabama." Bee then asked, "Will you follow me?" Every man rose up and shouted their reply, "We will follow you to the death!" Facing toward Jackson's battling men, Bee stood up in his stirrups and while peering through the heavy smoke, pointed his sword toward Jackson's location and shouted, "Yonder stands Jackson like a stone wall; let's go to his assistance!"[58]

The 4th Alabama fell into column. Bee placed himself at their left and led them toward Jackson's position. It was nearly 3:00 P.M. when Jackson ordered his artillery to the rear because the guns could no longer serve their purpose due to the close fighting taking place along his lines. On their way to assist Jackson, the 4th Alabama came across a farm road that ran through the pine woods behind Jackson and continued northwestward past the southern approach to the Henry house. Bee's columns had just moved onto the road when the limbered train of the Alburtis battery came charging down the road at a gallop, cutting through their ranks. To avoid being run down, the columns dispersed to the left and the right of the road into the thickets, separating the left company from the rest of the regiment. Bee was eager to engage and continued on at the head of the left company, which "obliqued to the right upon the open plain and proceeded about 100 yards...."[59]

Jackson was heavily engaged all across his front. As Bee arrived with his meager force in the hottest moments of the fighting, he and his men became a part of Jackson's counterattack. While charging into the battle leading his gallant men, Bee took a Minié ball to the head and fell from his horse, mortally wounded. Some of his men quickly carried him to the rear and laid him in the shade next to the farm road in the pine woods.

Jackson's attacking force quickly swarmed over Ricketts's position as the Union gunners abandoned all six pieces. During the melee, Ricketts was shot from his saddle and Lieutenant Douglas Ramey, commander of Ricketts's right section, was killed.

Sometime during Jackson's initial countercharge, Heintzelman had ordered the brigades of Franklin and Willcox to move into position encompassing the western rim of Henry Hill along the Sudley Road.

A few men of the 2nd Virginia tried to drag one cannon to the rear, but they were forced to give it up by Union infantry fire enfilading their right. Franklin's and Willcox's brigades were resuming the Union attack, and Jackson's Virginians were driven from Ricketts's idle guns. Now Smith's 49th Virginia moved forward from the wood line and took possession of Ricketts's artillery pieces. Using the gun carriages to rest their rifles and steady their aim, they fired into Willcox's beleaguered Federals gathered in the Sudley Road depressions. Shortly, Colonel Ward's 38th New York of Willcox's brigade charged up from the Sudley Road and dispersed the 49th as it was turning the guns around. Unsupported, the 49th fell back. The 38th rolled three of the recovered cannons off the plateau to the Sudley Road. Men of the 5th and 11th Massachusetts also tried to remove some pieces, but without success.[60]

While regiments of Franklin's and Willcox's brigades were advancing from Sudley Road, Beauregard's reinforcements had been moving fast to Jackson's left. The rallied 7th Georgia came from behind the Robinson house and passed around Jackson's rear and to the left of the disengaged 33rd. Virginia. As the 7th Georgia arrived, the 49th Virginia was rallying on their left after being forced back by the 38th New York.

While the fight ensued around the far right of what had been Ricketts's right section, Griffin's two howitzers were retaken by the 14th New York (Brooklyn). By this time, Colonel W.C. Fisher's 6th North Carolina had arrived from or near Portici. Making their way across open fields and through the woods, they emerged on the left of the rallying 49th Virginia, within eighty yards of Griffin's idle guns and the 14th New York's supporting line. Fisher led his regiment straight at the Zouaves, charging through a fire fight taking place between the Federals and the 4th Alabama engaged as part of Jackson's counterattack. The 6th North Carolina recaptured Griffin's guns and was passing over the battery when Fisher received a shot to the head and was killed.

Fisher was possibly killed by friendly fire when caught in the crossfire of the 4th Alabama and Willcox's forces. For decades, a historical plaque noted the spot where Fisher fell, but it was removed when the Visitor Center was built. The spot (south and west of the flagpole) is now covered over with asphalt in the parking lot.

Jackson continued to push forward, countercharging each time there was a Union charge, holding on to the Henry Hill plateau and depriving McDowell of a foothold. Major A.F. Bidwell's 1st Michigan of Willcox's brigade briefly retook some guns but could not hold them. In successive countercharges led by Heintzelman, the 1st Michigan and 14th Brooklyn attempted to press forward, but each time they were met by stiff resistance and repulsed. Ricketts's battery changed hands three times.

It was at this juncture that Beauregard decided to initiate a sweeping attack all across the Confederate front. As Jackson penetrated the center of the line, the Confederate right swept the area clear in the vicinity of the Robinson House.

A unit included in Beauregard's attack across the Confederate front was the 7th Georgia led by Colonel Francis Bartow. Bartow's horse had been shot out from under him, so he was afoot encouraging his gallant Georgians when he was struck down by Minié balls and died within a few minutes. He fell some one hundred yards to the right and rear of where Bee received his mortal wound.

Howard's Brigade Advances on Chinn Ridge

Union reinforcements of Hunter, Heintzelman, and Tyler were now moving up. Arnold's battery came racing forward to take position at the back of the Stone House at "left Center" as Sherman readied his brigade for an assault on Henry Hill. At about the same time, Howard's brigade swung farther to the south to occupy Chinn Ridge and threaten the Confederate left.[61] In Beauregard's Official Records report, he said, "The woods and fields were filled with their masses of infantry and carefully preserved cavalry. It was a truly magnificent spectacle as they threw forward in fine style on the broad, gentle slopes of the ridge...."[62]

SHERMAN'S ADVANCE ATTEMPTS MEET HEAVY ONSLAUGHT

Using the Sudley Road as their stepping-off point, Sherman then threw one regiment after another into the fray in a desperate effort to take the hill. First, he sent the "gray clad" 2nd Wisconsin. Moving out from Sudley road by the left flank, they advanced steadily to the crest of the hill. Just as they cleared the top, they received a heavy fire, which they returned before they broke and retreated in confusion. They rallied and charged the hill a second time, only to be forced back in disorder.[63]

Having swept the vicinity of the Robinson house clear, Beauregard now sent Hunton and Hampton from his right flank to attack Sherman's left as he attempted to establish a foothold along the northwest quadrant of Henry Hill.

Meanwhile, from Sherman's brigade, the 79th New York (Highlanders) led by Colonel James Cameron (brother of Lincoln's Secretary of War, Simon Cameron), swung into line and closed up. Using the Henry house to guide on, Cameron excitedly urged them on. Just as they reached the crest of the hill, their ranks were staggered by "incessant and severe musketry fire." They met Hampton's Legion as the Confederates were flank-attacking Ricketts's unsupported artillery position located near the Henry house. Hampton, leading his Legionnaires as they swarmed in and around the Henry house, was shot from his horse. Hampton's second in command, Capt. James Conner, immediately assumed command and led the Legion, capturing two of the guns while sending the Highlanders back to the Sudley Road along with the gunners. The 79th New York twice attempted to rally; Cameron desperately made a third try and finally a few did obey. As they charged up the hill, Cameron fell mortally wounded near the spot where Hampton was wounded only moments before. The Highlanders broke, leaving Cameron on the field where he fell.[64]

Markers are located near the Henry house identifying the spots where Cameron and Hampton fell. The Cameron marker is located about 125 feet northwest of the north side of Henry house, and the Hampton marker is located about 80 feet north of the north side of Henry house. The two markers are about 100 feet apart.

Sherman continued to launch his regiments into the fight one at a time. Next, he sent Colonel M. Corcoran's 69th New York forward. They reached the crest just to suffer the same fate of the regiments before them. Sherman later wrote, "The firing was very severe and the roar of cannon, muskets and rifles incessant."[65] For a short time only, they maintained their position and then retired in disorder. Farther to the left, Colonel Isaac Quinby's 13th New York was equally unsuccessful.[66]

However, Beauregard's left and right flanks became gravely endangered as Federal pressure continued to steadily mount. At about 3:15, Fisher's 6th North Carolina regiment rallied and moved to take position on the Confederate left. Beauregard swiftly ordered another general attack all along the line, and personally led a full assault that successfully cleared the field. The Confederates took final possession of the Henry and Robinson houses and the greater part of Ricketts's and Griffin's batteries.[67]

BEAUREGARD MOUNTS A COUNTERATTACK THAT DELIVERS A FINAL BLOW

Despite being denied the Henry/Robinson Hill plateau, McDowell still occupied a position of strength. From his right, which was anchored in the woods in the vicinity of the Chinn House, his line curved in a great arc from the back of the Stone House to a position near the Stone Bridge, occupied by Keyes's Brigade.[68] The Union right, held by Colonel Oliver Howard's brigade comprising the 3rd, 4th, and 5th Maine and the 2nd Vermont, plus Sykes's U.S. regulars, faced almost due east of the Sudley road. So extended, it invited an attack which Beauregard was quick to mount.

Johnston was fast moving reinforcements to Beauregard. In the lead were Colonel J.B. Kershaw's 2nd and Colonel E.G.B. Cash's 8th South Carolina regiments, followed by Captain D. Kemper's four-piece battery (Alexandria Light Artillery) and Colonel R.T. Preston's 28th Virginia. Rapidly moving up in close support was General Kirby Smith's brigade, 1,700 strong. The brigade, comprising the 1st Maryland Infantry Battalion, 3rd Tennessee Infantry, 10th Virginia Infantry, and Lieutenant R.F. Beckham's Culpeper Artillery, had only detrained a short time before and had quickly advanced "to the sound of the firing." Upon arriving, Smith immediately began moving his brigade into line of battle west of Sudley Road. While leading the 1st Maryland to the right of the 2nd South Carolina, he was struck from his horse by Union sharpshooters, seriously wounded.[69] The command of Smith's brigade was assumed by Colonel Arnold Elzey. Elzey and other units moved in an "irregular line" to blunt a Federal attack being led by the 1st Michigan.[70]

While leading the 1st Michigan against Elzey's Confederates, Colonel Willcox was struck down, seriously wounded by shrapnel from an artillery shell, probably fired from one of Beckham's guns.[71] Willcox was captured and later taken to Portici for medical attention. He was placed in a room along with Ricketts and subsequently the two were sent to Richmond and incarcerated. After several months, both were paroled and exchanged.

It was about 3:45 P.M. when Elzey decided to make a change of front and led his brigade into a wooded area not far from the Chinn House. Moving to form his line of battle, he placed his 3rd Tennessee on the right, the 1st Maryland in the center and the 10th Virginia on the left. Beckham's artillery went into battery to the left of the 10th Virginia and immediately began firing upon Howard's positions. Stuart's 1st Virginia Cavalry rode to the left in support of Beckham.

Meanwhile, the three-regiment brigade of Colonel Jubal Early moved north across the southern slopes of Chinn Ridge and to the left of Elzey. Early struck Howard's right flank and rear.[72]

A Demoralized Army Retreats and Panics

The weight of this last combined Confederate attack, delivered about 4 P.M., proved decisive. Exhausted and beaten, the Federal line staggered and fell back across Young's Branch. The contagion of retreat caught the other Union forces on Henry Hill and there was a general retirement from the field. This soon degenerated into panicked disorder. McDowell stated in his official report, "Every effort was made to rally them, even beyond the reach of the enemy's fire, but in vain." Taking a position on "the extreme

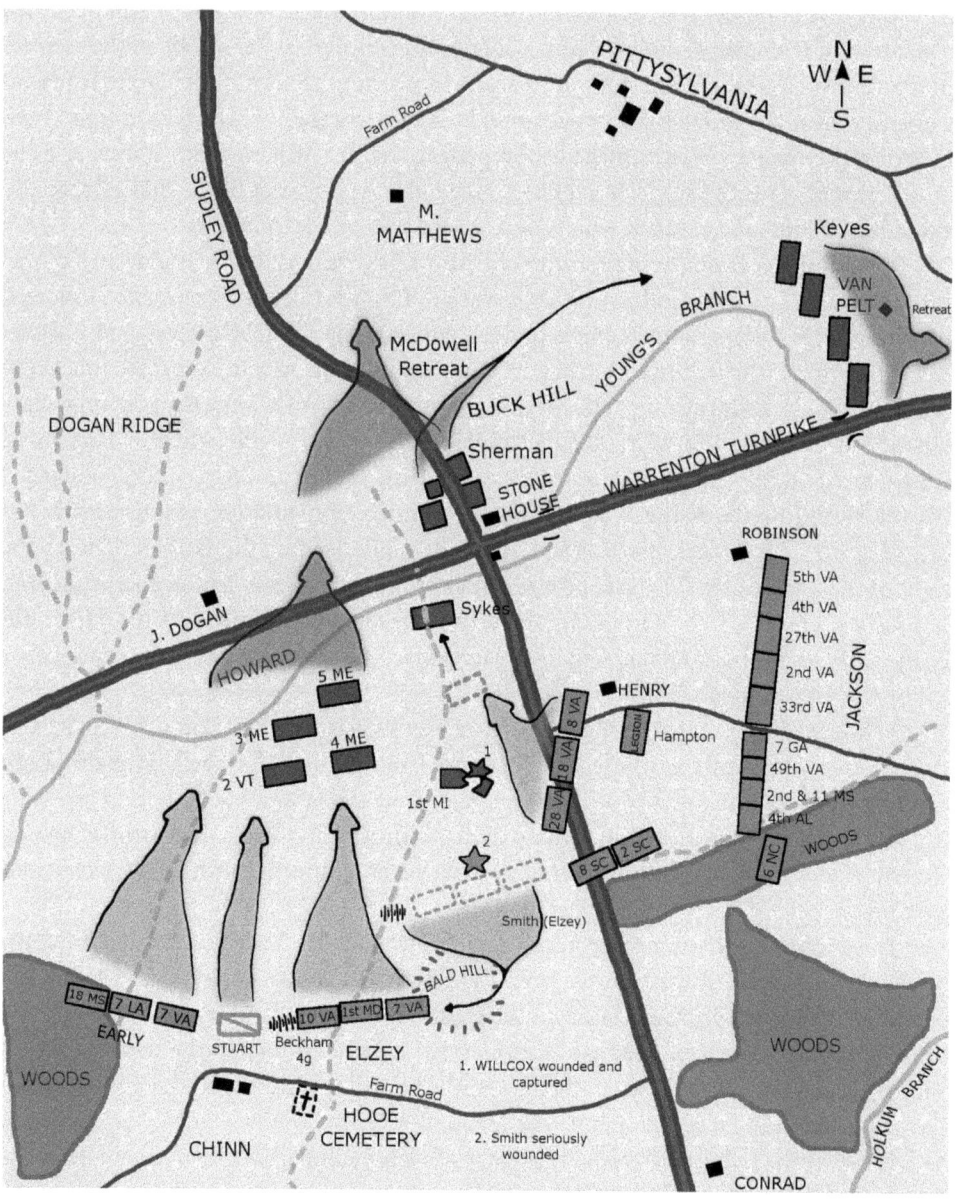

3:45–4:15 P.M.— The Final Blow (drawing by Rachael R. Johnson)

right (John Dogan House Hill), Sykes's U.S. Regulars attempted a stand but quickly joined the panic. The line of retreat followed closely the pattern of the morning's advance — the divisions of Hunter and Heintzelman retreating rapidly by Sudley Ford, while Sherman's and Keyes's brigades, of Tyler's command, crossed at the fords from whence they came, just above the Stone Bridge."[73]

KEMPER STOPS FOR A HITCHHIKER

Moving out in hot pursuit, Confederate units pressed the attack. Early moved forward with Beckham's battery and Stuart's 1st Virginia Cavalry along the Sudley Road, and Cash, Kershaw and Kemper's battery pressed along the turnpike. As Kemper's limbered artillery was passing the Stone House, an old man with long, stringy gray locks, wearing dusty, sweaty civilian clothes, and carrying a musket, stepped out from along side of the turnpike to hail him. It was 62-year-old Edmund Ruffin, weary and dusty from walking six miles from Manassas to the sound of battle. Kemper stopped and allowed the old man to straddle one of the cannons. Keeping a precarious seat on the cannon with his left hand and gleefully holding his musket high in the air with his right hand, Ruffin went flying east with the artillery past the Stone House.

Approaching the Cub Run Suspension Bridge, Confederate units of Cash, Kershaw and Kemper's battery were informed by advanced guards that Union troops were in sight and not far ahead. Ruffin wrote the following account in his diary[74]:

> The road was strewed with articles which were thrown away by the fugitives — arms, accoutrements, haversacks (mostly well filled with lard biscuits or crackers), Knapsacks filled and loose articles of clothing, blankets, drums & brass musical instruments, etc.... After our detachment, which consisted of Colonel Kershaw's then command, had followed a few miles, and it was after sunset (or when darkness was beginning to approach) that the foremost guards announced that the enemy's troops were in sight and not far ahead — cavalry as at first supposed. By order, two of Kemper's guns were unlimbered and quickly ready for firing. I having before obtained the captain's permission fired the first of these guns — either 10 or 12 thus directed and rapidly fired off.... The first wagon had just been driven upon the bridge to pass over when the first gun (my gun) was fired from Kemper's battery, leaded (as I learned afterwards) with shrapnel, or spherical case shell as the official reports of the Yankee commander afterwards stated. Some of the shots from this discharge ... struck one or more of the horses of the foremost wagon. In their pain and fright they suddenly turned upset the wagon so as to barricade the whole width of the bridge and effectively preclude any other wheel carriage and horses from passing. The whole mass of fugitives immediately got out of track and all escaped who could on foot and quickly as possible.

Confusion was compounded by the fact that two masses of Federal troops were converging on the bridge from different directions along the routes of the morning advance. With the blocking of the bridge (Cub Run Bridge), more panic seized the troops, causing them to abandon all vehicles and seek crossings to the right and left of the bridge. The panic was further heightened by continued discharges of the Confederate cannon and the charge of Stuart's 1st Virginia Cavalry.

Adding further to the demoralization of the men were the crowds of sightseers and fugitives who crowded the narrow roads. Throughout the night and the rain of the next day, the tide of half-crazed soldiers and civilians streamed into Washington. The Confederates were too battle-weary, disjointed, and exhausted to mount an effective pursuit into Washington.

Six

Interval of Occupation

Aftermath Events — The First Seven Months

THE CASUALTIES

In the initial aftermath of the battle, the disposition of the casualties was priority, determined by the victors. The dead needed to be buried as soon as possible and the wounded needed medical attention. In the case of captives, many were fortunate enough to be paroled, while the others were marched off for incarceration. The number of casualties that occurred in the first major battle of the Civil War was small in comparison to the number that were to occur in battles over the next four years. However, for those who fought at Manassas on July 21, 1861, the families living in the area, and the nation, both North and South, the numbers were horrific and staggering. There had never been carnage like this on the North American continent.

Casualty Numbers[1]

	Casualties	Killed	Wounded	Captured/Missing
Union	3,333	470	1,070	1,793
Confederate	2,306	387	1,906	13
Total	5,639	857	2,976	1,806

Abstract of Captured Ordnance and Prisoner Disposition

Beauregard assigned E.P. Alexander (then captain of engineers on general staff) to prepare a report of all captured ordnance turned in to the Ordnance Department, Army of the Potomac. Alexander's report also included prisoner dispositions. His report, dated October 12, 1861, included all ordnance turned in as of August 16, 1861.[2]

Artillery — Small Arms & Muskets

- 1 — 30-pounder Parrott gun, with 300 rounds of ammunition
- 9 — 10-pounder Parrott guns, with 100 rounds of ammunition each
- 3 — 6-pounder brass guns, with 100 rounds of ammunition each
- 3 — 12-pounder brass howitzers, with 100 rounds of ammunition each
- 2 — 12-pounder boat howitzers, with 100 rounds of ammunition each
- 9 — 14-pounder brass James rifles, with 100 rounds of ammunition each

(Alexander reported that one 6-pounder gun and one 12-pounder howitzer were found spiked, but they were easily withdrawn, bringing the total of captured artillery pieces to 29.)

3–caissons
6–traveling forges
4–battery wagons, fully equipped
64–artillery horses, with harness
500,000 rounds small-arms ammunition
4,500 sets of accouterments (cartridge boxes, etc.)
4,000 muskets

Quartermaster Stores

33 — horses
21 — wagons
25 — trunks and carpet-bags
870 — axes, spades, and entrenching tools
2 sets—carpenters' and blacksmiths' tools
12 sets— harness
23–extra traces for artillery
7 — platform and other scales
1,650 camp cooking utensils

Hospital Equipment

7–ambulances
5 — medicine chests, partially filled
6 —cases surgical instruments
2 sets— panniers

(Alexander reported that other hospital items, i.e., litters, instruments, and supplies, had been appropriated by surgeons of regiments, besides the loss from plundering by individuals and citizens.)

Miscellaneous Articles

Miscellaneous, i.e., pistols, swords, drums, knapsacks, canteens, bridles, etc.

(Alexander reported it was impossible to provide a count of these items because for the most part they were carried off by individuals.)

Other Miscellaneous items, i.e., bed ticks, buckets, coffee mills, picket pins, halters, saddles and bridles, 10 barrels commissary stores, and handcuffs. (Alexander noted that large numbers of these items had been carried off by individuals and civilians and he was not able to provide an accounting.)

Abstract Numbers and Disposition of Union Prisoners[3]

Non-wounded sent to Richmond	871
Wounded sent to hospitals at Richmond and other locations	550
Total	1,421

(Alexander noted that the prisoners represented themselves as belonging to 47 different volunteer regiments, 9 regiments of regular Army, and the Marine Corps. Alexander provided no number of prisoners paroled at Manassas.)

JACKSON GETS MEDICAL ATTENTION

While McDowell's forces wildly retreated back to Washington, Jackson was denied permission to join in the pursuit, as Beauregard had ordered him to get medical attention for his wounded hand. On his way to the rear, the wound pained him so much that he stopped at the first regimental hospital he came to; the surgeon there proposed to cut the injured finger off. Jackson must have had different thoughts about that, for while the doctor turned his back a few moments to look for his instruments, Jackson silently mounted his horse and rode off.

Jackson soon came upon his own medical doctor, located near Portici. As Jackson initially arrived on Henry Hill and deployed his brigade into position, his brigade medical director, Dr. Hunter Holmes McGuire, set up a field hospital situated along a small stream, a short distance north of Portici. Years later, McGuire described the encounter:

> I was busily engaged with the wounded, but when I saw him coming, I left them and asked if he was seriously hurt. "No," he answered, "not half as badly as many here, and I will wait." And he forthwith sat down on the bank of a little stream near by and positively declined any assistance until "his turn came." We compromised however, and he agreed to let me attend to him after I had finished the case I was dressing when he arrived. I determined to save his finger if possible, and placed a splint along the palmar surface to support the fragments, retained it in position by a strip or two of adhesive plaster, covered the wound with lint, and told him to keep it wet with cold water.[4]

Jefferson Davis Arrives

President Davis had detrained with his staff at Manassas Junction about the time McDowell was in heavy retreat. He was immediately taken to Liberia, where Colonel Jordan of Beauregard's staff gave him a horse. Riding hard to the field of battle, he had been told by stragglers along the six-mile ride that they were defeated. Approaching near Portici at a gallop, he came down a little hill and stopped when he got to the stream where McGuire had set up his hospital. Davis's face was a "deadly pale and his eyes were flashing" as he glanced over the area, seeing a great crowd of soldiers. McGuire described the scene:

> The enemy had been routed and the wounded brought back to the field hospital which I had made for Jackson's brigade. Out of about eighteen hundred shot that day in our army, six hundred or more were out of Jackson's brigade, and he himself had come to the hospital wounded. Hundreds of men had come back, the fight being over, to see about their wounded comrades, so there were really several thousand people gathered in and about that hospital.[5]

Davis was still with the understanding of what the stragglers had told him, that they had been defeated. McGuire continues to describe the scene:

> He [Davis] stood up in his stirrups, glanced over the crowd, and said: "I am President Davis; all of you who are able, follow me back to the field." Jackson was a little deaf, and didn't know who Davis was or what he had said until I told him. He stood up at once, took off his cap and saluted the President and said: "We have whipped them; they ran like dogs. Give me ten thousand men and I will take Washington city tomorrow."[6]

Council of War

The late evening hours found the Confederate leaders at Liberia. First came Davis and Johnston, and later, Beauregard rode in to join them. This was actually a council of war to decide the next course of action for the Confederacy. There was no official written account of this meeting, but no pursuit of McDowell was mounted. Controversy arose as a result of not following up the victory with a move on Washington, and it soon became a subject of contention. In addition, mistrusts, misunderstandings, egos, and differences in command decisions became a growing cause of animosity between the three leaders, played out in newspapers and the Confederate Congress for the remaining war years and after.[7]

In 1874, writing in his *Narrative of Military Operations* about the situation in the aftermath of the battle, Johnston had this to say[8]:

> All the military conditions we knew forbade an attempt on Washington. The Confederate army was more disorganized by victory than that of the United States by defeat. Many [volunteers] in ignorance of their army obligations left the army. Besides this the reasons for the course condemned by the non-combatant military critics were: The unfitness of our raw troops for marching or assailing entrenchments. The want of the necessary supplies of food and ammunition and means of transporting them. Until near the 10th of August we never had rations for more than two days, and sometimes none; nor half enough ammunition for a battle. The fortifications upon which skilful engineers ... had been engaged since April, manned by at least fifty thousand Federal troops.... The Potomac, a mile wide, bearing United States vessels-of-war, the heavy guns of which commanded the wooden bridges and southern shore."

RECOVERY OF THE WOUNDED

Night fell across what had once been "a typical peaceful country-side," but was now a scene of horror with the scattered dead lying among wounded soldiers and the dead and wounded horses. Amplifying the scene were mixed screams and moaning of many of the wounded soldiers and horses. While the cries for help, whimpering, and pleas for water could be heard across the battlefields, details using lanterns picked up the wounded and took them to places set up for their care. Most of the dwellings throughout the battlefield area were used for attending the wounded in some manner or form, while personal possessions of the residents were subject to confiscation or forced requisition.

The largest of the hospitals initially set up by the Union was at the Sudley Church. As soon as the engagements on Matthews Hill began, Union medical personnel started preparing the church to receive the wounded. Church pews were removed, blankets were spread out over the floor, hay was brought in for bedding, and buckets of water were carried down from the Sudley Spring (located near the ford on Catharpin Run). In addition, the communion table was made ready as an improvised operating table while instruments and dressings were arranged for immediate use.

Those arrangements were hardly completed when the ambulances began arriving. Most Union ambulances were canvas-topped, four-wheel vehicles pulled by two horses, but many single-axle, two-wheel ambulances were still in service which had been devised in the Crimean War. Assistant Surgeon D.L. Magruder described the scene:

> In about two hours, the church, both upon the main floor and in the gallery, was completely filled, and I was obliged to take possession of three other unoccupied buildings, which are situated about seventy-five paces further down and on the opposite side of the road towards the creek. So soon as I could get them cleared out, wounded men were carried into

Six. Interval of Occupation

them until they were filled also. For want of other buildings, I was obliged to order many of the wounded to be laid under the trees, in the grove immediately around the church.

The number swelled to some 250, according to Magruder's estimate. Several capital operations, namely amputations, were performed before the rush of retreating columns crowded their makeshift facilities so completely that work for the time being was suspended.

As the battle intensified throughout the day, the surgeons became aware that their capture was imminent, and a number of them volunteered to remain in order to care for the wounded. The number included Assistant Surgeons Gray and Sternberg of the regular army, Surgeon Swift and Assistant Surgeons Winston and DeGraw of the 8th Regiment, New York Militia.[9]

In the afternoon, as McDowell's army was pursued through the Sudley area in their frantic retreat, the Sudley Church was overrun. The wounded and all medical personnel fell into Confederate hands, notably by the command of Colonel J.E.B. Stuart of the First Virginia Cavalry Regiment. After Stuart passed through Sudley, he followed the retreating Federal columns some twelve miles from Manassas, and after having returned to the Sudley area, "encamped that night on Sudley farm, where there was a large church (the Sudley Church), used as a hospital by the enemy, containing about 300 wounded, the majority mortally."[10]

Four days later, a visiting minister, Charles Wesley Andrews, from Shepherdstown, Virginia, wrote of this tragic scene:

> The communion table was taken for amputations and was literally dripping with human blood. Many had died. One had a frightful wound in the hip from a cannon shot and was calling for chloroform. I called to see him the next day but found that his leg had been taken off at the hip joint and he died a few minutes after. Another was dying in all the contortions of lockjaw, another was undergoing an amputation. Some with death upon their faces spoke of wives and children who they were no more to see....[11]

Following the taking of the Sudley Church hospital by Confederate forces, Union and Confederate surgeons worked side by side. Prisoner Edward P. Doherty, Co. A, Seventy-first New York, recorded the names and regiments of a large number of the prisoners held at Sudley Church, both wounded and non-wounded. Doherty's account and list of names was printed in the *New York Times* on Tuesday, August 6, 1861. Doherty states that in all, there were 286, of whom 32 died up to the time that he left. Doherty and two other prisoners successfully escaped their captors during the night of Friday, July 26, 1861.

During the time the church was being used as a hospital, local families came to assist in the care of the wounded, providing food and other needs. As further reported by Doherty: "Ladies and farmers of the surrounding country visited our hospitals, bringing them milk, soup, and cakes."[12]

The three buildings opposite the church that Magruder referred to were the Thornberry home and two of Thornberry's outbuildings. A testimonial letter written years later by John Thornberry's daughter, Laura Thornberry Fletcher, who was 6 years old at time of First Battle of Manassas, describes in detail the devastation and sorrow that confronted the Thornberry family: "Ten men had bled to death in her mothers bedroom ... carpets and all furniture were out and gone. We never saw any of it again, or anything else. The old farm well in the back yard was almost full of everything that would go into it. Such as china ware, cooking utinsels [sic], flat irons, and every thing you can imagine used in a family was thrown in it. How we all cried over it; and no prospects of replacing any of it."[13]

Resting at the crossroads in the Valley of Young's Branch was the Stone House. It had the misfortune of being in one of the most strategic locations on the battlefield. During the midday phase of the battle, as the Confederates were being forced from Matthews Hill, the valley of Young's Branch fell into the hands of McDowell's invading army. Immediately, the Stone House was turned into an improvised hospital or aid station. Almost everything was removed, and very quickly every room from the basement to the top floor was crowded with wounded. Many were being carried from the field to the Stone House on muskets.

The need and want of water became an overpowering factor for the medical personnel and the wounded. A well that supplied the water for the Stone House was located in the front yard some forty paces away. In the heat of the battle raging around the valley of Young's Branch, getting to the well for water was a dangerous task. One of the wounded took it upon himself to fetch water for those inside. Although not able to walk, he crawled to the well carrying empty canteens and was able to return with the canteens filled with water. The well was like a beacon for thirsty soldiers in the valley, and it wasn't long before the well was dry.[14]

Later in the day, after the Union forces had retreated and the Confederates retook control of the area, they found thirty-two wounded, many of them "dreadfully mangled by cannon shot." In an after-battle report by Colonel Robert T. Preston of the 28th Virginia Regiment, he had this to say about the Stone House[15]: "In this house were found a large number of the wounded enemy, some dead, and thirty-six men, who surrendered themselves prisoners. Among them were two officers, a surgeon, and assistant surgeon. The latter was liberated on parole, and directed to take charge of and assist the enemy's wounded. There were also found in the house about one hundred arms."

The next day, General Beauregard sent word to Union commanders, inviting them to send "surgeons and attendants to administer to their relief." This was followed by the arrival of Union ambulances and surgeons from Washington. In a few days, the Stone House was being used as a parole station, placing large numbers of the wounded soldiers on parole.

All during the fighting, first on Matthews Hill and subsequently on Henry Hill, the Stone House was in the wake of the artillery duels taking place. Consequently, it was hit by several artillery shells and musket balls, causing considerable damage.

An Act of Compassion Saves the Life of a Young Union Soldier

On the day of battle and for several days afterward, Amos and Margaret Benson spent endless hours giving aid and comfort to the wounded at the Sudley Church. The Bensons' home was about 400 yards southeast of the church. In the late twilight hours of the second day, the Bensons were returning home after spending a long, exhausting day at the church. As they neared their home, they sighted a body clad in a blue uniform lying beside a fence. The young soldier had lain there for two days and was just now regaining consciousness. They could readily see that he was seriously wounded and should not be moved. This prompted Amos to run quickly back to the church for assistance. Within moments he was back and in the company of a Confederate surgeon. The wound was extensive; the young man had taken a bullet to the chest which tore through a lung. After a quick exam, the surgeon told the Bensons that nothing could be done.

Amos and Margaret were devout Christians and knew without hesitation that they were going to do all they could for the young man to make him comfortable. The young man's clothing was dirty and blood-stained; maggots had invaded his wound, and lice were crawling over his body. After removing his clothing, they washed him, cleaned and dressed his wound, dressed him in clean clothing, placed blankets on him, and nurtured him with food and water. As he couldn't be moved, they erected a tent-like shelter over him and for the next ten days continued to nurse him and attended to all his needs. At the end of the tenth day, he had improved enough to be carried to the church, where he received further attention. Over the course of several days, he was placed in a freight car at Manassas Junction with other prisoners and transported to Libby Prison in Richmond.

The young soldier was Private John L. Rice, who had been with the 2nd New Hampshire Infantry Regiment of Burnside's Brigade engaged in the fighting on Matthews Hill during the morning phase of the battle. Burnside's Brigade had stacked rifles after the fight on Matthews Hill but was caught up in the retreat during the Confederate pursuit. It was during that time that Rice went down with a musket ball through his lung.

In the retreat, two other New Hampshire boys bore him off the battlefield with the intentions of dropping him off at the Sudley Church hospital. Since they were being closely pursued, and Rice appeared dead or near death, they laid him under a fence and frantically continued their retreat.[16]

Later, Rice was paroled; he went back to his unit, and still later was commissioned to the rank of lieutenant colonel. Twenty-five years later, while on a trip to Washington, he took time out to travel to the Bull Run battlefield, seeking out information about the Bensons. After learning that both Amos and Margaret Benson were still living, he lost no time "in reaching their house and making myself known." They had a most enjoyable reunion, and he was most surprised to learn that "after Bull Run, Benson had enlisted in Stuart's Cavalry, and that we had literally fought face to face in a dozen desperate battles during the next twelve months, while his wife had remained at home and again succored our wounded, left there by Pope when he was driven from the same bloody field in '62."

As he was making his departure, Rice asked if there was any way by which he might repay them for saving his life. Their reply was "no, there was nothing." Rice was persistent, and finally Mrs. Benson said, "If you want to do that, our little church over yonder was destroyed during the war. It has cost us a severe struggle to rebuild it and we owe $200 on it yet—which is a heavy burden in this poor country." After Rice returned to his hometown of Springfield, Massachusetts, he told his story to the editor of the local paper, *The Republican*. After his story was printed, contributions flowed in and Rice was able to send $235 to the Sudley Church.[17]

Death and Interment of Mrs. Henry

Mrs. Henry died sometime during the afternoon of July 21, 1861, after the Federal army began their retreat. Before she died, one of James Robertson's daughters and her mother came to the Henry house and witnessed a grieving scene: the dying Mrs. Henry was trying to comfort "Miss Henry," telling her "not to weep for her."[18]

Caught up in the dismal scene on Henry Hill were two local civilians, the Wiginton sisters, Lucy and Susan. In the late dark hours, they crossed the fields from their home near Groveton to the ruins of the Henry house. Finding the dead Mrs. Judith Henry and her grieving son and daughter (John and Ellen), the sisters took charge of the situation and, while consoling the two, set about the task of preparing Mrs. Henry's body for burial.[19] Monday, the next day, Confederate soldiers assisted in the burial of Mrs. Henry. Sometime after the interment, a Confederate officer on horseback riding by the grave site saw a sobbing man lying prone across the grave. John Henry looked up and through sobs exclaimed, "They killed my mother!"[20]

The Henry house had been severely damaged and was no longer habitable. Sometime after the battle, Ellen went to live with her cousins, the Carters, at Pittsylvania.

Gravesite of Judith Henry — First Civilian Killed in a Civil War Battle. Modern-day view (2010) looking north (photograph by Jessica Johnson)
THE GRAVE OF OUR MOTHER
JUDITH HENRY
KILLED NEAR THIS SPOT BY THE EXPLOSION OF SHELLS IN HER DWELLING DURING THE BATTLE OF THE 21ST OF JULY, 1861. WHEN KILLED SHE WAS IN HER 85TH YEAR AND CONFINED TO HER BED BY THE INFIRMITIES OF AGE.
[the next two lines are illegible]
HER HUSBAND DR. ISAAC HENRY WAS A SURGEON IN THE UNITED STATES NAVY ON BOARD THE FRIGATE CONSTELLATION, COMMANDED BY COM TRUXTON, ONE OF THE SIX CAPTAINS APPOINTED BY WASHINGTON IN THE ORGANIZATION OF THE NAVY, 1794
OUR MOTHER THROUGH HER LONG LIFE, THIRTY FIVE YEARS OF WHICH WERE SPENT AT THIS PLACE, WAS GREATLY LOVED AND ESTEEMED FOR HER KIND, GENTLE, AND CHRISTIAN SPIRIT

Six. Interval of Occupation 97

BEE'S LAST REQUEST

At daylight on the day after the battle, Imboden was awakened by a messenger from ex–Governor Alston of South Carolina, summoning him to the side of his commander Brigadier General Bee. After being mortally wounded, Bee had been carried to a cabin to the east-northeast and across the Bull Run, not far from Portici. There, Imboden found his beloved commander unconscious. Writing for *Battles and Leaders* in 1883, Imboden provided the following account of his visit to see Bee:

> In a few minutes, while I was holding his hand, he died. Some one during the night had told him that I had reflected on him for leaving our battery so long exposed to capture; and, at his request, messengers had been for hours hunting me in the darkness, to bring me to him, that I might learn from his own lips that he had sent Major Howard to order me to withdraw, when he was driven back across Young's Branch and the turnpike. I was grieved deeply not to have seen him sooner.[21]

IMBODEN MAKES APOLOGY TO JACKSON

The second evening after the battle, Mrs. Jackson arrived. Jackson had taken up quarters in a little farmhouse near Centreville. Three days after the battle, on learning that Jackson's wound had become severely painful due to inflammation and swelling, Imboden rode out to see him. He arrived shortly after sunrise. Imboden found Jackson under some trees, slowly and diligently pouring cup after cup of cool spring water over his hand. Jackson was faithfully following McGuire's instructions. Imboden said regarding his visit:

Captain John D. Imboden. Virginia Light Artillery—Staunton Artillery; Army of the Shenandoah—Bee's 3rd Brigade (courtesy Library of Congress).

> Of course, the battle was the only topic discussed at breakfast. I remarked, in Mrs. Jackson's hearing, "General, how is it that you can keep so cool, and appear so utterly insensible to danger in such a storm of shell and bullets as rained about you when your hand was hit?" He instantly became grave and reverential in his manner, and answered, in a low tone of great earnestness; "Captain, my religious belief teaches me to feel as safe in battle as in bed. God has fixed the time for my death. I do not concern myself about that, but to be always ready, no matter when it may over-

take me." He added, after a pause, looking me full in the face: "Captain, that is the way all men should live, and then all would be equally brave."

Imboden added about his conversation with Jackson, "I felt that this last remark was intended as a rebuke for my profanity, when I had complained to him on the field of the apparent abandonment of my battery to capture, and I apologized. He heard me, and simply said, 'Nothing can justify profanity.'"[22]

Years later, McGuire had more to say about Jackson's wound and its treatment: "I think he had a kind of fancy for this kind of hydropathic treatment, and I have frequently seen him occupied for several hours pouring cup after cup of water over his hand with that patience and perseverance for which he was so remarkable. Passive motion was instituted about the twentieth day and carefully continued. The motion of the joint improved for several months after the wound healed, and in the end the deformity was very trifling."[23]

Victory and Defeat Reactions Across the Nation

Victory ... as Received in the South

News of the victory was received with feelings of great happiness and excitement throughout the South. As church bells rang, people congregated in their houses of worship to hear sermons praising God and to give thanks for their victory, while public officials issued congratulatory proclamations. Newspapers were at work throughout the days and nights following the victory, putting out detailed accounts as quickly as the news came in. President Davis of the Confederacy dispatched a victory wire from the Manassas battlefield that read: "We have won a glorious though dear-bought victory. Night closed on the enemy in full flight and closely pursued."

The South believed they had won tremendous prestige abroad, and that support from England and/or France would be forthcoming; however, over the next four years, it became apparent they had been lulled into a false sense of security.

Defeat ... as Received in the North

The news of the Union defeat quickly spread across the North, leaving it dismayed and disillusioned. Lincoln shared this feeling as he listened throughout the night in silence to the eyewitness description of the battle. In the immediate aftermath, all seemed lost for the North, but despair was soon replaced with hope and determination, as illustrated in an editorial that appeared in a Northern newspaper stating the need to follow a strong resolve[24]: "The nation has been shocked into an earnestness which nothing can lull, pervert or withstand. Those who have essayed the life of this great republic must give up theirs as the penalty. And with that perhaps will fall their cherished institutions. We know the high stake for which we are playing, and we shall carry it through to the end. The integrity of our country must and shall be preserved."

The Search for Fallen Loved Ones

For days, weeks, and months after the battle, Northern and Southern families from across the nation visited the Manassas Battlefield seeking information about a fallen son, husband, father, or other loved one. Those few who were fortunate enough to locate their loved ones' remains would return with them to their homes for reburial.

One such family from Georgia brought a white marble stone to mark where their beloved one fell. George T. Stovall of the 8th Georgia was carrying his wounded brother from the field of battle when he was mortally wounded. Originally, the stone was located where it had been determined he fell, but sometime later the stone was moved to the edge of the cornfield by the farmer so that he wouldn't have to plow around it.

Acting Captain Charles R. Norris of the 27th Virginia Regiment was another fallen Confederate soldier whose body was recovered by a family member. At only 17 years of age, he received acclaim after his death for his display of bravery while leading a company of the Virginia Regiment, a part of General Jackson's command. Norris was killed instantly while leading his company in a charge upon Ricketts's battery. On Monday, a day after the battle, his body was recovered by his older brother Joseph L. Norris and taken to his home and family in Leesburg, Virginia.

George T. Stovall Marker. Located on Matthews Hill, near the site of Matthews home. Modern-day view (2010) of the marker as one faces the east (photograph by the author).

THIS MARBLE MARKS THE SPOT WHERE FELL GEORGE T. STOVALL OF THE ROME LIGHT GUARDS 8TH REGT GEORGIA VOLUNTEERS IN THE BATTLE OF JULY 21, 1861 BORN AT AUGUSTA GA APRIL 7, 1835 HIS LIFE HE DEVOTED TO HIS GOD AND SACRIFICED IN HIS COUNTRY'S DEFENCE HIS LAST WORDS WERE I AM GOING TO HEAVEN

THE FIRST CIVIL WAR MONUMENT

Two months after the battle, two Confederate regiments that had suffered heavy losses, the 7th and 8th Georgia, erected and dedicated a monument amid great fanfare in honor of their beloved commander, Brigadier General (posthumous rank) Francis Bartow, on the spot where he fell. This was the very first Civil War monument. It was cylindrical in shape, five to six feet tall, and about 18 to 24 inches in diameter. Six months later the Confederates were preparing to abandon Manassas Junction, and, knowing Union forces would soon be occupying the area, the Georgians did not want to leave the monument behind. They believed the Yankees would most likely destroy it, so they took action to safeguard it. They broke the monument off at its base, presumably to move it to a place of safekeeping. No information has ever been found as to what happened to the monument after that. It was never seen again.

In early March 1862, the Confederates were fast moving out of the area and would soon be confronting their adversary. The weight and size of the monument would have made it very difficult to move any great distance. What if they never moved it? What if they buried it right there on the spot or close by? It seems plausible to this author that they just may have done that. If so, in this modern era, it is possible for ground-penetrating radar to detect it. The original Bartow monument was located approximately twenty-five feet to the east of Bartow's present-day monument. A tree is presently on the spot, but, remnants of the original monument's base can still be seen where the tree has grown up through it.

Confederate Camps

From July 1861 until March 1862, the Confederates built extensive lines of entrenchments and redoubts throughout the Manassas Junction area. Forts and gun emplacements were made along Bull Run and other streams along the Orange and Alexandria and Manassas Gap Railroads, and at Occoquan, Cockpit Point, Evansport, and Dumfries. In addition, heavy guns were set in place for the blockading of the Potomac.

Army camps sprang up throughout the Manassas area. Camp Pickens was in the town of Manassas. Camp Walker was along the line of the Orange and Alexandria Railroad, a short distance southeast of McLean's Ford. Camp Wigfall was midway between the town and Union Mills Ford. Camp Prior was on the road to Occoquan, southeast of Manassas. Camp Bradley was southwest on the road to Brentsville.

The area was practically left barren by the taking of timber used in constructing their huts for shelter, and to build fires for warmth and for cooking. Almost all farms with timberland suffered in this way, in addition to the loss of their split-rail fences. The cramped living quarters and poor sanitary conditions quickly brought on the rampant spread of contagious diseases. Soon typhus, typhoid, and especially measles critically reduced the Confederate army's effective strength in numbers. Measles became such an epidemic that a measles camp and cemetery were established near Bristow.

Later, when the Union Army returned after the Confederates abandoned the area, they were sorely surprised to find that some redoubts in the Centreville area had logs in place of guns, painted black to give the impression of cannon. The fake cannon were called "Quaker Guns."

Military Situations Intensify and Jackson Is Sent to the Valley

By October 1861, military situations throughout the Virginia frontier had heightened. Military activity stretching from the Washington/Manassas area to the west between the Blue Ridge and Allegheny Mountains, sweeping southeast beyond Richmond, excited both governments, bringing about more changes to their military dispositions. In Washington, full mobilization for war was well underway; in the three months since the Union defeat at the Battle of Manassas, new recruits had been pouring into Washington to undergo intensified training under General George McClellan. For the Union Army, reorganization and training were in earnest as they prepared for a new invasion attempt into Virginia to take place in the early spring of '62 with the goal of occupying Richmond.

During this time, a Union force under the command of Major General Nathaniel P. Banks had been sent into the Valley. The Confederate defenders of the Valley consisted of two militia brigades under the command of two former governors of Virginia, Brigadier General Henry A. Wise and Brigadier General John B. Floyd. In addition to the militia's being untrained, Wise and Floyd were so much at odds with each other that united action was impossible. While Union forces were building up strength in the Valley, Banks make raids upon the citizenry, resulting in overwhelming complaints to the Confederate government of "constant plundering, insulting females and keeping the whole border for miles in the interior in a state of uneasiness and alarm."[25]

On October 7, Jackson was promoted to the rank of major general along with General James Longstreet. On October 22, General Order No.15 from the Adjutant and Inspector General's Office in Richmond established the Department of Northern Virginia and designating its three districts. "Johnston was named to command the department, Jackson the Valley District between the Blue Ridge and the Alleghenies, Beauregard the Potomac District in the center, and Major General T.H. Holmes the Aquia District on the east. The special order assigning Jackson to the Valley district was dated October 28; the special order for him to leave for the district was dated November 4."[26] On November 8, Johnston was instructed by Confederate Acting Secretary of War Judah P. Benjamin to issue orders sending Jackson's old brigade (the Stonewall Brigade), including the Rockbridge artillery, to join Jackson in the Valley. Johnston reluctantly complied after furiously protesting, setting up another confrontation with Davis that added fuel to their ongoing discord.

CREATION OF THE CONFEDERATE BATTLE FLAG

It was quickly apparent to all who were present at the First Battle of Manassas that several contributing factors adversely affected the course of battle events. In addition to the inexperienced and undisciplined troops on both sides, no real uniform standards yet existed for either army; it is estimated that there were more than 200 different types of uniforms on the battlefield that day: there were Federals in gray and Confederates in blue and brightly colored Zouave uniforms on both sides. Aside from these factors, another major problem was the similarity between the U.S. flag (Stars and Stripes) and the CSA flag (Stars and Bars). During battle engagements, troops followed where they saw their flag, and trying to identify it through all the dust and smoke could be confusing. There was little or no wind that day to unfurl the flags as they hung from their staffs, and they both looked the same. The flag seen in that state, especially at a distance, was a cause of great confusion about who was who. Many casualties occurred as a result of "friendly fire."

The need for a distinctive flag was of utmost importance to Beauregard. While in winter quarters at Manassas during the interlude, Beauregard came up with a design for a flag to be used in battle. His design used a blue saltire (in heraldry, one of the basic designs used on coats of arms, consisting of a diagonal cross) reminiscent of the St. Andrew's cross, on which were situated 13 stars with the saltire edged in white, all on a red background. It was to be square for ease of handling and to conserve material.

The first three of these flags, made of silk material, were hand-sewn by three sisters, Constance, Jennie, and Hettie Cary, who presented them to Generals Beauregard, Johnston, and Earl Van Dorn from October through December 2, 1861.[27] The flag was adopted by many units of the armies. Initially it was to be issued in different sizes: 48 inches square for the infantry, 36 inches square for the artillery, and 30 inches square for the cavalry. Constance Cary presented her flag to Van Dorn, who reaffirmed a pledge he had made to "liberate Alexandria and her nearby home."

In time, Beauregard sent his flag to his wife in New Orleans. When Union forces occupied the city in the spring of 1862, Mrs. Beauregard became concerned for its safety and sent it to friends in Havana via a foreign ship. It remained there until after the war, at which time it was eventually returned to Beauregard. Beauregard's flag was still in his possession when he died in 1893. Today it resides in the Louisiana State Museum in New Orleans, Louisiana.

Beauregard Transferred to the Western Theater

In late January 1862, General Beauregard agreed to a transfer to the Western Theater to serve as second in command to General Albert Sidney Johnston, departmental commander in the West. The transfer was made in the backdrop of much speculation. An embittered and disgruntled

General Beauregard's Battle Flag. One of the first three Confederate Battle Flags made. Designed by Beauregard and hand-sewn by three sisters, Jennie, Hettie, and Constance Cary from Alexandria, Virginia. Beauregard's personal battle flag, sewn by Jennie Cary, was the first to be presented (courtesy of the Collections of the Louisiana State Museum).

Beauregard had been writing what could be described as outspoken and contentious letters to newspapers, government officials, and members of the Confederate Congress, causing Davis and his administration a great deal of embarrassment. Davis was glad to see Beauregard out of Virginia.[28]

The Next Six Months

CONFEDERATE ARMY MOVES TO REPULSE MCCLELLAN AND ABANDONS MANASSAS

In the North, months of relative inactivity following First Manassas brought sharp criticism of McClellan. A restless public and the press clamored for a forward movement; McClellan complied and moved to initiate his plan to move overland on Richmond via Urbanna, Virginia.

The Confederate command learned of McClellan's plan. On March 9, 1861, the Confederate Army of the Potomac under the command of General Joe Johnston withdrew with all its forces to take up positions south of the Rappahannock. In the seven months since the Union defeat at the Battle of Manassas, the civilians living in Manassas, Centreville, and the surrounding areas were deeply inconvenienced by the presence of the soldiers in gray, the Confederates. The color of the uniform would soon change to blue with the Union occupation. The civilian population would continue to endure stringent oppression and hardships inflicted upon their lives and land, now at the hands of their enemy.

GRUESOME DISCOVERIES MARK INITIAL INTERMENTS OF TWO 2ND RHODE ISLAND OFFICERS

Within days of the Confederate evacuation of the Manassas area, Rhode Island Governor William Sprague left Washington with a Rhode Island cavalry troop of seventy-one. They were on a mission to recover the bodies of fellow members of the 2nd Rhode Island Infantry Regiment that had fallen while fighting at First Manassas. What they discovered during their search would become one of the most intriguing and gruesome stories to come out of the Civil War.

On the day of battle, Union medical personnel were using the Sudley Church as a hospital and it was there that Colonel John Slocum and Major Sullivan Ballou of the 2nd Rhode Island Infantry Regiment were taken after being severely wounded on Matthews Hill. On the July 14, two days before McDowell began his march from Washington, Sullivan Ballou wrote a letter to his wife Sarah in which he spoke of a strong premonition of his death, a feeling that he wouldn't be coming back. Sullivan Ballou told of his love for Sarah and his family members. True to his premonition, Sullivan Ballou was killed, and about the same time as was his commander, Colonel Slocum. Later, his heart-rending letter was widely read after its publication in many Northern newspapers. Both bodies were wrapped in blankets, placed in wooden coffins, and buried next to each other in a ravine across the road from the Sudley Church, south of the Thornberry home.

Sprague had been present at First Manassas with the 2nd Rhode Island Infantry Regiment, but it is hard to determine what command role he played. Sprague was a chief organizer of the regiment, and he made a promise that one day, after the battle, he would return and bring the remains of those who died there back to his state for a decent burial. He had called upon Privates Josiah W. Richardson, Tristan Burgess, and John Clark to accompany them. Richardson had stayed behind that July day to nurse the wounded at the Sudley Church and was witness to Slocum's and Ballou's burials. He could lead the way to their graves. Clark had been wounded and taken to the Martin Matthews house, where he witnessed the burial of Captain Levi Tower. It was hoped that Burgess could help locate where Captain Samuel James Smith of Company I was killed during the retreat from the battlefield.

As they approached the Stone Bridge across the Bull Run, they found that the Confederates had blown it up before evacuating Manassas just weeks before. A search on both sides of the Bull Run failed to find any trace of Smith's burial spot. Burgess recalled, "I was a hasty affair." While approaching the Sudley Ford from the north, they came across a skeleton leaning against a tree, a grisly reminder of what had taken place there seven months earlier.

Shortly, they were at the Sudley Church. After gazing at the church for several moments, Sprague called upon Richardson to lead the way to the spot where Slocum and Ballou were buried. Richardson turned down a wooded ravine near the road leading from the church and, after traveling a few hundred yards, pointed out two graves. Richardson advised Sprague that they "shouldn't have much trouble; he believed the top of either coffin would not be over two feet under ground."

As groups of men gathered around the grave sites, two troopers came forward with shovels. The earth was damp and soggy. As the two troopers were sinking their shovels into the muddy earth, a Negro girl wearing a gaudy dress came forward to within a few feet of where they were digging. She was most likely from one of the five free Negro families living in cabins located along the Sudley-Manassas Road, south of the Sudley Church. After engaging in a conversation about what they were doing, she readily informed them, "You ain't go' find him. Dem Georgia boys dug him up weeks ago. Dey cut his head off and carried it away and dey done burnt his body down in de hollow dere." Thereupon, she led a stunned Sprague and his party to a bank along a brook and pointed to a pile of ashes nearby. Not far from the ashes lay a blanket, described as sodden and muddy. One of the troopers kicked it and it fell open, exposing several tufts of hair.

Sprague had also included a surgeon in his party, Dr. James B. Greeley. Greeley began going through the ashes, examining several objects he had uncovered. He concluded they were human and identified a femur, thighbone, backbone (vertebra), and parts of the pelvis bones. They were placed in a blanket. Not far away, the searchers discovered two shirts, one of silk and the other a striped calico, caught in some bushes in the brook. Those items were also gathered up, and as they were placing them in a blanket, a trooper noticed that the collars were buttoned and sleeves were unbuttoned. Greeley immediately concluded "they cut his head off" and further noted that it "wasn't burned with the rest of the body" and "no skull was in the ashes—no teeth, or anything." After studying the shirts, Sprague exclaimed, "Those aren't Slocum's shirts," that he "knew him well," that "he never wore a shirt like that," and so "they must be Ballou's."

Excitedly, they returned to the grave sites. Digging was extremely difficult; the soggy soil clung to the shovel and they had no luck in locating a coffin. Since they believed that the top of the coffin(s) were only about two feet under the ground, they decided to run a saber down to see if they could strike it. After plunging the saber to its hilt into the other grave site, they concluded that the grave was empty. Then they sank the saber into the other grave site and struck a hard object. Hurriedly they dug out the coffin from the second grave. They opened it anxiously and found a body rolled in a blanket. As the face was uncovered, Sprague was the first to speak. He said solemnly, "That's him all right. I recognize him by his mustache." They had found Slocum's body.

Sprague and Greeley thought it obvious what had happened. They concluded: "The 2nd Regiment (Second Rhode Island) cut up those Georgia boys rather badly, and they were sore at Slocum, the commanding officer. They just got the wrong body." Before leaving the area, Sprague, accompanied by his aide and some of his officers, set about the Sudley neighborhood to gather what information they could. A fourteen-year-old boy eagerly spoke with them. He told them that he was sure it was done by the Twenty-first Georgia and that he had watched. He then added that they soon put out the fire because of the horrible stench it created. The boy most likely was Samuel Thornberry, the oldest son of John Thornberry.

Sprague and his detail then stopped at a large home that belonged to 82-year-old Burkett Newman. Newman explained that he had not seen the actual burning, but three or four days later he had gone down to see the ashes and the bones and the coffin. Newman led them back to the spot and described things as they were when he made his visit. He told Sprague and the others: "It was an awful thing—barbaric," and quickly added, "But no Virginians did it. Virginians wouldn't do such a thing. I'm sure it was the Georgians. They were terribly mad at Colonel Slocum."

The next witness they spoke to was a white woman. They learned that she had nursed the sick and wounded at Sudley Church after the battle. Most likely they were speaking with Margaret Benson, wife of Amos Benson. Tearfully, she told them that she had witnessed the whole affair. She had begged and entreated that the dead be held sacred, but the "savages" had mocked her; so she had saved a lock of hair—a lock for friends she was confident someday would come along. A member of Sprague's detail gingerly accepted it from her fingers and added it to the tuft collected earlier.

Back at the grave site once more, the search party readied to move on to the burial site of Captain Levi Towers. Sprague's entourage included his private two-horse wagon and two baggage wagons loaded with forage, rations, and empty coffins. Two of these coffins would no longer be empty, as one now contained the body of Slocum and another held what remains they were able to collect of Ballou.

Having led the search party to the Matthews house, Private Clark pointed out a large mound at the side of the yard. The men went about unearthing the site, and seven bodies were exhumed from the mass grave before the body of Captain Towers was uncovered.[29]

At the conclusion of the search, all the remains were returned to Rhode Island and reinterred. Ballou's head was never recovered. In addition, the original of the famous last letter that Sullivan Ballou wrote his wife on July 14, 1861, has never been found. Sometime later, a story circulated that Mrs. Ballou placed it inside his casket on his reinterment, but that has never been verified.

News of the discoveries and the shocking details of what took place after the initial burials of Colonel John Slocum and Major Sullivan Ballou did much to inflame the hatred toward the South. It has never been established which Georgia regiment those who committed the heinous act belonged to.

Union Army Moves into Vacated Confederate Camps

Prior to his departure for the Peninsula, McClellan sent an expeditionary force out to the Centreville and Manassas areas, which they found deserted. Manassas was promptly taken over and the Confederate camps were soon occupied by Union soldiers. Later, Manassas was used as a store and quartermaster depot to supply the Army of Virginia after it was created under the command of Maj. Gen. John Pope.

Terror Comes to John Thornberry and Family

The families within the Sudley-Groveton area were subjected to countless hardships and horrors, simply because they had the misfortune to live in a place that was occupied by both friendly and unfriendly forces at different times. During the time the Confederates occupied the area, the families were often forced to give up farm grain, timber on their land, or fence rails. Sometimes they were compensated for these losses, but that was not always the case. When the Union forces came back to occupy the area, the civilians' difficulties only increased. Farm animals, chickens, horses, and mules would be taken from their farms, in addition to raids on their smokehouses and food stocks with no compensation. Returning seven months later after suffering their defeat, many of the new occupiers committed acts of cruelty.

One such act befell the John Thornberry family. Thornberry had been with the 49th Virginia Infantry Regiment during the fighting on Henry Hill and was wounded. Afterwards he was taken to his father's home. There he became sick with typhoid fever and was subsequently removed to a hospital in Orange, Virginia. Eight weeks later he was medically discharged from the Confederate army and able to return to his home.

Sometime after the Union forces returned and occupied the area, a cavalry unit of ten troopers smashed through Thornberry's front door about 2 o'clock one morning. A piece of the splintered door struck Mrs. Thornberry in the face. In a testimonial letter written years later by Laura Thornberry Fletcher, daughter of John Thornberry, she stated her mother was "disfigured very badly" from the incident.

She continued to describe the incident: "They arrested my father and oldest brother, who was 16 years old, for spies. They were not spies and never had been." The brother was Samuel Thornberry, who would have been 13, possibly 14 years old at the time. The troopers took John outside under a tree in the front yard and placed a rope around his neck. They were going to hang him. Crying hysterically, young Samuel and the family were pleading, "He didn't do anything." Most likely someone of the family then said something about a diary, and one of the troopers spoke out to "search his pockets before you draw that rope." In going through John's pockets, they found a diary that John kept, which gave an accounting of his activities and his whereabouts. That saved his life, but it didn't stop them from taking him off to Capitol prison in Washington.

During the next few agonizing weeks and months, Mrs. Thornberry made several trips to Washington to plead for his release. Finally, after three months, he was released.[30]

Seven

Prelude to Second Manassas

McClellan Advances on Richmond

After evacuating the Centreville/Manassas Junction area to take up a position south of the Rappahannock, Johnston aligned his forces with his right resting at Fredericksburg and his left at Culpeper Court House. This action forced McClellan to modify his original plan to move on Richmond, taking an overland route via Urbanna. He now decided to advance on Richmond, moving by water to Fortress Monroe and up the Peninsula. On March 17, McClellan's Army of the Potomac embarked from Alexandria.[1]

McClellan had envisioned that with his army encircling the greater portion of Richmond and the armies of Banks and Fremont moving in from the west and south, Richmond would be taken, thus bringing down the Confederacy. However, Jackson's successes in the Valley over the next three months greatly alarmed Lincoln. Although severely outnumbered, Jackson's division of just 17,000 was winning battles over Banks's and Fremont's two armies in the Valley, thus keeping them in check.

Lincoln became afraid for the safety of Washington. For the city's defense, Lincoln pulled 40,000 troops from McClellan's army and placed them under the command of Major General Irving McDowell. This decision was to reduce McClellan's anticipated striking force by approximately one-third, thus seriously impairing his plans against Richmond. Lincoln, however, believed that the four armies of McClellan, McDowell, Fremont and Banks would circle Richmond. The main force of McClellan would move in from the east, with a strength of 105,000, McDowell with a force of 40,000 from the north, and Banks's and Fremont's armies with a combined strength of 63,000 encircling from the west and south.[2] This strategy failed to materialize; the armies of McDowell, Fremont, and Banks were scattered over the northern part of Virginia, with little or no communication or purpose of action with one another.

Johnston, in the meantime, had reinforced Major General John Bankhead Magruder at Yorktown. On May 4, however, the decision was made to evacuate the town, and the next day a successful rearguard action was fought at Williamsburg to cover the Confederate withdrawal to Richmond. The Federal army pursued Johnston over land and water to White House on the Pamunkey, where McClellan established his headquarters on May 16. The next day, McClellan resumed his advance on Richmond.[3]

Johnston Severely Wounded and Lee Takes Command

On June 1, with a force of 63,000, Johnston attacked McClellan's forces, and the battles of Seven Pines and Fair Oaks ensued. The Confederates were repulsed and Johnston was severely wounded. The command of the Army of Northern Virginia now fell to Robert E. Lee.

The Emergence of General John Pope

In early June, Lincoln and Secretary of State Stanton brought in Major General John Pope from the Army of Mississippi to reorganize the armies of McDowell, Fremont, and Banks into a new army. A West Point Graduate, class of 1842, Pope fought under Zachary Taylor in the Battles of Monterrey and Buena Vista during the Mexican War. Just weeks prior to being summoned to Washington, he had obtained a minor victory at Island 10 in the Mississippi and received much media attention.

Pope had a reputation for being smug, pompous and a braggart. While commander of the District of North and Central Missouri in July, his relationship with Fremont was strained as he cunningly worked to get Fremont removed from his command. Fremont accused Pope of having treacherous intentions toward him, demonstrated by his lack of action in following Fremont's offensive plans in Missouri.

Lincoln brought Pope in under great expectations, believing he had found the general he had long sought. On June 26 Pope assumed command of the Army of Virginia with a movable army strength of 49,500 as follows: Fremont (Sigel), First Corps, 11,500; Banks, Second Corps, 14,500; McDowell, Third Corps, 18,500; and cavalry numbering 5,000 men.[4] Fremont resigned in protest of Pope, stating he would not take orders from him; General Franz Sigel assumed command of the First Corps.

Jackson Ordered to Join Forces with Lee

Jackson's successes in the Valley received much acclaim throughout the South; he was their hero. Historians have made much of his accomplishments. Pulitzer Prize winner and noted historian author Douglas Southall Freeman made this assessment of Jackson's Valley Campaign:

> With a force that never had exceeded, if indeed it reached, 17,000 men of all arms, he had cleared the enemy from the greater part of the Shenandoah. What was far more important, he had used this small force so effectively that he had forced President Lincoln to change the entire plan for the capture of Richmond. At a time when the junction of McDowell with McClellan would have rendered the defense of the Confederate capital almost hopeless, Jackson temporarily had paralyzed the advance of close to 40,000 Federal troops. Rarely in war had so few infantry achieved such dazzling strategic results.[5]

Between June 6 and June 17, Jackson and Lee exchanged several means of correspondences, by way of letters, emissary Colonel A.R. Boteler (congressman), and telegraph, expressing their views and decisions, culminating in Jackson's movement from the Valley to unite with Lee. At the time, Jackson had just won the actions at Cross Keys and Port Republic and believed that, with more men, he could drive Fremont and Shields down the Valley as he had driven Banks. Lee agreed, but the final conclusion was conveyed to Jackson via Boteler that the pressure on Richmond prevented the detachment of enough troops to make a large-scale offensive possible. Lee wrote Jackson that the course to pursue was to conceal all movement and to start for Richmond as soon as practicable. Moving in secrecy by marches and rail, Jackson's command started out from Staunton on June 18, and on Monday morning, June 23, Jackson was sitting down at Lee's headquarters in a council of war with Lee, Longstreet, A.P. Hill, and D.H. Hill.[6]

On June 26, Lee launched his great counteroffensive, which, within seven days of desperate fighting, forced McClellan back upon Harrison's Landing on the James. Lee's success had saved Richmond.

Pope Concentrates Along the Rapidan River

At the time of Lee's counteroffensive against McClellan, Pope's orders for his new command were to demonstrate with his army toward Gordonsville and Charlottesville and draw off as much of the force as possible in front of General McClellan, distracting the enemy in his front so as to reduce the resistance opposed to his advance on Richmond as far as possible.[7]

Lee Reorganizes the Army of Northern Virginia

Failure of the Confederate Congress to act upon the needs of their military limited the operational effectiveness of the Confederate armies. Under Confederate law, there were no provisions for any units larger than a division, and the rank of lieutenant general had not been authorized; thus no corps could be established. This created many problems for brigade and division commanders and ultimately the army chief. Lee experienced the problems firsthand as the system proved nearly ruinous for him during the Seven Days Battle.[8] Historian Douglas Southall Freeman described it as a "system of semi-autonomous, frequently jealous and often uncooperative divisions."[9] Under the system, each division was acting like a small independent army on the battlefield.

Until such time as the Confederate Congress would make appropriate provisions in the law to rectify the situation, Lee was forced to revolutionize the organization of his Army of Northern Virginia to succeed the system. After the Seven Days Battle, Lee established two different command units above the division level and simply called them wings (vice-corps) and assigned his two major generals, Longstreet and Jackson, to command. "The system worked, mainly because he had two good cooperating Major Generals."[10]

On September 18, 1862, the Confederate Legislature changed the law providing for the organization of Divisions into Corps, and the units were to be commanded by officers of the new grade of Lieutenant General.[11]

Halleck Changes McClellan's Plans for Richmond

After a brief few days in office as general-in-chief of all the Union land forces, Halleck overruled McClellan's plans for another try against Richmond and proposed that Pope's new Army of Virginia and McClellan's army unite at Fredericksburg, thereby protecting Washington while remaining a threat to Richmond. McClellan accepted Halleck's proposal with displeasure.[12]

On July 14, Pope ordered an advance on Gordonsville, but Lee, anticipating the movement, had detached Jackson to this point the day before. On August 7, Jackson, having been reinforced by A.P. Hill, moved upon Culpeper, hoping to crush Banks before Pope could consolidate his forces. Two days later, eight miles to the southwest of Culpeper, Jackson attacked Banks at Cedar Mountain and managed a hard-fought victory.[13]

Later, Lee learned that McClellan had been ordered to reinforce Pope and that Reynolds's and Porter's corps would arrive in support of Pope between August 19 and 21. For McClelland, he was all the more incensed by these changes, as they placed him in a secondary role. For Lee, he realized that he must move on Pope as quickly as possible and destroy him before Pope and McClellan's forces joined. Lee then ordered Longstreet to join Jackson. At this time the center of Pope's army was at Cedar Mountain with his right at Robinson's River and his left at Raccoon Ford on the Rapidan. Thus stationed, his army was directly opposite Gordonsville. Massing his troops behind Clark Mountain, Lee planned to attack Pope's left at Somerville Ford and cut off his retreat to Washington. A copy of Lee's orders detailing his plans, carried by a courier who was captured by Union cavalry scouts, fell into Pope's hands.[14]

2nd Battle of Manassas Campaign Begins

Warned of the move by the capture of Lee's orders, Pope withdrew to the Rappahannock. Lee followed and spent the next five days probing Pope's positions. In the meantime, Stuart had learned from dispatches captured in a raid on Pope's train-car headquarters at Catlett Station that Heintzelman, Porter, and Reynolds of McClellan's army were within two days' march of Pope. In addition, Reno, with 8,000 of Burnside's men, had already joined Pope behind the Rapidan.[15] Soon Pope would have approximately 130,000 men. Quick planning and action on Lee's part was now of the utmost importance.

In one of the most daring exploits of the war, he decided to split his forces in an effort to get around to the rear of Pope's army and move Pope off the Rappahannock. Confederate General James Longstreet with 30,000 men would demonstrate along the west bank of the Rappahannock, keeping Pope's attention. At the same time, Jackson would march north with a force of 24,000 and cross over the Rappahannock, making a wide arcing rush over the Bull Run Mountains through a pass called Thoroughfare Gap. In getting Pope's attention behind his forces, Lee hoped to wedge Pope from the Rappahannock. This done, Longstreet would march to join Jackson, taking the same route as Jackson through the Thoroughfare Gap.[16]

Unknown to him at the time, Lee's daring plan to split his forces and wedge Pope off the Rappahannock, thereby putting himself in a position of his choosing to do battle against him, marked the start of the campaign leading to the 2nd Battle of Manassas.

Jackson's "Foot Cavalry" Makes History — August 25–26

Starting from Jeffersonton on August 25, Jackson moved through Amissville and Orlean to bivouac that night at Salem. The next day he pushed through the Thoroughfare Gap and Gainesville to Bristow. Upon reaching Bristow, he captured and destroyed Pope's communications and supply lines there. During the night of August 27, Jackson's cavalry and infantry detachments were sent to Manassas Junction to capture Pope's great base of supplies. Within a 48-hour period, he had completed a 54-mile march while destroying Pope's supply base and supply lines, a feat unparalleled in military history.

Jackson's reputation for swift movement and rapid response, which had gained his command the sobriquet "Jackson's Foot Cavalry," began one year earlier when he moved his brigade 57 miles in twenty-five hours from Winchester to reinforce Beauregard at the First Battle of Manassas. His reputation was reinforced just months later when he demonstrated extraordinarily swift movements numerous times during the Valley campaign, successfully overcoming Union forces of overwhelming odds.

Bristol Station Raid — August 26

Jackson's assault on Manassas Junction began only hours after he had destroyed Pope's communications and supply lines at Bristow Station in the late hours of August 26. During the taking of Bristow Station, the Confederates encountered four trains moving from the southwest on their way to pass through Manassas Junction. Before Jackson's main column, led by Colonel Thomas T. Munford's 2nd Virginia Cavalry and Ewell's division, could take action to stop the trains, the first train, "No. 6 train, engine Secretary," was able to escape through a hail of Confederate musket fire. The second train crashed after Munford's 2nd Virginia Cavalry succeeded in removing rail tracks. A third train crashed into the rear of the second train, while the fourth train escaped to Warrington Station: its crew was able to reverse the train upon seeing the destruction in its path.[17]

Capture of Pope's Supply Depot at Manassas Junction

Jackson was aware that Pope's huge "stores of great value" were located just five miles to the north of Bristow Station. He knew they would be guarded but did not know at what strength, and he did not want to lose any time in capturing the depot before the Yankees could destroy the stores. He gave this task to one of Ewell's brigade commanders, Brigadier General Isaac Trimble. Trimble suggested that he only take his 21st North Carolina and the 21st Georgia, which he proudly referred to as his "two twenty-ones." The two regiments totaled about 500 men. Jackson agreed, but then ordered Stuart and his cavalry to go along.[18]

The moment the bullet-riddled Secretary rolled into Manassas Junction, the Union garrison was immediately made aware of the Confederate presence at Bristow Station. At 8 P.M. telegraph messages reporting Jackson's movements were sent to Pope's headquarters along the Rappahannock. At the same time, they were also received by Union general-in-chief Major General Henry W. Halleck and by Colonel Herman Haupt's headquarters in Alexandria. For some unknown reason, Jackson's men at Bristow Station had failed to cut Pope's communications lines for at least an hour.

The garrison commander, Captain Samuel Craig, immediately set about the task of placing his men in defensive positions around the supply depot in anticipation of a possible Confederate foray. Craig didn't have long to wait. In the dead of night, Trimble and Stuart's commands moved swiftly upon the depot and captured Craig within minutes, along with three hundred men of his garrison, all their equipment, a large herd of horses, several artillery pieces, and tons upon tons of stores. Trimble's command suffered only four casualties: two killed and two wounded.[19]

As soon as Haupt and Halleck received the news of Jackson's Bristow Station Raid, they set about quick preparations for assembling an attack force of four thousand men and moving them by train to confront the raiders. Before their plans were completed, they received another message that the Secretary had crashed into another train just east of the bridge over the Bull Run, blocking the track entirely. At about 6 A.M. on August 27, Brigadier General George W. Taylor's brigade, consisting of four New Jersey regiments and two Ohio regiments of Colonel E. Parker Scammon's brigade of Brig. General Jacob D. Cox's command, was headed toward Bull Run.[20]

Meanwhile, back at Bristow Station, Jackson and the remainder of his command had rested and were up at dawn on the 27th. He gave orders for Ewell to remain at Bristow Station with three brigades as rear guard. Jackson, never one for tarrying, was now more stimulated to act, as he had received reports from Trimble indicating that attack upon his position from nearby Union forces was imminent. In quick response, by 9 A.M., Jackson had reached Manassas Junction and had several of his brigades and over two dozen cannon in place around the depot and surrounding areas. A Yankee infantry regiment, the 2nd New York, and several artillery pieces had moved up from along the Bull Run. In a short time, as the Confederate guns opened up on them, they quickly dispersed.

About this time, General Taylor and his New Jersey Brigade had detrained east of the Bull Run bridge near the crash site of the Secretary. Taylor had unwittingly marched his infantrymen directly into the arc of the Confederate lines. As they closely approached, Jackson gave the order to open fire. The results were staggering losses, as Taylor's men were ripped apart. Jackson, seeing the deadly results, pulled out a white handkerchief and rode out in front of Taylor's troops to seek their surrender.[21] The Yankees' answer was a musket shot that swished by Jackson's head, fired by one of Taylor's troops. The Confederates responded with intense, deadly fire that ripped through Taylor's ranks. Taylor finally realized his predicament and ordered a retreat, which was short-lived, as they were quickly pursued; General Taylor was mortally wounded, 339 of his attack force were killed or wounded, and 201 were captured. Taylor's foray against Jackson was over in less than 45 minutes from the time they had detrained.[22]

When the fight was over, the men of Jackson's command swarmed over the captured stores. The capture of Pope's stores, which amounted to hundreds of tons, was the largest capture of its kind during the entire Civil War. Jackson's men saw before them "two tracks for a distance of half a mile each, freight car after freight car, more than 100 of them, all new, all loaded with supplies of a variety that out scaled imagination." Jackson had one concern about the stores: alcohol. Before he allowed the men to go about their plundering, he ordered that "every drop" of alcohol be located and spilled out.[23] Jackson had no time to take inventory of the stores, and transporting them away was out of the question except for what the men could carry with them.

After a day of great feasting, the stores were destroyed. Jackson then marched his men to Stony Ridge, a wooded area north of the Unfinished Railroad cut of the Manassas Gap Railroad, about one and one-half miles southwest of the Sudley Church. Arriving in the early morning hours of August 28, they bivouacked to await the arrival of Lee and Longstreet.[24]

Battle of Kelly Run — August 27

While Jackson's men were feasting at Manassas Junction, Major General Joseph Hooker's 2nd Division of McClellan's Army of the Potomac Third Corps was on the march from Warrenton Junction, having been sent by McClellan to assist Pope. During the morning of the 27th, the 72nd New York from Hooker's division was running reconnaissance of Bristow Station when they were detected by Ewell's pickets. Ewell was quick to respond and deployed his three brigades in strong positions to await the enemy, whom he was sure would be returning in force. At the same time, Ewell sent his aide and soon-to-be stepson, Campbell Brown, to Jackson, asking him what he should do if the Federals returned in force.

Before Jackson's response was received, troops from Hooker's division were on the scene. Ewell directed his forces to fall back across Kettle Run and burn the bridge. As Hooker's forces advanced across Kettle Run, they were immediately pounded by Ewell's artillery. As the fighting progressed, it became apparent to Ewell that he was greatly outnumbered. By 4 P.M., Ewell had not yet received an answer from Jackson; he was faced with a situation where his command was in danger and knew he had to withdraw to save it. While he was starting to make those preparations, Campbell Brown arrived with a response to Ewell's message from Jackson. Jackson stated that Ewell was to "determine the strength of the enemy's advance ... if they came in force ... to ... fall back fighting to the rest of the corps at Manassas ... in any event ... to avoid an entangling engagement." Ewell was doing exactly as Jackson would have wanted him to do.[25]

In the next two hours, Ewell's three brigades held off Hooker's strong division while skillfully disengaging under heavy fire without encountering a devastating attack. Upon leaving Bristow to rejoin the rest of Jackson's command at Manassas Junction, Ewell's men destroyed the railroad bridge across Kettle Run.[26]

Army of Virginia Order of Battle

MAJOR GENERAL JOHN POPE

FIRST CORPS
MAJOR GENERAL FRANZ SIGEL

FIRST DIVISION
MAJOR GENERAL ROBERT C. SCHENCK

First Brigade Brig. Gen. JULIUS STAHEL
27th Pennsylvania, Col. Bushbeck
8th New York, Col. Hedterich
41st New York, Lieut. Col. Holmstedt
45th New York, Lieut. Col. Wratislaw

Second Brigade Col. NATHANIEL C. McLEAN, 75th Ohio
25th Ohio, Col. Richardson
55th Ohio, Col. J.C. Lee
3rd Ohio, Col. O. Smith
75th Ohio, Major Reilly

SECOND DIVISION
BRIGADIER GENERAL A. VON STEINWEHR

First Brigade
Col. JOHN A. KOLTES

29th New York, Major Hartman
68th New York Lieut. Col. Kleefisch
73rd Pennsylvania, Lieut. Col. Muhleck

THIRD DIVISION
BRIGADIER GENERAL CARL SCHURZ

First Brigade
Col. A. SHIMMELPFENNIG
61st Ohio, Lieut. Col. McGroarty
74th Pennsylvania, Major Blessing
8th W. Virginia

Second Brigade
Col. W. KRYZANOWSKI
54th New York, Lieut. Col. Ashby
58th New York Major Henkel
75th Pennsylvania, Lieut. Col. Mahler

INDEPENDENT BRIGADE
Brig. Gen. ROBERT H. MILROY
2nd W. Virginia
3rd W. Virginia
8th W. Virginia
5th W. Virginia, Col. Zeigler
82nd Ohio

ARTILLERY OF THE FIRST CORPS
New York Light Artillery, 2d Battery, Lieutenant Blume; 1s Div. 1st Brigade
New York Light Artillery, 13th Battery, Captain J. Dieckmann; Reserve Art.
1st New York Light Artillery, Battery I, Captain M. Wiedrich; Reserve Art.
2d New York Light Artillery, Battery L, Captain J. Roemer; 3rd Div. 2nd Brigade
Pennsylvania Light Artillery, Battery F, Captain R.B. Hampton; 3rd Div. 1st Brigadier
Ohio Light Artillery, 12th Battery, Captain A.C. Johnson; Independent Brigade
1st Ohio Light Artillery, Battery I, Captain H. Dilger; Unattached
1st Ohio Light Artillery, Battery K, Captain Lieutenant G.B. Haskins; 1st Div. 2nd Brigade 3d W. Virginia Light Artillery, Battery C, Captain F. Buell; Unattached

SECOND CORPS
MAJOR GENERAL NATHANIEL P. BANKS

FIRST DIVISION
BRIGADIER GENERAL ALPHEUS S. WILLIAMS

First Brigade
Brig Gen. SAMUEL W. CRAWFORD

10th Maine, Colonel George L. Beal
46th Pennsylvania
28th New York
5th Connecticut

Second Brigade
Merged in the others

Third Brigade
Brig. Gen. GEORGE H. GORDON

2d Massachusetts, Colonel George L. Andrews
3d Wisconsin, Colonel Thomas H. Ruger
27th Indiana, Colonel Colgrove

SECOND DIVISION
BRIGADIER GENERAL GEORGE S. GREENE

First Brigade
Col. CHARLES CANDY
5th Ohio
7th Ohio
66th Ohio
29th Ohio
28th Pennsylvania

Second Brigade
Col. M. SCHLANDECKER
111th Pennsylvania
109th Pennsylvania
3d Maryland
102d New York
8th U.S. Infantry Battalion, Capt. T.M. Anderson
12th U.S. Infantry Battalion, Capt. T.M. Anderson

Third Brigade
Col. JAMES A. TAIT

1st Division of Columbia
78th New York
60th New York
Purnell Legion, Maryland
3d Delaware

ARTILLERY OF THE SECOND CORPS
Capt. CLERMONT L. BEST
Maine Lt. Art'y, 4th Batt'y, Robinson's
Maine Lt. Art'y, 6th Batt'y, McGilvery's
Penn. Lt. Art'y, Battery E, Knap's
N.Y. Lt. Art'y, 10th Batt'y
1st N.Y. Lt. Art'y, Batt'y M, Cothran's
4th U.S. Art'y, Batt'y F, Best's

THIRD CORPS
MAJOR GENERAL IRVIN McDOWELL

FIRST DIVISION
BRIGADIER GENERAL RUFUS KING
BRIGADIER GENERAL JOHN P. HATCH

First Brigade
Brig. Gen. JOHN P. HATCH
Col. T. SULLIVAN

2nd U.S. Sharpshooter, Col. Post
30th N.Y., Col. Frisby

Second Brigade
Brig. Gen. ABNER DOUBLEDAY

56th Pennsylvania, Lieut. Col. Hoffman
76th New York, Col. Wainwright
95th New York

84th New York (14th N.Y. Militia), Lieut. Col. Fowler
    22nd New York
    24th New York

Third Brigade	Fourth Brigade
Brig. Gen. MARSENA R. PATRICK	Brig. Gen. JOHN GIBBON
80th New York (20th N.Y. Militia), Col. Pratt	2nd Wisconsin
21st New York	6th Wisconsin
23rd New York	7th Wisconsin
35th New York	19th Indiana, Col. S. Meredith

Artillery
Capt. Joseph B. Campbell

New Hampshire Light Artillery, 1st Battery
1st New York Light Artillery, Battery L
1st Rhode Island Light Artillery, Battery D
4th U.S. Artillery, Battery B

SECOND DIVISION.
BRIGADIER GENERAL JAMES B. RICKETTS

First Brigade	Second Brigade
Brig.-Gen. ABRAM DURYEE	Brig. Gen. ZEALOUS B. TOWER
97th New York	94th New York, Col. Root
104th New York	26th New York
105th New York	88th Pennsylvania
107th Pennsylvania	90th New York

Third Brigade	Fourth Brigade
Col. ROBERT W. STILES	Col. J. THORBURN
11th Pennsylvania, Col. Coulter	1st W. Virginia
83d New York (9th Militia)	84th Pennsylvania
12th Massachusetts, Col. F. Webster	110th Pennsylvania
13th Massachusetts Col. Leonard	7th Indiana

PENNSYLVANIA RESERVES
BRIGADIER GENERAL JOHN F. REYNOLDS

First Brigade	Second Brigade
Brig. Gen. GEORGE G. MEADE	Brig. Gen. TRUMAN SEYMOUR
3d Pennsylvania Reserves, Col. Sickles	1st Pennsylvania Reserves, Col. Roberts
4th Pennsylvania Reserves, Col. Magilton	2d Pennsylvania Reserves, Col. McCandless
7th Pennsylvania Reserves, Lieut. Col. Henderson	5th Pennsylvania Reserves, Lieut. Col. Dare
8th Pennsylvania Reserves, Capt. Lemon	6th Pennsylvania Reserves, Col. Sinclair
13th Pennsylvania Reserves (1st Rifles), Col. McNeil	

Third Brigade
Brig. Gen. CONRAD F. JACKSON

9th Pennsylvania Reserves, Col. Anderson
10th Pennsylvania Reserves, Col. Kirk
11th Pennsylvania Reserves, Lieut. Col. Jackson

12th Pennsylvania Reserves, Col. Hardin

ARTILLERY OF THE THIRD CORPS
MAJOR TELLSON, CHIEF OF ARTILLERY

1st N.Y. Lt. Art'y, Batt'y L, Reynolds's
1st R.I. Lt. Art'y, Batt'y D, Munroe's
1st Penn. Lt. Art'y, Batt'y A
1st Penn. Lt. Art'y, Batt'y B, Cooper's
1st Penn. Lt. Art'y, Batt'y F, Matthews's
1st Penn. Lt. Art'y, Batt'y G
Penn. Lt. Art'y, Batt'y C
Maryland Lt. Art'y, 2d Batt'y, Thompson's
Maine Lt. Art'y, 2d Batt'y, Hall's
Maine Lt. Art'y, 3d Batt'y, Pontoniers
Maine Lt. Art'y, 5th Batt'y, Leppien's
N. H'shire Lt. Art'y, 1st Batt'y, Gerrish's
4th U.S. Art'y, Battery B
4th U.S. Art'y, Battery E
5th U.S. Art'y, Battery C, Ransom's

CAVALRY OF THE ARMY OF VIRGINIA

FIRST CORPS	SECOND CORPS
Beardsley's Brigade	Buford's Brigade
Brig. Gen. J. BEARDSLEY	Brig. Gen. JOHN BUFORD
9th New York	1st Vermont
4th New York, Lieut. Col. F. Nazet	5th New York
6th Ohio, Col. W.R. Lloyd	1st West Virginia
1st Maryland, Lieut. Col. Wetschky	1st Michigan
1st Connecticut Battalion	
THIRD CORPS	
	Unattached
Bayard's Brigade	
Brig. Gen. GEORGE D. BAYARD	2d New York
	3d Indiana–Detachment
	Various detached companies at headquarters and elsewhere
1st New Jersey, Lieut. Col. Karge	
1st Pennsylvania, Col. Owen Jones	
1st Rhode Island, Col. Duffle	
1st Maine, Col. Allen	

ARMY OF THE POTOMAC

THIRD CORPS
MAJOR GENERAL SAMUEL P. HEINTZELMAN

FIRST DIVISION
MAJOR GENERAL PHILIP KEARNY

First Brigade	Second Brigade
Brig. Gen., JOHN C. ROBINSON	Brig. Gen., DAVID B. BIRNEY
20th Indiana, Col. William L. Brown	88th New York

63d Pennsylvania, Col. Alexander Hays
105th Pennsylvania, Capt. Craig
30th Ohio (5 companies)

40th New York, Col. Egan
101st New York, Lieut. Col. Gesner
57th Pennsylvania
3d Maine, Col. Champlin
4th Maine, Col. Walker

Third Brigade
Col. O.M. POE

2d Michigan Volunteers
37th New York
2d Michigan
3d Michigan
5th Michigan
99th Pennsylvania

SECOND DIVISION
MAJOR GENERAL JOSEPH HOOKER

First Brigade
Brig. Gen. CUVIER GROVER

Second (or Excelsior) Brigade
Col. TAYLOR, 72d New York

1st Massachusetts, Col. R. Cowdin
2d New Hampshire, Col. O. Marston
11th Massachusetts, Col. W. Blaisdell
16th Massachusetts, Maj. O. Banks
96th Pennsylvania, Maj. R.L. Bodine

70th New York
71st New York
72d New York
74th New York

Third Brigade
Colonel JOSEPH B. CARR, 2d New York

2d New York, Capt. Park
5th New Jersey, Lieut. Col. W.J. Sewell
6th New Jersey, Lieut. Col. G.C. Burling
7th New Jersey, Col. Joseph W. Revere
8th New Jersey, Capt. D. Blauvelt, Jr.
115th Pennsylvania, Lieut. Col. Robert Thompson

ARTILLERY OF THE THIRD CORPS, A.P.

Graham's Battery,
Randolph's Battery E, 1st Rhode Island Artillery

FIFTH CORPS, ARMY OF THE POTOMAC
MAJOR GENERAL FITZ JOHN PORTER

FIRST DIVISION
MAJOR GENERAL GEORGE W. MORELL

First Brigade
Col. JAMBS BARNES, 18th Massachusetts

Second Brigade
Brig. Gen. CHARLES GRIFFIN
Not in action

Maine, Col. Charles Roberts
18th Massachusetts, Capt. Stephen Thomas
22d Massachusetts, Major Mason W. Burt
25th New York
13th New York
1st Michigan, Col. H.S. Roberts

Third Brigade
Brig. Gen. DAN BUTTERFIELD

17th New York, Col. Lansing
44th New York
12th New York
16th Michigan
83d Pennsylvania, Lieut. Col. Campbell
1st U.S. Sharpshooters, Col. Berdan

SECOND DIVISION
BRIGADIER GENERAL GEORGE SYKES

First Brigade	Second Brigade
Lieut.-Col. R.C. BUCHANAN, 4th Infantry	Lieut.-Col. WILLIAM CHAPMAN, 3d Infantry
3d Infantry, Capt. John D. Wilkins	2d Infantry, Major C.S. Lovell
4th Infantry, Capts J.B. Collins and H. Dryer	10th Infantry, Major C.S. Lovell
12th Infantry, 1st battalion, Capt. Blunt	6th Infantry, Capt. L.C. Bootes
14th Infantry, 2d battalion, Capt. J.D. O'Connell	11th Infantry, Major D.L. Floyd-Jones
14th Infantry, 2d battalion, Capt. D.B. McKibben	17th Infantry, Major G.L. Andrews
Third Brigade	Piatt's Brigade
Col. GOUVERNEUR K. WARREN, 5th New York	Brig. Gen. A. SANDERS PIATT
5th New York, Capt. C. Winslow	86th New York, Col. Bailey
10th New York, Col. Bendix	63d Indiana, Capt. Bruce

ARTILLERY OF THE FIFTH CORPS

Smead's Battery, 5th U.S. Artillery
Weed's Battery, U.S. Artillery
Van Reed's Battery, U.S. Artillery
Hazlett's Battery, U.S. Artillery
Randol's Battery, 1st U.S. Artillery
Martin's Massachusetts Artillery
Battery C, Rhode Island Artillery

NINTH CORPS, ARMY OF THE POTOMAC
BRIGADIER GENERAL J. L. RENO

FIRST DIVISION
BRIGADIER GENERAL ISAAC I. STEVENS

First Brigade	Second Brigade
Col. CHRIST	Col. LEASURE
8th Michigan	100th Pennsylvania
50th Pennsylvania	45th Pennsylvania
45th New York	

Third Brigade
Col. FARNSWORTH

Seven. Prelude to Second Manassas

79th New York

28th New York
28th Massachusetts

SECOND DIVISION
MAJOR GENERAL JESSE L. RENO

First Brigade	Second Brigade
Col. NAGLE	Col. FERRERO, 51st New York
48th Pennsylvania	51st New York
2d Maryland	51st Pennsylvania
9th New Hampshire	21st Massachusetts
6th New Hampshire	

ARTILLERY OF THE NINTH CORPS

Massachusetts Light Artillery, 8th Battery

Battery E, 2d U.S. Artillery, Captain Benjamin Others

CAVALRY

There was no cavalry in the Army of the Potomac.

Army of Northern Virginia Order of Battle[27]
General ROBERT E. LEE

RIGHT WING, Maj. Gen. JAMES LONGSTREET

ANDERSON'S DIVISION
Maj. Gen. R.H. ANDERSON

Armistead's Brigade	Wright's Brigade
Brig. Gen. L.A. ARMISTEAD	Brig. Gen. A.R. WRIGHT
9th Virginia	3d Georgia
14h Virginia	22d Georgia
38th Virginia	44th Alabama
53d Virginia	48th Georgia
57th Virginia	
	Artillery
Mahone's Brigade	Maj. JOHN S. SAUNDERS
Brig. Gen. W. MAHONE	
6th Virginia	Grimes' (Virginia) battery
12th Virginia	Huger's (Virginia) battery
16th Virginia	Moorman's (Virginia) battery
41st Virginia	

JONES' DIVISION
Brig. Gen. D.R. JONES

Toombs' Brigade	Jones' Brigade
Col. H.I. BENNING	Col. GEORGE T. ANDERSON
Brig. Gen. R. TOOMBS	

2d Georgia
15th Georgia
17th Georgia
20th Georgia

1st Georgia (Regulars)
7th Georgia
8th Georgia
9th Georgia
11th Georgia
Wise (Virginia) Artillery

Drayton's Brigade
Brig. Gen. T.F. DRAYTON

50th Georgia
51st Georgia
15th South Carolina

Phillips' Legion
Leake's (Virginia) battery

WILCOX'S DIVISION
Brig. Gen. C.M. WILCOX

Wilcox's Brigade
Brig. Gen. C.M. WILCOX

Pryor's Brigade
Brig. Gen. R. A. PRYOR

8th Alabama
9th Alabama
10th Alabama
11th Alabam
Anderson's battery, Thomas (Va.) Art'y

14th Alabama
5th Florida
8th Florida
3d Virginia
2d Florida

Maurin's battery, Donaldsonville (Louisiana) Artillery

Featherston's Brigade
Brig. Gen. W.S. FEATHERSTON
Col. CARNOT POSEY

12th Mississippi
16th Mississippi
19th Mississippi
2d Mississippi Battalion
Chapman's battery, Dixie (Virginia) Artillery

HOOD'S DIVISION
Brig. Gen. John B. HOOD

Hood's Brigade
Brig. Gen. JOHN B. HOOD

Whiting's Bridge
Col. E.M. LAW

18th Georgia
Hampton (South Carolina) Legion
1st Texas
4th Texas
5th Texas

4th Alabama
2d Mississippi
11th Mississippi
6th North Carolina

Artillery
MAJ. B.W. FROBEL
Bachman's battery, German (South Carolina) Artillery
Garden's battery, Palmetto (South Carolina) Artillery
Reilly's battery, Rowan (North Carolina) Artillery

KEMPER'S DIVISION
Brig. Gen. JAMES L. KEMPER

Seven. Prelude to Second Manassas

Kemper's Brigade
Col. M.D. CORSE

1st Virginia
7th Virginia
11th Virginia
17th Virginia
24th Virginia 56th Virginia
Rogers' battery, Loudoun (Virginia) Artillery

Jenkins' Brigade
Brig. Gen. M. JENKINS
Col. JOSEPH WALKER

1st South Carolina (Volunteers)
2d South Carolina Rifles
5th South Carolina
6th South Carolina
4th South Carolina Battalion (?)
Palmetto (South Carolina) Sharpshooters
Stribling's battery, Fauquier (Virginia) Artillery

Pickett's Brigade
Col. EPPA HUTTON

8th Virginia
18th Virginia
19th Virginia
28th Virginia

Evans' Brigade
Brig. Gen. N.G. EVANS
Col. P.F. STEVENS

17th South Carolina
18th South Carolina
22d South Carolina
23d South Carolina
Holcombe (South Carolina) Legion
Boyce's battery, Macbeth (South Carolina) Artillery

ARTILLERY OF THE RIGHT WING

Washington (Louisiana) Artillery
Col. J.B. WALTON

Eshleman's (4th) company
Miller's (3d) company
Richardson's (2d) company
Squires's (1st) company

Lee's Battalion
Col. S.D. LEE

Eubank's (Virginia) battery
Jordan's battery, Bedford (Va.) Artillery
Parker's (Virginia) battery
Rhett's (South Carolina) battery

LEFT WING, Major General T.J. JACKSON
JACKSON'S DIVISION

Brig. Gen. WILLIAM B. TALIAFERRO
Brig. Gen. WILLIAM E. STARKE

First Brigade
Col. W.S.H. BAYLOR
Col. A.J. GRIGSEY

47th Alabama
2d Virginia
4th Virginia
5th Virginia

27th Virginia
33d Virginia

Second Brigade
Col. BRADLEY T. JOHNSON

Third Brigade
Col. A.G. TALIAFERRO

48th Alabama
10th Virginia
23d Virginia
37th Virginia

Fourth Brigade
Brig. Gen. W.E. STARKE
Col. LEROY A. STAFFORD

1st Louisiana
2d Louisiana

21st Virginia
42d Virginia
48th Virginia
1st Virginia Battalion

9th Louisiana
10th Louisiana
15th Louisiana
Coppen's (Louisiana) battalion

ARTILLERY
Maj. L.M. SHUMAKER

Brockenbrough's (Maryland) battery
Carpenter's (Virginia) battery
Caskie's battery, Hampden (Virginia) Artillery
Cutshaw's (Virginia) battery
Poague's battery, Rockbridge (Virginia) Artillery
Raine's battery, Lee (Virginia) Artillery
Rice's (Virginia) battery
Wooding's battery, Danville (Virginia) Artillery

HILL'S LIGHT DIVISION
Maj. Gen. AMBROSE P. HILL

Branch's Brigade
Brig. Gen. L. O'B. BRANCH

7th North Carolina
18th North Carolina
28th North Carolina
33d North Carolina
37th North Carolina

Archer's Brigade
Brig. Gen. J J. ARCHER

5th Alabama Battalion
19th Georgia
1st Tennessee (Provisional Army)
7th Tennessee
14th Tennessee

Pender's Brigade
Brig. Gen. W.D. PENDER

16th North Carolina
22d North Carolina
34th North Carolina
38th North Carolina

Field's Brigade
Brig. Gen. C.W. FIELD
Col. J.M. BROCKENBROUGH

40th Virginia
47th Virginia
55th Virginia
22d Virginia Battalion

Gregg's Brigade
Brig. Gen. MAXCY GREGG

1st South Carolina
1st South Carolina Rifles
12th South Carolina
13th South Carolina
14th South Carolina

Thomas' Brigade
Brig. Gen. E.L. THOMAS

14th Georgia
35th Georgia
45th Georgia
49th Georgia

ARTILLERY
Lieut. Col. R.L. WALKER

Braxton's battery, Fredericksburg (Virginia) Artillery
Crenshaw (Virginia) Battery
Davidson's battery, Letcher (Virginia) Artillery
Fleet's battery, Middlesex (Virginia) Artillery

Latham's battery, Branch (North Carolina) Artillery
McIntosh's battery, Pee Dee (South Carolina) Artillery
Pegram's battery, Purcell (Virginia) Artillery

EWELL'S DIVISION
Maj. Gen. R S. EWELL
Brig. Gen. A.R. LAWTON

Lawton's Brigade
Brig. Gen. A.R. LAWTON
Col. M. DOUGLASS

13th Georgia
26th Georgia
31st Georgia
38th Georgia
60th Georgia
61st Georgia

Early's Brigade
Brig. Gen. J.A. EARLY

13th Virginia
25th Virginia
31st Virginia
44th Virginia
49th Virginia
52d Virginia
58th Virginia

Trimble's Brigade
Brig. Gen. I.R. TRIMBLE
Capt. W.F. BROWN

15th Alabama
12th Georgia
21st Georgia
21st North Carolina
1st North Carolina Battalion

Hays' Brigade
Brig. Gen. HARRY T. HAYS
Col. HENRY FORNO
Col. H.B. STRONG

5th Louisiana
6th Louisiana
7th Louisiana
8th Louisiana
14th Louisiana

ARTILLERY

Balthis' battery, Staunton (Virginia) Artillery
Brown's battery, Chesapeake (Maryland) Artillery
D'Aquin's battery, Louisiana Guard Artillery
Dement's (Maryland) battery
John R. Johnson's (Virginia) battery
Latimer's battery, Courtney (Virginia) Artillery

CAVALRY
Maj Gen. J.E.B. STUART

Hampton's Brigade
Brig. Gen. WADE HAMPTON

1st North Carolina
2d South Carolina
10th Virginia
Cobb (Georgia) Legion
Jeff. Davis Legion

Lee's Brigade
Brig. Gen. F. LEE

1st Virginia
3d Virginia
4th Virginia
5th Virginia
9th Virginia

Robertson's Brigade
Brig. Gen. B.H. ROBERTSON

2d Virginia
6th Virginia

Artillery

Hart's (South Carolina) battery
Pelham's (Virginia) battery

7th Virginia
12th Virginia
17th Virginia Battalion

ARTILLERY
First Virginia Regiment
Col. J.T. BROWN

Coke's battery (Williamsburg Artillery)
Dance's battery (Powhatan Artillery)
Hupp's battery (Salem Artillery)
Macon's battery (Richmond Fayette Arty)
Smith's battery (3d Company, Richmond Howitzers)
Watson's battery (2d Company, Richmond Howitzers)

Sumpter (Georgia) Battalion
Lieut. Col. A.S. Curtis

Blackshear's battery (D)
Lane's battery (C)
Patterson's battery (B)
Ross' battery (A)

Miscellaneous Batteries

Ancell's battery, Fluvanna (Virginia) Artillery
Huckstep's (Virginia) battery
Milledge's (Georgia) battery
Page's (R.C.M.) Morris (Virginia) Artillery
Peyton's battery, Orange (Virginia) Artillery
Turner's (Virginia) battery

Eight

August 28, 29, 30 — Second Battle of Manassas

August 28 — The First Day's Battle Draws Near

Pope was stunned by the news of Jackson's raid on his base and responded as Lee expected. Upon learning that Jackson had cut his communications and supplies, he ordered a turnaround of his army and started a northeastward movement to Manassas Junction. Later, Pope boastfully vowed he would get Jackson and "bag the whole crowd."[1]

In the late hours of August 27, Jackson left Manassas Junction, moving north up the Sudley Manassas Road, and in the early morning hours of August 28 went into bivouac on Stony Ridge. Captain Blackford gave a brief description of Jackson's position:

> The position was a wonderfully strong one along the line of an old railroad where there were successive cuts and fills of from eight to fifteen feet, making most formidable breast works for infantry both in the cuts and behind the banks, while the elevated ground in rear gave position for artillery to fire over their heads. The left flank was covered by Bull Run and the right rested on the crest of a ridge which could be crowned with batteries to enfilade the whole front. The high ground was wooded, and in these woods Jackson massed his corps, hiding them completely, while Stuart surrounded them by a curtain of cavalry to keep off their scouting parties who were in search of Jackson's dreaded men.[2]

While Jackson was on Stony Ridge, scouts of Stuart's cavalry had captured a Union courier, and in the courier's pouch they found a copy of Pope's orders directing his army to converge on Manassas. Jackson was concerned about Pope's movements, which were placing the Union army closer to Washington. There were breastworks around Centreville that the Confederates had constructed a year earlier during the Confederate occupation, and he didn't want Pope moving into those defenses. In addition, he didn't want to engage Pope at any place on the other side of the Bull Run and was looking for an opportunity to let Pope know where he was. Events were quickly unfolding that would soon accord Jackson that opportunity. Through couriers, Jackson was in constant contact with Lee and Longstreet and knew exactly where they were. Longstreet had left Major General R. H. Anderson's Division, including Colonel Stephen D. Lee's Artillery

Battalion, at the Rappahannock, and with his remaining 25,000 was on the march to join Jackson. They were following Jackson's route and would reach Thoroughfare Gap in the late hours of August 28.[3]

When Pope moved his army off the Rappahannock, the 1st Corps, commanded by General Franz Sigel, and his 3rd Corps, commanded by General Irvin McDowell took a route via Gainesville to reach Manassas Junction. By midmorning of August 28, the two corps reached Gainesville. At Gainesville, Sigel moved down the Wellington Road and McDowell continued west on the Warrenton Turnpike after sending General James Ricketts's Division to guard Thoroughfare Gap in anticipation of Longstreet's arrival. McDowell's route to Manassas Junction would take him to the intersection of Warrenton Turnpike and Pageland Road, turning south down Pageland.[4]

General John F. Reynolds's Pennsylvania Reserves were the first of McDowell's corps to reach the intersection. While Reynolds was moving south down Pageland, he was fired upon by artillery placed near the Brawner Farm by Jackson, about one-half mile to the north. Reynolds rushed an artillery battery to an area north of the Warrenton turnpike and east of Pageland Road.[5]

An artillery duel ensued, and after a few shots were fired, the Confederates limbered their artillery and withdrew. As this action faded away, McDowell rode up Monroe Hill (modern Stuart Hill) to an apple orchard and sat under one of the trees. While he was studying his maps, Reynolds and Division Commander General Rufus King joined him. Reynolds reported seeing a wagon train on the Sudley-Manassas Road and the three concluded that the Confederate artillery battery they engaged must have been there to protect the train. Reynolds then continued his march down Pageland towards Manassas Junction and was soon out of sight.[6]

Following Reynolds were the four brigades of Brigadier General Rufus King's division. When the first three brigades of King's division had turned south down Pageland from the intersection, his fourth brigade was still on the turnpike facing east. At that point, the division was halted and disbursements of rations were made. King and some of his staff had their dinner alongside the pond located in the southeast quadrant of the intersection.[7]

Meanwhile, moving with Kearny's division, Pope arrived in Manassas at noon to find his massive supply depot in embers, but no Jackson. There he was informed by captured stragglers of Jackson's command that Jackson was at Centreville. Pope then sent out orders to his corps redirecting them to move on Centreville. The corps of Heintzelman and Reno moved along the Centreville Road, Sigel and Reynolds along the Manassas-Sudley Road, and King's Division of McDowell's corps along the Warrenton Pike. After receiving his orders, McDowell ordered King to countermarch to the Warrenton Turnpike and advance on Centreville. McDowell then rode off to find Reynolds and Pope.[8] It would be twelve hours before McDowell was heard from again as he became disoriented in the dark and got lost.

The intersection became a mass of confusion. King's three brigades that were stretched out to the south for a mile became jumbled while reforming for the countermarch. As this confusion was in motion, King had an epileptic seizure and was placed in an ambulance in the rear of Brigadier General Marcena Patrick's brigade. King's division was now without a commander.[9] After some delay, the division headed east on the Warrenton Turnpike.

Nearing 5 P.M., Jackson and some of his commanders were conversing when Stuart's engineer officer, Captain William W. Blackford came galloping into their camp. Blackford had just come from a farmhouse where he had gone with a party of three other soldiers to obtain some buttermilk, and in doing so, he had encountered five Union soldiers that were part of King's advance guard. They managed to capture four. Blackford then observed the forward columns of Hatch's brigade coming down the turnpike with a heavy line of flankers out. He reported the capture of the prisoners to Jackson and the presence of infantry in large force. Jackson calmly fastened on his sword, mounted his horse and rode out onto the ridge that extended east of the Brawner Farmhouse.[10]

Battle of Brawner Farm (Groveton)

Only within the past four decades have historians recognized the significance of the battle at the Brawner Farm on August 28, 1862. Brawner Farm was actually as much a part of the 2nd Battle of Manassas as the engagements that occurred on the subsequent two days. Confusingly, the battle has been identified in the official records, other official correspondence, and soldiers' letters as the Battle of Groveton and the Battle of Gainesville.[11] Remarkably, the Brawner Farm afterward remained in a pristine state of preservation even though it did not come under National Park protection until May 21, 1985.

The Brawner family home (owned by a family named Douglas) was a log farmhouse located deep within the northeast quadrant of the Warrenton Turnpike and Pageland Lane intersection. It was about one-quarter of a mile north of the turnpike and about equal distance east of Pageland Lane. Near the farmhouse were a few outbuildings, and in the back, peach and lemon trees; some 70 yards east and south of the home was a large apple orchard.[12] The farm land was about 320 acres with a small barn located some distance to the east-northeast of the farmhouse. The farm fields were separated by split-rail fences and a few haystacks were present in the hayfields. Some distance below the apple orchard was woodland (Brawner Woods) that stretched further south, separated by the turnpike. The woods continued south of the turnpike and were a part of the Cundiff farm. The terrain had significant features, including a ridge that ran east of the house for almost one-half mile, gently sloping downward as far as Groveton. To the northeast of the house was another ridge (given the name Douglas Heights) that ran north all the way to the Unfinished Railroad cut. Near the north side of the turnpike and about 200 yards east of Brawner Woods emerged another ridge that stretched from the south-southwest to the north-northeast for about 600 yards; it was later known as Battery Heights.

"Bring out your men, gentlemen"

Some of King's soldiers marching in the columns along the turnpike spotted the lone figure riding up and down the ridge and assumed it to be a Confederate scout, unaware that it was Jackson himself who was observing them. After studying the Union columns, Jackson wheeled his horse and galloped back to his encampment. Reining in his horse, he simply said to his commanders, "Bring out your men, gentlemen."[13]

King's 7,500 men of his four-brigaded division were isolated from all other Union forces as they marched through the intersection and headed east on the turnpike in response to Pope's orders to converge on Centreville. Leading the forward brigade with four regiments and closely followed by Captain John A Reynolds's Battery L, 1st New York Light Artillery, was Brigadier General John Hatch, whose forward columns were just moving across the Groveton intersection. Next in line was the brigade of Brigadier General John Gibbon with four regiments, closely followed by Joseph Campbell's Battery B, 4th U.S. Artillery. Gibbon's forward columns had just passed the Brawner Woods. Following Gibbon was Brigadier General Abner Doubleday's brigade of three regiments, and his forward columns were about 500 yards west of the Brawner Woods. General Marsena Patrick led the fourth brigade with four regiments, and his forward columns were a quarter of a mile to the west, extending beyond the Pageland Road intersection.[14]

At about 5:30, a quarter of a mile north of the Groveton intersection, the Confederate artillery battery of Asher Barber's Staunton Artillery from Ewell's division rolled into battery and opened fire on Hatch's forward columns. Hatch was surprised; the 14th Brooklyn of his brigade was out as flankers reconnoitering the ground in their front and he had received no report of any enemy presence.[15] After two volleys, the guns were on target and the shells exploded in the middle of the columns. Hatch's men were near panic as they took cover on both sides of the road. Hatch ordered up his 1st New York Light Artillery, but the Confederate artillery was coming in hot and heavy, "making it almost impossible for the cannoneers to man their pieces." King's Division came to a complete halt.[16]

Upon hearing the cannon fire, General Gibbon rode out onto the ridge later to be known as Battery Heights to see where the cannon fire was coming from. As he was turning to leave and looking to his left while viewing the area north of the Brawner farmhouse, he saw limbered Confederate artillery getting ready to go into battery.[17] Gibbon rushed back to his brigade and sent Joseph Campbell's Battery B, 4th U.S. Artillery, consisting of six twelve-pounder Napoleons, onto the ridge at Battery Heights to counter the Confederate fire. Within moments an artillery duel was underway between a section of Captain George Wooding's Danville Artillery and Campbell's Battery B artillery.[18]

Very shortly, a second section of Wooding's artillery joined the Confederate guns on the ridge behind the Brawner farmhouse and began firing upon the brigades of Doubleday and Patrick. Patrick quickly moved his excited columns into the wooded area south of the turnpike. To his regimental commanders, Doubleday shouted out, "Bring the men forward at double quick," and his equally excited regiments dashed the 500 yards into the Brawner Woods south of Gibbon's regiments and the turnpike. Doubleday located Gibbon, and after assessing their situation, they erroneously concluded it was part of Stuart's cavalry and mere horse artillery without infantry support that was firing upon them. All of King's division was now under artillery fire.[19]

At this time, the brigade commanders were unaware that they had no division commander; any decisions to be made would be made by the individual brigade commanders. The two commanders did not know where King was; what they did know was that they had to act quickly on a decision. Doubleday suggested they should storm the battery, and Gibbon replied, "By heaven, I'll do it."[20]

The forward regiment of General Gibbon's brigade was the 6th Wisconsin led by Col. Rufus Dawes, followed by the 7th Wisconsin led by Col. William Robinson. Third in line was the 2nd Wisconsin, followed by the 19th Indiana led by Col. Solomon Meredith. Campbell's artillery was next in line behind the 19th Indiana.[21] Gibbon's brigade wore distinctive uniforms: knee-length dark-blue frock coats, sky-blue pants, white leggings, and plumed black felt hats that had wide brims with one side pinned to a high crown. They first became known as "The Black Hat Brigade." Later, they would be known as "The Iron Brigade."

The 2nd Wisconsin was one of only two regiments in King's Division that had seen action. They were the veterans of Gibbon's brigade. Gibbon's 2nd Wisconsin commander was 29-year-old Colonel Edgar O'Connor, who at the time could not speak above a whisper due to a recent illness. His commands had to be relayed by his adjutant.[22] To capture the artillery battery, Gibbon accompanied his 2nd Wisconsin through the Brawner Woods. It was about 6 P.M. when the 2nd Wisconsin emerged from the woods and went into a line of battle formation. They marched forward across the fields toward the artillery battery on the ridge northeast of the Brawner farmhouse.[23]

Before the regiment's skirmishers got within musket range of the Confederate guns, the artillerymen limbered their pieces and galloped away. Coming into view a quarter of a mile away in the distance was a huge mass of Confederates in line of battle with their battle flags out front. They marched head-on towards Gibbon's startled columns. It was the Stonewall Brigade, about 800 strong, but to the 2nd Wisconsin it looked like thousands.[24] At the 1st Battle of Manassas, the strength of the Stonewall Brigade was 2500. During the thirteen months between the two battles, the Stonewall Brigade had engaged in many battles, including Jackson's Valley campaigns, the Peninsular campaign, and more recently, Cedar Mountain. Coming into action at the 2nd Battle of Manassas, their strength had been reduced to 800, and before the next three days were over, their strength would be less than half of that number.

The skirmishers from both sides exchanged shots, and then the 2nd Wisconsin skirmishers broke and ran back to the flanks of their regiment. When the two forces were about 150 yards apart, the commands to fire were given. The 2nd Wisconsin advanced to the mid–slope of the ridge, and many fell under the Confederates' thunderous hail of fire. Instantly, the regiment fell back to the position of the 2nd Wisconsin's present-day plaque. From that location, the 2nd Wisconsin's left flank extended about 50 yards and their right flank about 75 yards. The Stonewall Brigade advanced and took a position behind a split-rail fence. The two opposing forces were less than 80 yards apart.[25] It was during this time, while leading his men into line of battle, that the 2nd

Wisconsin's Colonel Edgar O'Conner was mortally wounded. He was shot twice, once in the arm, and once in the groin, from which wound he died on the field within an hour.[26] His command now fell upon Lt. Col. Lucius Fairchild.

Gibbon now knew this was no mere horse artillery he had encountered, and his situation was such that he could not disengage; he sent for Meredith's 19th Indiana. The 19th Indiana came forward using the same route through the woods as did the 2nd Wisconsin. Emerging from the woods about 6:20 P.M., in quick time, they went into a line of battle and formed on the 2nd Wisconsin's left. The 19th Indiana's left flank was anchored 30 yards south of the southeast corner of the Brawner farmhouse, its right flank next to the 2nd Wisconsin's left flank.[27]

Next, Gibbon sent for Robinson's 7th Wisconsin. The 7th Wisconsin came forward using the same route through the woods as the two previous regiments. Emerging from the woods in line of battle, they deployed on a slight slope to the right of the 2nd Wisconsin.[28]

Gibbon next sent for Dawes's 6th Wisconsin. The 6th Wisconsin moved from the turnpike, through the fields behind Campbell's artillery on Battery Heights and on forward until they occupied a wet weather bed.[29]

While Gibbon was anxiously engaged in bringing up his brigade, Jackson was vigorously urging the deployment of brigades from Taliaferro's and Ewell's divisions. From the time that Jackson had made the decision to bring on a fight, his men were not initially in a posture to expediently commit to a full-scale battle.

As the Stonewall Brigade deployed along a fence line, Jackson was desperately trying to hurry other units into battle. It was getting dark, and the opportunity for decisive action was waning. Jackson became anxious and he took to the field, where he found only two regiments of Lawton's brigade were ready to move. Not waiting for the rest of the brigade to form, Jackson personally led the two regiments and they joined the fight, lining up along the fence rails on the left flank of the Stonewall Brigade. By 6:30, four of Lawton's regiments were engaged. By 7 P.M., four regiments of General Trimble's brigade were engaged, forming along the fence rails on the left flank of Lawton's brigade, for a total of thirteen Confederate regiments now engaged. They were in an almost straight line that extended from the west to the east for one-half a mile with no more than 80 yards' separation from Gibbon's and Doubleday's forces to the south. From the Confederate right to left were Baylor's Virginians: the 4th, 27th, 5th, 33rd, and 2nd. Next came Lawton's Georgians, the 26th, 31st, 61st, and 38th, followed by Trimble's 21st Georgia, 21st North Carolina, 15th Alabama, and 12th Georgia.[30]

While Jackson was trying to bring up brigades from Taliaferro's and Ewell's Divisions, Gibbon's difficulties were more exasperating for him. He had no other regiments to bring up; his whole brigade was engaged, and several times he sent aides to look for King. They were unable to locate him or any of his staff. It is interesting to note that there was animosity among the brigade commanders of King's Division. Much of the criticism was toward Gibbon. Nicknamed the "Southern Renegade," Gibbon had been raised in North Carolina and had three brothers fighting for the Confederacy. He sent word to Hatch for help but Hatch responded that he was pinned down by artillery fire. He sent word to Patrick for help, but Patrick did not respond. Later, at the court of inquiry investigating the conduct of Irving McDowell, Patrick stated, "He had no orders to commit his regiments."[31] Doubleday did respond, and sent forward two of his three regiments: the 76th New York, commanded by Colonel William Wainwright, and the 56th Pennsylvania. After all, it was Doubleday who made the suggestion that they should storm the Confederate artillery battery. Shortly, Campbell shifted his artillery forward and asked for infantry support. In response, Doubleday sent his last regiment, the 95th New York, to support Campbell.[32]

When the 6th Wisconsin moved into position, they left a gap of two hundred and fifty yards between their left flank and the right flank of the 7th Wisconsin. Following the same route as the 6th Wisconsin, the 76th New York and 56th Pennsylvania moved from the turnpike, crossed the fields of Battery Heights, and filled the large gap between the 7th and 6th Wisconsin.[33] During most of the battle, Gibbon directed the Union brigades from the left flank of the 19th Indiana, most probably on or near the right side of Brawner Lane leading to the house from the turnpike. (The original Brawner Lane, going to the Brawner house from the turnpike, was located about 50 feet to the east of the present-day lane.)

By 7 P.M., all the Union regiments taking part in this battle were engaged and it was getting dark. The six Union regiments were in a line of battle that extended west to east for one-half mile, almost in a straight line. Their deployment, from the Union's left to right, was the 19th Indiana, 2nd Wisconsin, 7th Wisconsin, 76th New York, 56th Pennsylvania, and the 6th Wisconsin. As darkness spanned over the evening, diffusing the silhouette of the masses on the killing field, each army was firing at the flashes of the other's musket fire.

Lt. Col. Lucius Fairchild of the 2nd Wisconsin describes what next took place after his regiment had deployed into line of battle: "While we were arranging ourselves in line we could see their line which looked like a black mass ... we were then ordered to lie down and fire. My God, what a slaughter! No one seemed to know the object of the fight, there we stood one hour the men falling all around; we got no orders to fall back, and Wisconsin men would rather die than fall back without orders."

Lawton and Trimble's brigades were with the division commanded by Major General Richard S. Ewell. Ewell was also desperately trying to hurry and engage his units and as Trimble's regiments were moving into position, Ewell personally led the 12th Georgia to the far left flank of the Confederate line. As they were approaching a fence line, they came under heavy fire from Dawes's 6th Wisconsin and the 56th Pennsylvania. Seeing that it was crossfire they were receiving, he attempted to get a better look and was seriously wounded by a musket ball, which struck him in his left knee.

Ewell knelt down on his left knee near a pine tree. He had his left hand on a low limb, and was studying the area to see where the crossfire was coming from. A musket round hit him, striking him in the knee he was kneeling on. The round went through the kneecap and traveled down through the bone marrow of the tibia, lodging in his calf muscle. Later that night, he was taken back to Sudley Church. Next day he was moved to the Buckner house, where his leg was amputated.[34] Ewell wouldn't be heard of again until Gettysburg; however, lost were the qualities of leadership he had shown under Jackson.

While Lawton and Trimble's Brigades were being deployed, Jackson ordered Brigadier General William B. Taliaferro to send one of his brigades to strike the left flank of the Union line. One of Taliaferro's brigade commanders was his uncle, Col. Alexander G. Taliaferro. General Taliaferro accompanied his uncle in leading three Virginia regiments: the 10th, 23rd, and 37th. Marching across the southern portion of Stony Ridge, Taliaferro moved his three Virginia regiments into position in the immediate area of the farmhouse.[35]

At the time Taliaferro was given the order to strike the Union left flank, a Confederate artillery battery under the command of young Capt. John Pelham of Stuart's horse artillery was rushing three, 3-inch rifled artillery pieces to the battlefield from the Sudley Church area. As previously noted, darkness was setting in. En route in the darkness, one of Pelham's guns took a wrong turn and was lost. Traveling west and then south from the area of the Unfinished Railroad, Pelham arrived with two artillery pieces and went into battery south and west of the Brawner farmhouse.[36]

In previous battles, beginning with 1st Manassas, the boyish-faced 23-year-old Pelham had gained fame as an outstanding artillery officer. He was the apple of the eye of his commanders, including Lee, Jackson, and J.E.B. Stuart. Later in the war, Pelham was mortally wounded near Kelly's Ford, and it is said that Lee and Stuart both wept when he died.

By 7:30 P.M., Col. Taliaferro's Virginians and Pelham's artillery were fully engaged. Somewhere near the farmhouse, General Taliaferro took three musket balls. Although seriously wounded, he remained on the field until the battle ended.[37]

Jackson was desperately trying to finish the battle before total darkness. About 8 P.M., he ordered an attack, but only four of the thirteen regiments got the word, including Lawton's 26th and 31st Georgia and Trimble's 21st Georgia and 21st North Carolina. The four regiments charged over the fence line. The 26th and 31st Georgia hit the 2nd Wisconsin, and the 21st Georgia and 21st North Carolina struck the 56th Pennsylvania. Lawton's two regiments were repulsed by the combined massive firing of the 2nd and 7th Wisconsin. Trimble's two regiments were repulsed by the combined firing effect from the 56th Pennsylvania and the 76th New York. The Confederates made it to within 30 yards of the Union regiments, sustaining heavy casualties.[38]

Meanwhile, on the Confederates' right flank, Taliaferro's Virginians pressed forward and attacked from in and around the farmhouse, while Pelham's guns enfiladed the ranks of the 19th Indiana at an artillery range of only 50 to 60 yards away. Pelham states: "After remaining in position about half an hour, Major Shumaker ordered me to fall back. Owning to the pole of one of my guns being broken I could not obey the order, and continued firing with one gun until the enemy was driven back."[39] During the melee, the Brawners' home and personal property suffered heavy damage.

Shortly after Lawton's Georgians and Trimble's two 21sts made their fatal attack, the 19th Indiana began to crumble, and the regiment began falling back to the turnpike; in moments the rest of the Union regiments also fell back and left the battlefield.

IN THE AFTERMATH

After Jackson's Confederates were committed, with exception of the Stonewall Brigade, his artillery and other infantry were slow going into action. By the time darkness had settled over the battlefield, only three of his fourteen brigades were engaged. Jackson had succeeded in letting Pope know where he was; however, it was very costly. All told, Jackson had engaged about 3000 and had 1026 casualties, or 34 percent of his attacking force. His Stonewall brigade had 51 percent casualties (411 casualties out of strength of 800). Two of his Georgia regiments, the 26th and the 21st, lost 70 percent between them. In addition, two of Jackson's division commanders fell, seriously wounded: Brigadier Generals William B. Taliaferro and Richard S. Ewell. Adding to those losses, two of the Stonewall Brigade's regimental commanders were killed: Colonel John Neff of the 2nd Virginia and Colonel Lawson Botts of the 33rd Virginia.

For the Union, six regiments successfully held off three of Jackson's brigades, although it was almost equally costly. All told, Gibbon and Doubleday had engaged

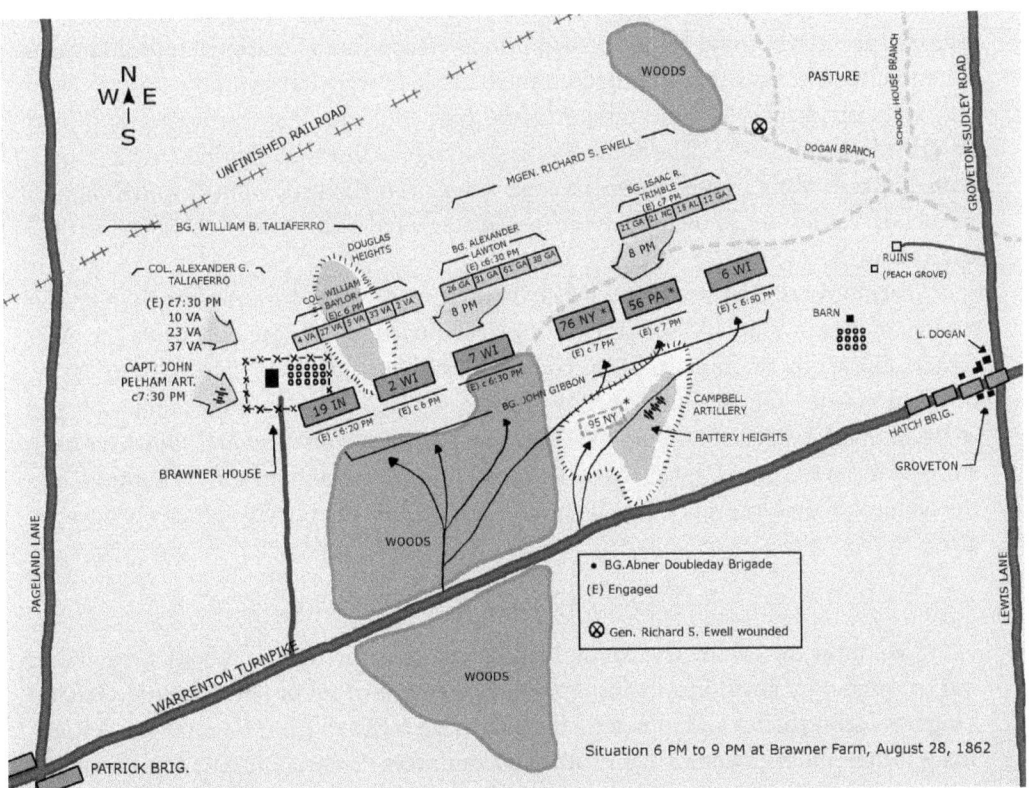

Situation 6 P.M. to 9 P.M. at Brawner Farm, August 28, 1862 (drawing by Rachael R. Johnson).

about 2800 and had 1229 casualties or 44 percent. Gibbon's 2nd Wisconsin went in with strength of 430 and lost 276, or 64 percent. The 19th Indiana's strength was 423 and lost 259, or 61 percent. In addition, adding to Gibbon's losses, his 2nd Wisconsin Regiment lost their "Little Colonel," Edgar O'Conner. Gibbon stated, as recorded in the *Official Record*, that O'Conner's "major (Allen) was wounded in two places, but kept the field. Colonel Cutler, Sixth Wisconsin, whilst bravely moving up to the assistances of his comrades, was badly wounded in the leg. Every field officer of the Seventh Wisconsin (Colonel Robinson, Lieutenant-Colonel Hamilton, and Major Bill) remaining on the field and bringing off his regiment in the best possible manner. The major of the Nineteenth (May) fell mortally wounded whilst his regiment was sustaining a destructive fire on the left of the line."[40]

Later, Major Rufus Dawes of the 6th Wisconsin wrote these chilling words: "The best blood of Wisconsin and Indiana was poured out like water, and it was spilled for naught."[41]

After the battle, the night was filled with the screaming, moaning, and crying of the wounded. Both sides sent units out to carry off the wounded; however, the darkness and the great numbers made it difficult to locate all of them. Most Union wounded lay exposed to the elements throughout the night and many throughout the next day. Very quickly after the first casualties began to mount, the Union set up a hospital at the Cundiff farmhouse located a few hundred yards south of the turnpike, and the Confederates set up a hospital at the Sudley Church. When King's Division left for Manassas Junction, their remaining wounded on the battlefield were left behind.

Captain Blackford rode out onto the battlefield the next morning and later described what he saw[42]: "The bodies lay in so straight a line that they looked like troops lying down to rest. On each front the edge was sharply defined, while towards the rear of each it was less so, showing how men had staggered backward after receiving their death blow."

Blackford recalled hearing the "shrill voice of a young boy apparently not over fifteen or sixteen years old sobbing bitterly. He moved to help the boy, when the boy's father, apparently the captain of his company came up and said, "'Hello, Charley, my boy, is that you?' 'Oh yes,' said the boy. 'Father, my leg is broken, but I don't want you to think that is what I am crying for; I fell in a yellow-jackets' nest and they have been stinging me ever since. That's what makes me cry — please pull me out.' The stings and the wound proved too much for the plucky boy and he died in his father's arms soon after."[43]

King's Council of War

Soon after the battle, the Union brigade commanders met and held a council of war to assess their position and decide their next course of action. By this time, General King was feeling better and joined them. A message received from General James Ricketts was their only contact with any other Union forces. Earlier, Ricketts's Division had been sent by Corps Commander General Irvin McDowell to Thoroughfare Gap to stop Longstreet in the event he was on his way through the pass. Ricketts did encounter

Longstreet but was unable to block his way. Ricketts's message to King stated he was retiring to Manassas Junction. Having had no contact with any of his commanders, King was in a quandary as to what to do. He knew that they had located Jackson and believed if they stayed, Jackson would hit them in full force the next morning. With the urging of his brigade commanders, he decided to withdraw to Manassas Junction.[44]

Throughout military history since the conclusion of this battle, King's withdrawal from the field after the Brawner Farm battle has come under heavy scrutiny. The controversy became public beginning in the autumn of 1862 when a court of inquiry was convened to investigate the conduct of Irving McDowell during the Second Battle of Manassas. Several months later in 1863, during the court-martial of Fitz John Porter, it again came under question. Then, fifteen years later, at the retrial of Porter in 1878, it again came under scrutiny. Later, in 1896, much of the controversy accumulated after Charles King, son of Rufus King, wrote his book, *Gainesville, 1862*, in which he sought to answer and put to rest the scrutiny raised by his father's detractors. What is certain is that King's Division did withdraw to Manassas from the field, moving south down the Pageland Road.

Longstreet had reached Thoroughfare Gap at about 3 A.M. only to find his way blocked by Federal troops under Ricketts. Outmaneuvering his opponent by way of Hopewell Gap, Longstreet forced Ricketts to fall back to Gainesville. That night Ricketts, like King, moved toward Manassas. This enabled Longstreet to affect an easy junction with Jackson's right flank before noon of the following day.[45]

Late in the night, Pope learned of King's fight with Jackson and of Jackson's whereabouts. Discounting all reports of Longstreet's approach, Pope began preparations to go after Jackson the next day, saying he would take care of Longstreet later and repeating his prior vow he would "bag the whole crowd."

Jackson's Deployment Along the Unfinished Railroad

During the evening of the 28th and early morning of the 29th, Jackson took up a position along the Unfinished Railroad bed, which extended two miles southwesterly from near Sudley Springs to Groveton. The grades and cuts of this road provided ready-made entrenchments and formed a very strong position.[46]

Now with an effective strength of about 18,000 infantry and 40 guns, Jackson deployed his divisions of Brigadier General William E. Starke (W.B. Taliaferro), Brigadier General A.R. Lawton (Ewell), and Major General Ambrose P. Hill in strong positions along the Unfinished Railroad. Along his right flank, he formed a double line of battle, with Starke's Division on the right and Lawton on the left. Starke had in his front line from left to right the old Stonewall Brigade, now commanded by Colonel William Baylor, the brigade of Colonel Alexander G. Taliaferro, and in rear, Starke's old brigade, now commanded by Colonel Leroy A. Stafford. His fourth brigade, commanded by Colonel Bradley Johnson, was temporarily deployed near the crossing of the Groveton-Sudley Road and Unfinished Railroad. It was detached and in observation. Lawton had in his front line from left to right, his old brigade now commanded by Colonel M. Douglass and the brigade of Colonel Isaac Trimble. For his second line, Lawton placed the brigades of Brigadier General Jubal Early and Colonel Henry Forno.

On the 29th, the positioning of Hill's six brigades (Jackson's left flank) was in constant change of troop movements as they were subjected to many Union attacks throughout the day, from early morning to late evening. They changed positions several times from one to another. Initially, Hill had in his front line, from his left to right, the brigades of Brigadier General Maxcy Gregg, Brigadier General C.W. Field, and Brigadier General E.L. Thomas. In support north of the Groveton-Sudley Road (later known as Featherbed Lane) were Brigadier General L.O'B. Branch, Brigadier General W.D. Pender, and Brigadier General J.J. Archer.[47] These positions changed throughout the day, beginning with the attacks by brigades of Brigadier General Carl Schurz's division of Sigel's corps.

August 29 — Second Day

POPE PREPARES TO ATTACK JACKSON

By 9:30 P.M. of the 28th, Pope had been made aware of the battle at Brawner Farm and erroneously concluded that King met the head of Jackson's column in retreat from Centreville.[48] In addition, he falsely concluded that King had remained at Groveton and now stood between Jackson and Lee's main body, which he believed was more than a day's march away.

On the bases of his erroneous assumptions, Pope made preparations to attack the "retreating" Jackson the next morning. Dawn of August 29 would see the beginning of disastrous failures for Pope, brought on for the most part by Pope himself. His faulty decisions proved to be based on miscalculations, bad judgments, and poor generalship driven by an inflated ego.

While King's division was approaching Manassas in the early morning hours of the 29th, Gibbon was having second thoughts about the decision he and the other commanders had persuaded King to make: to withdraw from Groveton. Setting out on his own, he rode hard in search of Pope. Before Gibbon's arrival, Pope had learned that King's Division had left the field near Groveton and was withdrawing to Manassas Junction, as was Ricketts, and he was furious. Pope's first words when he saw Gibbon were, "Where is McDowell? ... He is never where he ought to be!" Of course, Gibbon didn't know; McDowell had been lost for the past twelve hours.[49]

After Gibbon reported the events at the Brawner Farm to Pope, Pope initiated an order for Gibbon to deliver to Porter at Manassas. The order directed Porter to "push forward with your corps and King's division, which you will take with you, upon Gainesville. I am following the enemy down the Warrenton Turnpike. Be expeditious, or we will lose much."[50] During this time, King decided to give over his command to Hatch because of ill health. Gibbon met Porter on the outskirts of Manassas and conveyed Pope's orders to him. In obedience to his orders, Porter reversed his march to Centreville, and at about 10:00 A.M., had reached Dawkins Branch, about 3 miles north of Gainesville. He halted there after finding Confederates posted in his front. He then sent a brigade of his leading division forward on reconnaissance and waited.[51]

While Porter deployed a brigade from Major General George W. Morell's division, McDowell arrived, having found his way after being lost for hours. McDowell showed Porter a dispatch he had received a few minutes before from Brigadier General John Buford, the commander of the Union cavalry on the right. The dispatch stated that 17 Confederate regiments, 1 battery, and 500 cavalry had passed through Gainesville at about 8:45 A.M.[52] This was the advance of Longstreet's command, which had left Thoroughfare Gap early that morning and now, unbeknownst to Porter, was at that moment moving into position on Longstreet's developing right flank (Porter's front).

McDowell had also received a joint order from Pope that called for an attack on Jackson, based on the assumption that Jackson had been stopped in attempting to retreat through Thoroughfare Gap. Pope did not know the position of his own troops, much less those of Jackson.

McDowell and Porter discussed the order, which read as follows:

Headquarters Army of Virginia
Centreville, August 29, 1862

Generals McDowell and Porter:
You will please move forward with your joint commands toward Gainesville. I sent General Porter written orders to that effect an hour and a half ago. Heintzelman, Sigel, and Reno are moving on the Warrenton turnpike, and must now be not far from Gainesville. I desire that as soon as communication is established between this force and your own the whole command shall halt. It may be necessary to fall back behind Bull Run at Centreville to-night. I presume it will be so, on account of our supplies.... If ay [sic] considerable advantages are to be gained by departing from this order it will not be strictly carried out. One thing must be had in view, that the troops must occupy a position from which they can reach Bull Run to-night or by morning. The indications are that the whole force of the enemy is moving in this direction at a pace that will bring them here by to-morrow night or the next day. My own headquarters will be for the present with Heintzelman's corps or at this place.

Jno. Pope,
Major-General, Commanding

The two generals concluded that Buford's report of Longstreet's passing through Gainesville had not reached Pope. In view of this, McDowell exercised the discretionary latitude authorized by the order and cautioned Porter against a farther advance. McDowell told Porter that he would be taking King's division with him and would move northward on the road leading out from Bethlehem Church to Sudley Road, taking position between Porter and the commands operating along the turnpike.[53]

THE JUNCTION OF LONGSTREET AND JACKSON'S COMMANDS

Jackson knew of Longstreet's progress, having been kept apprised by couriers. Knowing that Longstreet would be arriving sometime that morning, Jackson sent Stuart to meet him. About mid–morning, Stuart set out, riding hard with a regiment of cavalry. In his book, *War Years with Jeb Stuart*, Blackford described the meeting:

> Two or three miles from the battlefield we came in sight of Longstreet's dust. The weather had been very dry and the roads very dusty and the march of large bodies of troops raised a cloud that could be seen for miles as it rose above the tops of the trees. At this welcome sight, Stuart, accompanied by his staff only, galloped ahead to meet the long expected column. To keep his dust from annoying the troops General Lee and staff were riding a hundred yards in advance of the column, and here General Stuart joined him. Generals Lee, Longstreet and Stuart then rode on still further in advance, so as to confer freely, and General Stuart explained all that had happened and the position Jackson then held. When within about half a mile of the battlefield General Lee and General Stuart rode off to one side of the road, dismounted and sat down on the grass. General Stuart, taking out his map of the country, spread it out and proceeded to explain the position of affairs more fully for about a quarter of an hour.[54]

While Lee and Stuart conferred, Longstreet's Corps of 25,000 passed by, and as the columns approached the Turnpike and Pageland intersection, the junction between the two wings of Longstreet and Jackson began. Toward the end of the conference between Lee and Stuart, and while the juncture was taking place, Lee sent for Jackson. No record exists of those historical discussions between Lee, Longstreet, Stuart and Jackson that took place along the Warrenton Road. A marker, not on the battlefield, indicates the place where Lee, Jackson, and Longstreet met. It is located approximately four-tenths of a mile west of the Warrenton Turnpike and Pageland Road Intersection and approximately 100 yards north of the Turnpike (modern Rte. 29).

Stuart and his cavalry moved off to the right while Blackford rode ahead to reconnoiter. He rode three miles south to Dawkins Branch, where he observed Porter's approach, half a mile beyond. Blackford continued to describe what next took place:

> I reported the result of my reconnaissance to General Stuart and he at once informed General Lee, who sent some infantry over to confront Porter. While awaiting this reinforcement, General Stuart, with that fertility of resource which characterized him in emergencies, caused his cavalry to get branches of pine trees and, after tying them to their halter straps, to gallop backwards and forward, dragging them on a dusty road which led through some old fields grown up in bushes, where the clouds of dust rose up in sight of the enemy. Seeing this long, heavy cloud of dust rising above the trees, Porter naturally thought it was heavy bodies of troops and was no doubt influenced by it in advancing no further than Dorkins [sic] Branch....[55]

Positioning of Longstreet's Wing

While Longstreet made his juncture and deployed into a defensive posture east of Pageland Road, Jackson's command warded off attacks from brigades of Franz Sigel's corps against his center and left flank. Jackson was anxious that Longstreet occupy the area adjacent to his far right flank, considering it a priority. Prior to Longstreet's arrival, Jackson had deployed the brigades of Early and Forno along the Pageland Road to guard his right flank. Hood's division was the van of Longstreet's command, and his infantry was directed to take position from the Brawner farmhouse and on south near the Cundiff farmhouse beyond the turnpike. As Hood's infantry moved onto the battlefield of

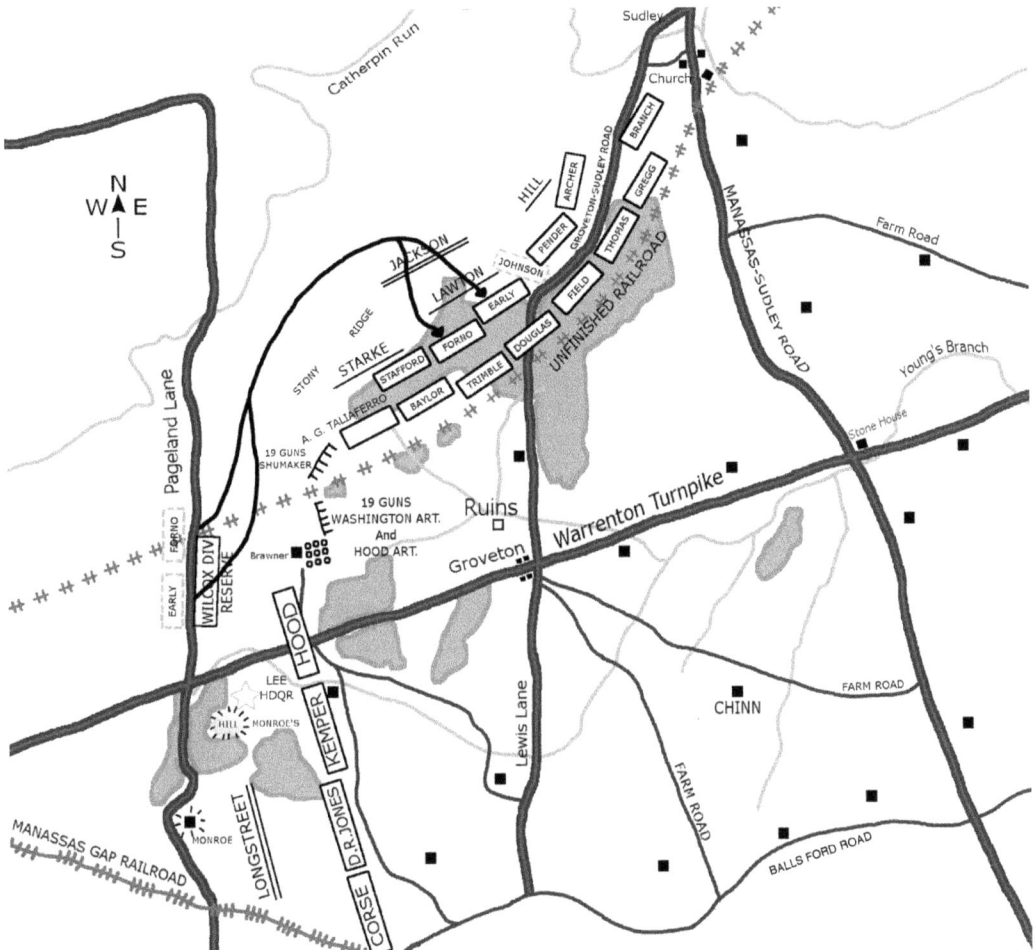

10:00–11:30 A.M. August 29 — Juncture of Longstreet's and Jackson's Wings (drawing by Rachael R. Johnson).

the previous afternoon's fighting, they picked their way over bodies and wounded left on the field by Gibbon's and Doubleday's brigades. Lee and Longstreet led the rest of Longstreet's columns onto the field. Continuing south and facing east, Kemper's division went into position, with his left flank next to Hood's right flank, Jones's division on Kemper's right flank, and Corse's division to the right of Jones. Initially, Wilcox's division was held in reserve along Pageland Road behind Jones and Corse. Sometime later, Wilcox was sent to Corse's right, Longstreet's right flank.

To complete the junction and cover the ridge north of the Brawner farmhouse and Jackson's far right flank (Douglas Heights), Longstreet instructed Colonel J.B. Walton, commander of the Washington Artillery, to place artillery batteries on that location. From the three batteries of Hood's division and two batteries of his own Washington Artillery, Walton placed a total of nineteen guns into battery on Douglas Heights.

Lee set up his tent headquarters on Monroe Hill (later known as Stuarts Hill), located about 800 yards east of Pageland Road and about 400 yards south of the turnpike. By 2 P.M., Lee had completed a study of his situation and "expressed his wish" to Longstreet that he immediately advance on his front and strike Pope's left. Longstreet did not feel that was plausible, stating that reconnaissance was needed, which he took care of personally. After one hour of reconnoitering his front, he reported to Lee that Union forces (Reynolds's Pennsylvania Reserves and Schenck's divisions) extended for almost one mile south of the Warrenton Turnpike, adding that the ground in his front was "not inviting." In addition, he made it known that he was very concerned about the force off his right flank and its strength. This unknown factor was clarified by Stuart as he shortly arrived from a reconnaissance of the Union force (Porter's Corps) along the Manassas-Gainesville Road and reported that it was "threatening and it was large."[56] Lee decided to hold off any action and await further developments by those forces.[57]

Pope's Plan to "Bag Jackson"

Under the illusion that Jackson was retreating, Pope continued to discount reports of Longstreet's movements, assuming that Lee's main body would not arrive for at least another one or two days. In addition, for inexplicable reasons, he believed that Porter would attack Jackson's right flank, while at the same time getting behind and attacking his rear positions. With these assumptions in mind, Pope had massed eight brigades that extended from the Sudley-Manassas road below the Unfinished Railroad and continued for almost one mile to the southwest near the Warrenton Turnpike. Pope's plan was to have Major General Franz Sigel attack Jackson's defenses and keep him busy while Porter advanced on Jackson's right flank and rear positions.

In the early morning hours, Pope sent orders to Sigel to advance and attack Jackson. Sigel's brigades began preparations between 5:30 and 7 A.M. Although several engagements nipped at Jackson's front throughout the day and into the late evening hours of August 29, there were a total of five major uncoordinated attacks against Jackson's defensive position along the Unfinished Railroad.

First Major Assault — Schurz's Attack

Sigel's orders to his Third Division commander, Brigadier General Carl Schurz, were to connect his left line of battle with Brigadier General Robert H. Milroy's Independent Brigade and locate and attack Jackson's left flank. Milroy was to move northeast out of the Groveton Woods as Schurz's two brigades, led by Colonel W. Krzyzanowski and Colonel A. Schimmelpfennig, would move northeast across the J. Dogan fields while aligning parallel to the Unfinished Railroad in their front. With Krzyzanowski on the left and Schimmelpfennig on the right, Krzyzanowski connected with Milroy's skirmishers, but they soon became disjointed, forcing Krzyzanowski and Schimmelpfennig to continue alone.[58] The result was that two separate attacks at two different locations against Jackson's defenses followed. Schurz's attack developed into a series of attacks that swung back and forth, lasting almost seven hours.

Schurz's division, advancing in line of battle upon Jackson's front from left to right, consisted of Krzyzanowski's 75th Pennsylvania, the 58th New York, and the 54th New York, Schimmelpfennig's 8th West Virginia, 74th Pennsylvania, and the 61st Ohio. As the two brigades advanced through the woods, Schimmelpfennig and Krzyzanowski lost contact with each other. Schimmelpfennig had moved off to the far right of Krzyzanowski.[59]

As Krzyzanowski's three regiments moved through the woods, led by his skirmishers, their rustlings were heard by Gregg's brigade. Opposite the oncoming Yankees were Gregg's five South Carolina regiments, closely aligned together in a small area on a stony shelf, located about 60 yards behind and parallel with the Unfinished Railroad cut. "At this point, the ground rising to some extent, the grade of the road immediately in our front rendered the depth of the cut about 6 feet; but the ground sloping to our right and left, reduced this depth to about one or two feet upon our flanks."[60] The Confederates left to right were posted Colonel Dixon Barnes's 12th, Lt. Colonel Edward McCrady's 1st, and Colonel O.E. Edwards's 13th. In reserve behind the center was Colonel Foster J. Marshall's Orr's Regiment of Rifles. Posted along a fence line perpendicular and to the left of the 12th was Colonel Samuel McGowan's 14th. General Gregg and his staff and all the field officers were on foot.[61]

Gregg sent McCrady's 1st South Carolina regiment forward to "ascertain the enemy's location and number." As they crossed over the railroad grade and pressing forward, the heavy woods and thick undergrowth limited their visibility. Shortly they came under fire from Krzyzanowski's skirmishers in their front. At this time Krzyzanowski forwarded his two New York regiments, the 54th and 58th, in quick-time. Advancing further into the thick woods, McCrady's Carolinians continued down a slope. The ground around formed a hollow at the bottom of the slope. Krzyzanowski's New Yorkers were in the hollow; waiting for the Rebels to come into range. A heavy firefight ensued. McCrady sent a messenger to Gregg reporting the force he had encountered. In response, Gregg sent Barnes's 12th and Edwards's 13th South Carolinians to assist McCrady, and the New Yorkers were driven back.[62] Krzyzanowski hurriedly brought up his last regiment, the 75th Pennsylvania Volunteers, and placed them to oppose Gregg's right flank.

As the fighting continued on for the next two hours, Gregg became aware that three of his five regiments had advanced more than 100 yards forward of their defensive post along the Unfinished Railroad, having pushed Krzyzanowski back. Earlier, he had been reminded by Hill of Jackson's orders to "not advance, and in so doing bring on a general engagement, but to hold the position and act on the defensive."[63] Gregg recalled the three South Carolinian regiments to their initial postings and readied for more attacks from Schurz's brigades.

During the time of Krzyzanowski's initial assaults, other developments were taking place near the Unfinished Railroad cut on Jackson's left. About mid-morning, a Union division from Major General Samuel P. Heintzelman's Third Corps of McClellan's Army of the Potomac, and commanded by Major General Philip Kearny, arrived on the far right flank of Sigel's corps. Shortly after Kearny's arrival, Schurz and Kearny had a meeting in which they discussed their situation: "General Kearny requested me to shorten my front and condense my line by drawing my right nearer to the left, so as to make room for him on the right."[64]

During the short lull created when Gregg fell back, Schimmelpfennig posted his three regiments to the right of Krzyzanowski; from left to right, they were the 8th West Virginia, the 74th Pennsylvania and the 61st Ohio. The 61st Ohio's far right flank was very near the Sudley-Manassas Road. In the posting of Schimmelpfennig's brigade, a gap emerged between the right flank of Krzyzanowski's 54th New York and the left flank of Schimmelpfennig 8th West Virginia. In addition, it was during this time that the 29th New York from Sigel's First Division was sent to assist Schurz. Schurz sent them to the rear of the 54th New York. In the course of shifting his regiments to the left in compliance to Kearny's request, the 1st New York of Brig. General David B. Birney's brigade from Kearny's division formed in the gap between Krzyzanowski and Schimmelpfennig. Schurz described the move: "I gave my orders to Colonel Schimmelpfennig accordingly. A short time afterward I discovered that two small regiments sent to my support had slipped in between my two brigades, and were occupying part of my line in the woods."[65] One of those regiments reported by Schurz would have been the 1st New York. It is not known what other regiment Schurz was referring to.

Gregg's brigade now faced a force in his front of some two thousand. Barnes was one of the first to see Schimmelpfennig's forward movements. Gregg's official report, written later by Brigadier General Samuel McGowan, reads: "The Twelfth being pressed by a heavy column on its left flank, Colonel Barnes changed front to the left, and charging in the most spirited manner drove the enemy down the railroad, breaking and routing them as often as they attempted to make a stand. When he had driven off the enemy and was returning Colonel Barnes was joined by Colonel Marshall (Orr's Rifles), who had been sent to his assistance, and the two regiments again charged and drove a heavy body massing near the railroad."[66]

Schurz reported that when Colonels Barnes and Marshall charged them, the two regiments that had slipped into the gap between Krzyzanowski and Schimmelpfennig, as well as the 54th New York "broke and were thrown out of the woods in disorder, the enemy advancing rapidly and in great force to the edge of the forest. The Twenty-ninth New York poured several volleys into them, checking the pursuit of the enemy only for a moment, and then fell back in good order."[67] Gregg recalled all his regiments at this time, in accordance with the order "not to advance, and in so doing bring on a general engagement."

After speaking with Kearny, Schurz was of the impression he could depend upon him for support. Following their meeting, Schurz received a dispatch from one of Sigel's aides advising him of a dispatch that Sigel had sent Kearny. In his official report, Schurz recalled the contents of Sigel's dispatch, "requesting him [Kearny] to attack at once his whole force, as the rebel general Longstreet who was expected to re-enforce the enemy during the day, had not yet arrived upon the battle-field, and we might hope to gain decisive advantages before his arrival."[68] From the time that Kearny arrived on the field, Schurz was heavily engaged for all of three hours, and Kearny provided him no support except for the 1st New York of Birney's brigade, the regiment that had slipped into Schimmelpfennig's line.

By 2 P.M., Gregg's and Schurz's brigades had been fighting continuously for most of six hours. When Schurz finally retired from the field after being relieved by units of Major General Joseph Hooker's Second Division of Heintzelman's Corps, Gregg's brigade had successfully fought off seven attacks against his position from Schurz's division of overwhelming numbers.

Second Major Assault — Milroy's Attack

Initially, Milroy's Independent Brigade was located in the Groveton Woods east of the Groveton-Sudley Road during the time Schurz's brigades, led by Krzyzanowski and Schimmellpfenig, were near the Unfinished Railroad preparing for their attacks on Jackson's left flank. Siegel's plan had been for Milroy and Schurz to connect, supposedly to make joint attacks against Jackson's defenses.[69] Milroy was unsuccessful in closing the connection, and no documentation has been found to explain his actions or whether or not he misunderstood Schurz's intentions.

While Schurz's command was engaged on Jackson's left, Milroy moved out of the woods, crossing over the Groveton-Sudley Road and advanced to the northwest instead of northeast. Milroy's brigade had a combined strength of about 1500, comprising the 2nd, 3rd, and 5th West Virginia and the 82nd Ohio regiments.

Milroy immediately came under some artillery fire from the left of his front, during which time he heard the sounds of muskets firing on Schurz's front, a half a mile to his right. He made a decision to send his 82nd Ohio and 5th West Virginia through the woods to help Schurz and hold his 2nd and 3rd West Virginians in the Groveton Woods. His idea was to charge the Confederate artillery battery. In Milroy's official report, he stated that the artillery "was a short distance over the top of a hill to our left...."[70] Most likely, this was Brockenbrough's (Maryland) Battery, located above the railroad cut about 200 yards north of what would become famously known the next day as the "Deep Cut."

While turning to the right to move toward Schurz, the two regiments sent to assist Schurz got directions confused in the woods and accidentally wandered into Jackson's defenses at a place known as the "dump," a 100-yard gap in the railroad grade. For defense of the "gap" area, Jackson had his stragglers, slackers, and other miscreants sent to defend the ground of that area.[71] The slackers failed to hold their positions, and the 82nd Ohio, led by Colonel James Cantwell, including the 5th West Virginia led by Colonel John L. Zeigler, breached Jackson's first line of defense. Within moments, regiments of Lawton's division in Jackson's second line of defense fell upon Cantwell's Ohioans and the West Virginians, almost entrapping them in the dump area. Milroy then sent his 2nd West Virginia to assist his two regiments at the "dump." Hurrying into the fight, they moved to the left of the 82nd. Their assault met with heavy response from Lawton's and Starke's Confederates, devastating the regiment in just a short few minutes. Milroy then sent his 3rd West Virginia forward and they met the same fate as his other three regiments. In complete disarray, the brigade retreated back to the Groveton Woods. In the onslaught, Cantrell took a musket ball to the head, which killed him instantly. Oddly enough, the casualty numbers for both the 2nd West Virginia and the 82nd Ohio were the same: each had twenty-four killed and one hundred fourteen wounded and missing. Losses to Milroy's Independent Brigade amounted to more than 300 casualties, almost one-fourth of his command.[72]

During this time, other developments took place. Reynolds's Pennsylvanians, along with a part of Schenck's division, were moving along the south side of the turnpike with the purpose of reaching Jackson's right. Sometime in the mid–morning, Reynolds had reached the battle area of the previous day. The Union commanders were unaware that by this time, Longstreet's wing had arrived and was busily engaged in moving into position. Here, Reynolds came under heavy fire from the Confederate artillery concentrated on Brawner heights, the juncture of Lee's two wings. At about 11 A.M., Reynolds's and Schenck's commands returned to their positions one-half mile south of Groveton and the turnpike along Lewis Lane.

On Jackson's right flank, sometime in the afternoon during a nonengagement period, Brigadier General Isaac Trimble of Lawton's (Ewell) division was seriously wounded from a musket ball to his left leg fired by a Union sharpshooter. Command of Trimble's brigade fell to Captain W.F. Brown.[73] Years later, in his autobiography, Early stated: "Trimble had been wounded by an explosive ball."[74] Ironically, 11 months later at the Battle of Gettysburg, Trimble was wounded again in the same leg, requiring amputation performed by Dr. Hunter McGuire.

While Sigel was making attacks on Jackson's positions, Pope arrived from Centerville about noon and rode north across John Dogan's fields, inspecting the positioning of his army. Initially he sat up his headquarters north of the Warrenton Turnpike near Dogan's farmhouse; however, sometime later they were relocated to Buck Hill, east of the Sudley Road and about 200 yards north of the Stone House.[75] It is interesting to note that while Pope was busy initiating his attack plans against Jackson's positions, Lee and Longstreet arrived with some 25,000 Confederates, and the junction of Jackson and Longstreet's wings took place less than two miles west of Pope's headquarters.

About this time, Federal reinforcements of Heintzelman's and Reno's corps were reaching the field. At 2:00 P.M., Hooker's division of Heintzelman's corps began relieving Schurz's troops on the Federal right. In addition, from the Army of the Potomac's Ninth Corps, Steven's and Reno's divisions of the Second Corps (both units theoretically under Reno's command) had come into supporting distance of the field.

THIRD MAJOR ASSAULT — GROVER'S ATTACK

The third assault took place at about 3:00 P.M. First Brigade Commander Brigadier General Cuvier Grover of General Joseph Hooker's 2nd Division, Heintzelman's Third Corps, Army of the Potomac was ordered to "go into the woods and charge." Observing that there was nobody in the area to support him, he asked about his support and was advised that it was on the way. Grover's brigade consisted of five regiments: three from Massachusetts, the 1st, 11th, and 16th; the 2nd New Hampshire; and the 26th Pennsylvania. This gave him a combined strength of about 1500. His line of battle extended for about 600 yards. The 2nd New Hampshire spearheaded the attack, with the 11th

Massachusetts to their left and 1st Massachusetts on their right. The 16th Massachusetts and the 26th Pennsylvania were in line of battle in the rear.[76]

In his official report, Grover reported his preparations: "Disposition for carrying out such orders were immediately made. Pieces were loaded, and bayonets fixed, and instructions given for the line to move slowly upon the enemy until it felt his fire, then close upon him rapidly, fire one well-directed volley, and rely upon the bayonet to secure the position on the other side."[77]

The attack along Jackson's left flank held by Hill's division was to the left of where Krzyzanowski's and Schimmellpfenig's brigades of Schurz's division had been fighting most of the morning and early afternoon against Gregg's brigade. Grover's attack struck at Gregg's right flank, held by Gregg's 13th and 1st South Carolinians and Brigadier General E.L. Thomas's brigade of Georgians: the 49th, 14th, and 45th. A gap in the railroad bed separated the two Confederate brigades, a "dump" area much like the one Milroy had encountered earlier in the morning, about three-quarters of a mile to the southwest.

As Grover's line of battle approached the railroad grade, they fired, and after the Confederates returned fire, his lead regiments charged up the embankments. Grover's right flank had no obstacle such as a high embankment to cross over, and his 1st Massachusetts charged through the railroad bed gap. With no time to reload, the Confederates were caught on the rear side of the embankment, hugging the rear slope. The charging troops stabbed with bayonets, crushed skulls with musket butts, and broke through to the next line of defenders.[78] Throughout all the battles of the Civil War, it was rare for opposing fighting forces to come close enough to each other for the bayonet, knives, or other physical contact to be used. The number of wounds contributed to the bayonet and knife for both Union and Confederate soldiers was small when compared to those inflicted by the musket, other small arms, and artillery. Grover's attack was a very bloody battle, resulting in heavy numbers of casualties, many attributed to hand-to-hand fighting.

Colonel William Blaisdell, leading the 11th Massachusetts, made this report:

> The Eleventh Regiment, being the battalion of direction, was the first to reach the railroad, and of course received the heaviest of the enemy's fire. This staggered the men a little, but, recovering in an instant, they gave a wild hurrah and over they went, mounting the embankment, driving everything before them at the point of the bayonet. Here for two or three minutes the struggle was very severe, the combatants exchanging shots their muskets almost muzzle to muzzle and engaging hand-to-hand in deadly encounter. Private John Lawler, of Company D, stove in the skull of one rebel with the butt of his musket and killed another with his bayonet."[79]

Another report, which demonstrates the prevalence of the power of human compassion, describes a similar incident:

> After charging up the embankment and reaching the rear side, a 2nd New Hampshire Sergeant encountered a 49th Georgian and the two clashed, wrestling each other to the ground. In the struggle, the Sergeant grabbed a huge bowie knife from the Confederate's belt and was in a movement to plunge it into the Confederate when the young Georgia boy gasped, "Oh, for God's sake — don't!" Their faces were just inches apart and in that one quick moment of staring into the eyes of the young lad, the Sergeant stopped the blow and said, "All right Johnny,"–stuffed the knife in his belt and then scrambled on."[80]

The swiftness of Grover's attack overwhelmed Thomas's three front line regiments and drove them through the Confederates' second line of defense to the Groveland-Sudley Road in their rear. Grover ruptured Jackson's line, pushing it into a horseshoe-like configuration.

The horseshoe-like configuration developed after Maxcy Gregg realigned his South Carolinians, swinging the 13th and 14th facing west between the railroad grade and Groveton-Sudley Road, while rushing his 1st and 12th to their support. Thomas was fast to rally his Georgians. The 49th quickly moved to link up with McGowan's 14th South Carolinians and then he hurriedly moved to align the 14th, 45th and 35th near the Groveton-Sudley Road.

During this time, Brigadier General William D. Pender and his brigade of four North Carolina regiments were placed north of the Groveton-Sudley Road in supporting distance of Thomas's right flank with orders to support him:

> Finally, it seeming to me to be the time to go to his assistance, I ordered my brigade forward, moving just to the right of Colonel Thomas. My men moved forward very gallantly, driving the enemy back across the railroad cut, through the woods on the opposite side, and beyond their batteries in the adjoining field. A battery of the enemy which was on the right of this wood as we advanced was flanked by my command and the cannoneers deserted their pieces."[81]

Thomas's 35th Georgia joined Pender's North Carolinians in pursuing Grover's brigade back across the railroad cut and beyond.

Brig. Gen. Cuvier Grover. Commander, First Brigade Hooker's Second Division Heintzelman's Third Corps, Army of the Potomac (courtesy Library of Congress).

Grover believed that he would receive support for his attack from Kearny; he hung on for as long as he possibly could, but help never came.

The Confederates flanked Grover's units and forced them out of the area in mass retreat. In the 20 to 30 minutes' duration of this engagement, Grover's brigade suffered 486 casualties (41 killed and 445 wounded and missing), almost one-third of his brigade's strength.[82]

Fourth Major Assault — Nagle's Attack

Having received no word of Porter attacking Jackson's right flank and rear, Pope ordered a fourth assault against Jackson. By this time, Brigadier General Reno's Ninth Corps of McClellan's Army of the Potomac had arrived on the field. At about 4:00 P.M., the 1500-man brigade of Col. James Nagle of Reno's Second Division made the attack

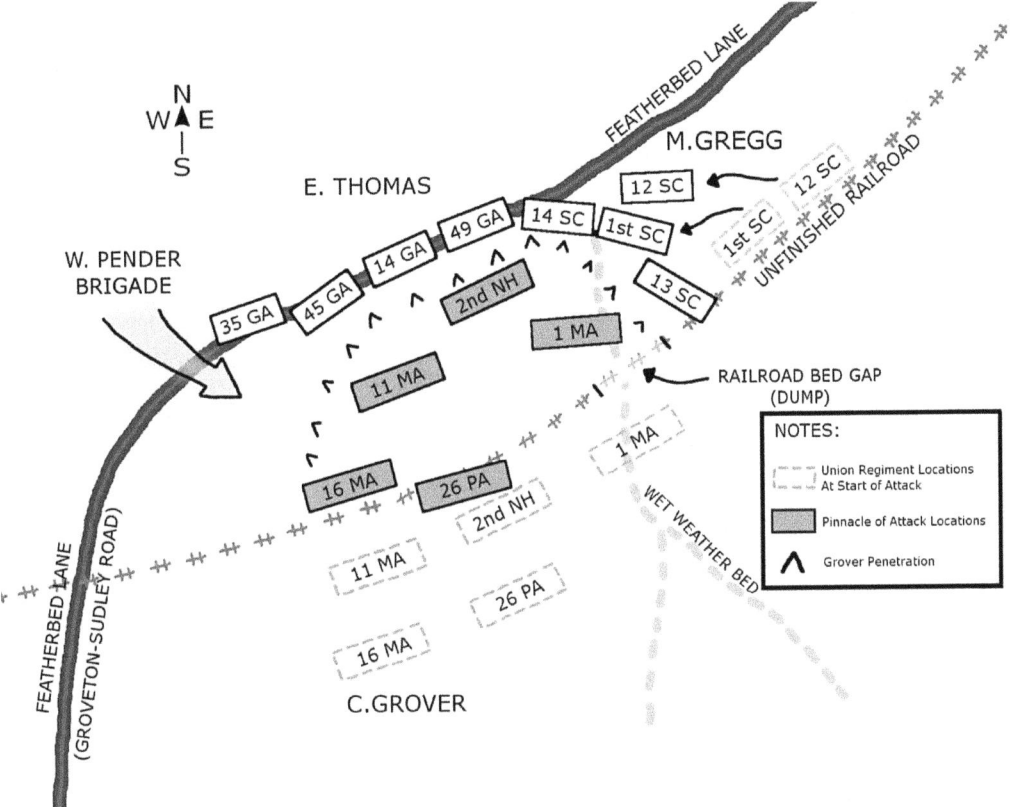

August 29, 1862 — 3:00 to 3:30 P.M.— Grover's Attack (drawing by Rachael R. Johnson).

against Jackson's center west of the Groveton-Sudley Road. Spearheaded by the 6th New Hampshire, with the 48th Pennsylvania on the left and the 2nd Maryland on the right, Nagle's line of battle extended almost 700 yards. Nagle's brigade swept into the Confederate first line of defense held by three regiments of Brown's (Trimble) brigade and three regiments of Lawton's brigade. Nagle's brigade breached the Confederate defenses and was able to carry its assault nearly 100 yards into Brown and Lawton's second lines of defense.

The Confederates recoiled, flanking Nagle's regiments, and after forcing them into a retreat, they pursued them south through the Groveton Woods. The brigades of Colonel's Bradley T. Johnson and Leroy A. Stafford joined Brown's and Lawton's jubilant Confederates in the pursuit. While passing through the Groveton Woods, General Milroy's Independent Brigade posted there was also overrun, and they too quickly retreated headlong to the south. Troops of Stafford's 2nd Louisiana overran Milroy's artillery and captured one of his pieces. As all the artillery horses had either been killed or wounded, the Louisianans harnessed some of their Union captives to the cannon, using them to move it into the Confederate defenses. The Confederates ended their pursuit and settled back into their defenses.

The initial assault extended on the right into the Confederate defenses held by

Field's Brigade. While attempting to rally his men as part of Nagle's 2nd Maryland struck Field's far right, Brigadier General C.W. Field was seriously wounded when a Minié ball entered his left thigh and passed upward, lodging in his right hip. His command fell upon Colonel J.M. Brockenbrough. The assault lasted about 20 minutes, and Nagle lost more than 500 men, one-third of his command.[83]

POPE PLANS TO TURN BOTH FLANKS OF JACKSON'S LINE

Pope rode out to the front, and after conferring with Heintzelman and Sigel, he inspected the line from right to left. By late afternoon plans were formulated to turn both flanks of Jackson's line. The attack on Jackson's Confederate left was to be executed by Heintzelman and Reno, that on the right by Porter.[84] Pope's next action clearly reveals that he continued to ignore the arrival of Longstreet. Shortly after 4:30 P.M., the following dispatch was sent to Porter[85]:

> Headquarters in the Field
> August 29 — 4:30 P.M.
>
> Major-General Porter
>
> Your line of march brings you in on the enemy's right flank. I desire you to push forward into action at once on the enemy's flank, and, if possible, on his rear, keeping your right in communication with General Reynolds. The enemy is massed in the wood in front of us, but can be shelled out as soon as you engage their flank. Keep heavy reserves and use your batteries, keeping well closed to your right all the time. In case you are obliged to fall back, do so to your right and rear, so as to keep you in close communication with the right wing.
>
> John Pope
> Major-General, Commanding

Pope's order, sent at 4:30 P.M., was received by Porter at Bethlehem Church at about 6:30 P.M. Upon its receipt, Porter immediately ordered Morell's division to attack. Shortly thereafter Porter rode to the front to find Morell's preparations complete, but by this time it was so late that darkness was upon them, and Porter decided to rescind the order.

This action became one of the most controversial issues of the war, resulting in Porter's court-martial. Sixteen years later, Porter finally received a re-trial and vindication. In the opinion of the Board in the re-trial "the order was based upon conditions which were essentially erroneous and upon expectations which could not possibly be realized."[86]

FIFTH MAJOR ASSAULT — KEARNY'S ATTACK ON JACKSON'S LEFT FLANK

By 5 o'clock in the afternoon of August 29, regiments of Hill's division along Jackson's left flank had beaten off severe Union assaults for most of nine hours at a cost of heavy casualties. The combined assaults especially took their toll on the five exhausted regiments of Gregg's brigade. Over the course of the day up to this time, Gregg's brigade had suffered more than 500 casualties, about one-third of its strength. In a reply to Hill in answer to a question regarding his condition, Gregg said, "Tell General Hill that my ammunition is exhausted, but that I will hold my position with the bayonet."[87]

As part of his plan for turning both of Jackson's flanks while continuing to believe that Porter would be attacking Jackson's right flank, Pope ordered what would be the fifth major assault against Jackson's defenses, four of which were against Jackson's left flank. Following the defeat of Nagel's assault, General Kearny sent eight regiments of his ten-regiment force of 2,700 on a diagonal course from the Sudley-Manassas Road to sweep westerly along the railroad cut, Hill's left flank. Kearny had detached Brigadier General John C. Robinson to lead the two Pennsylvania Volunteer regiments, the 63rd and 105th, the 12th Indiana, and the 3rd Michigan Marksmen.

Initially, Robinson succeeded in pushing Gregg and Thomas back several hundred yards, but then was stopped by Archer's flank fire. Most of the Confederates were now down to only one cartridge. Kearny then brought up most of Birney's brigade, the 4th Maine, 40th New York, 1st New York, and the 101st New York. In addition, Colonel Daniel Leasure's 100th Pennsylvania regiment of 577 men from Brigadier General Isaac I. Steven's Division of Reno's Ninth Corps had moved up on his left to give support. Shortly, Kearny was temporarily successful in rolling up Gregg's South Carolinians and Thomas's Georgians onto their right. The attack drove the Confederates to the rear and almost beyond the Groveton-Sudley Road.

By this time, Jackson had given Hill the brigade of Brigadier General Jubal A. Early, who had been deployed to the north and west of the Groveton-Sudley Road. While moving to assist Hill, Early received the 13th Georgia from Lawton and the 8th Louisiana from Forno. With his force of about twenty-five hundred, Early passed through Thomas's and Gregg's battered ranks and charged into Kearny's attacking columns, exercising the "rebel yell." In a short span of time, Kearny's attack was arrested and quickly repulsed. By 6:30 P.M., the Union forces had retreated from the Unfinished Railroad. Causalities of both Kearny and Hill amounted to one-fourth the total strength of those engaged. On August 29, casualty numbers for Jackson's three divisions were staggering. Hill's combined casualties over the entire day were devastating, while Gregg sustained 613, about half his total strength.[88]

HOOD'S AND HATCH'S DIVISIONS COLLIDE ALONG THE TURNPIKE

By 4 o'clock in the afternoon, conditions on Longstreet's right flank had changed. Reconnaissance had reported troop movement within the Union forces in front of Longstreet's right (Porter's corps) to Lee and Longstreet. They had been seen moving off to the northeast. No doubt the movement of troops reported to Lee and Longstreet was McDowell departing from Porter as he took King's (Hatch) division with him and moved northward to Sudley Road. Since leaving Thoroughfare Gap, Lee had been anxious to arrive at the battlefield so that he could speedily engage Longstreet's command. Now with the report that troops were drawing off in Longstreet's front, Lee wanted Longstreet to do what he had wished of him since their arrival: attack Pope's left along the turnpike. Longstreet argued that it was late and suggested, "The day being far spent, it might be as well to advance just before night upon a forced reconnaissance, get our troops into the most favorable positions, and have all things ready for battle at daylight the next morning." In the end, Lee consented.[89]

About dusk, McDowell arrived upon the field, having received an order from Pope to send a division after the enemy that was in "full retreat" down the Warrenton Turnpike. A hurried conference was held at the intersection of the turnpike and the Sudley Road, whereupon Hatch was ordered "to fall upon the enemy." Pope continued to believe Jackson was retreating toward the pike from the direction of Sudley Springs.

As the sun set, two of Hatch's brigades plus Captain George A. Gerrish's battery of howitzers moved westward along the turnpike, with the 2nd U.S. Sharpshooters out as skirmishers. Brigadier General Abner Doubleday's three-regiment brigade marched in the front ranks, followed by Hatch's old brigade, consisting of four regiments led by Colonel T. Sullivan plus the 2nd U.S. Sharpshooters. Patrick's brigade, which had been trailing far behind McDowell's march to the battlefield, was absent.

Simultaneously, Longstreet ordered Brigadier General John Bell Hood's division of two brigades to push eastward as "reconnaissance in force" from the vicinity of Groveton. Hood's brigade, commonly referred to as the Texas Brigade, consisted of three Texas regiments, the 1st, 4th and 5th, along with the 18th Georgia and the Hampton (South Carolina) Legion was aligned with its left resting along the turnpike. Colonel Evander Law's brigade of four regiments, the 4th Alabama, 2nd Mississippi, 11th Mississippi, and the 6th North Carolina, were aligned to the left of the Texas Brigade with its right resting on the turnpike. Longstreet brought Evans's South Carolinians forward as a reserve and ordered Colonel Eppa Hunton's brigade from Kemper's division to act as support for Hood's right. In addition, Wilcox's division was sent to Hood's left in reserve.

About one mile west of the Stone House, the two commands collided near the Groveton-Sudley Road and Warrenton Turnpike intersection. During the initial clash between the skirmishers of both divisions, Hatch ordered Gerrish's battery of howitzers onto a ridge off to his right and about 400 yards east of Lucinda Dogan's home. Doubleday's brigade felt the initial stunning fire coming from Hood's brigade, whose line of battle extended most of 700 yards and overlapped his left. Very quickly it was clear to Hatch that this was not a rear guard force of a retreating army. The fight became hot and furious, and as darkness was fast arriving, Hatch became alarmed, believing he needed to break off the fight while he could. He sent his adjutant Captain J.A. Judson to seek out McDowell. Finding McDowell near the Stone House, Judson described his commander's situation.[90] McDowell was furious and after going through a torrid of words, contradicted Hatch's assessment, telling Judson to "tell him [Hatch] the enemy is in full retreat and to pursue him!"[91] Hatch dejectedly received McDowell's orders, but by the time his adjutant had returned, the fighting was too close and heavy to break off anyway.

In the darkness of night, the visibility soon decreased to only a few yards, each side firing at the other's musket flashes. The fighting quickly became intense and heavy as the regiments of both divisions became engaged. Hood's brigades continued to advance and Hatch's forward units became disorganized in the darkness and began to fall back. Meanwhile, Patrick's brigade had arrived and was moving up from the rear through units of Hatch's brigade, which was falling back. Within moments, they had advanced too far and came into contact with units of Evans's brigade. Recognizing his precarious position, Patrick began to fall back.[92]

With his units badly disorganized in the darkness and falling back, Hatch decided to withdraw. Hood halted his advance and his Confederates bivouacked on the battlefield for a few hours. They then returned to their initial positions, taking many prisoners with them.[93]

By the time McDowell arrived on the field, it had been almost nine hours since he had received the intelligence witnessed by Buford detailing the numbers and strength of the Confederate force (Longstreet's command) that had moved through Thoroughfare Gap at 8:45 that morning. One has to ask the question, why was that information withheld from Pope, or was it?[94]

August 30 — Third Day

EARLY MORNING

During the night, the Confederates on Jackson's left retired from the advance positions taken during the day of August 29. At sunrise, two brigades of Ricketts's division took over part of Kearny's sector and began a vigorous reconnaissance in their front. Prior to this, Gregg had temporarily fallen back to replenish ammunition; hence, when Pope learned of this movement, it further supported his assumption that the Confederates were deserting the field.[95]

In his official report, Pope stated his situation:

> Every indication during the night of the 29th and up to 10 o'clock on the morning of the 30th pointed to the retreat of the enemy from our front. Paroled prisoners of ours taken on the evening of the 29th, and who came into our lines on the morning of the 30th, reported the enemy retreating during the whole night in the direction of and along the Warrenton turnpike. Generals McDowell and Heintzelman, who reconnoitered the positions held by the enemy's left on the evening of the 29th, confirmed this statement.[96]

This only supported Pope's assumption that the Confederates were in retreat to Thoroughfare Gap.

At three o'clock in the morning of the 30th, Porter received Pope's dispatch, dated "August 29, 1862 — 8:50 P.M.," ordering him to march immediately to the field of battle of the previous day and report to him in person for orders. In prompt compliance with this order, Porter moved out, leaving the left flank of the Federal army vulnerable to attack by a greatly superior force. In the confusion of the night, one of Griffin's brigades, accompanied by Morell, missed the turn onto the Sudley Road and marched on to Centreville, followed by Brig. General A. Sanders Piatt's brigade of Brig. General Samuel D. Sturgis's Reserve Corps.[97] As a result of this confusion, Porter did not have Morell and two of his brigades to assist in the actions of the next day.

Lee Finalizes the Positioning of His Two Wings

With his two wings deployed in a wide obtuse angle along a four-mile front, Lee awaited the Union attack. Jackson held the two-mile sector along the Unfinished Railroad north of the turnpike to Sudley Church, and Longstreet held the two-mile sector to the south of the pike. After Hood's reconnaissance-in-force action along the turnpike, Lee realigned Longstreet's right flank, shifting Hood's left flank to the south of the turnpike. Then he deployed Wilcox to Hood's previous location, covering the area between the turnpike and Jackson's right flank. The nineteen guns of Major L.M. Shumaker's artillery remained on the high ground of Jackson's far right flank, their field of fire extending almost to his center.

On Longstreet's extreme left flank at the juncture of the two wings, the eighteen guns of Colonel Steven D. Lee's artillery battalion were in position on Douglas Heights facing east, having replaced the previously deployed batteries of Walton. The batteries of Captains Parker, Rhett, Jordan, Eubank and Taylor comprised S.D. Lee's Artillery Battalion, for a complement of sixteen smoothbores, plus a section of two Parrotts belonging to Grimes's battery under Lieutenant Oakum of Major General R.H. Anderson's division. S.D. Lee's Artillery Battalion had been attached to Anderson's division, which was left to demonstrate along the Rappahannock while Lee and Longstreet followed the same route of Jackson's march. Around midnight and on into the early morning hours of the 30th, Anderson's division and S.D. Lee's Artillery Battalion arrived to rejoin Longstreet, having completed an extraordinary march which rivaled Jackson's.

S.D. Lee positioned his guns at about dawn after consulting with General John Bell Hood, at that time the division commander on Longstreet's left flank. S.D. Lee immediately reported his location to General Lee, and the general quickly sent his reply, "You are just where I wanted you; stay there."[98] Upon Anderson's arrival, his division was held in reserve along the Pageland Lane.

Colonel Stephen D. Lee. Commander, Lee's Artillery Battalion, Longstreet's Right Wing Stephen D. Lee's keen positioning of his eighteen guns on Douglas Heights was a paramount factor in the defeat of Union General Porter's Attack at the Deep Cut (courtesy Library of Congress).

Pope Orders an All-Out Pursuit of the Enemy

That morning, while Porter deployed in the Groveton Woods, Reynolds was making a personal reconnaissance of his front to the south of the turnpike. Riding to the fields west of Lewis Lane, he was fired upon by pickets of Longstreet's infantry. Reynolds ran a "gauntlet of a heavy fire" to gain the rear of his division. From there, he immediately communicated this intelligence to McDowell, who directed him to withdraw and form his division on Chinn Ridge.[99]

Immediately plans were initiated to press a vigorous pursuit. At midday the following Special Order was issued[100]:

> The following forces will be immediately thrown forward and in pursuit of the enemy, and press him vigorously during the whole day. Major-General McDowell is assigned to the command of the pursuit; Major-General Porters corps will push forward on the Warrenton turnpike, followed by the divisions of Brigadier-Generals King and Reynolds. The division of Brigadier-General Ricketts will Pursue the Hay Market road, followed by the corps of Major-General Heintzelman. The necessary cavalry will be assigned to these columns by Major-General McDowell, to whom regular and frequent reports will be made. The general headquarters will be somewhere on the Warrenton turnpike.

Pope's orders demonstrated that after three days, he continually failed to comprehend the precariousness of his situation.

Midafternoon — Porter Targets the "Deep Cut"

The target of the Union attack was the area known as the Deep Cut. Here the grade of the Unfinished Railroad ran below the surrounding area for several hundred yards, varying in depth from six to fifteen feet. As the grade continued to the northeast, it rose in height above the surrounding area for several hundred yards to almost fifteen feet in some places. Construction of this nature was necessary for the railroad grade itself to be level. Along the two-mile stretch of the railroad bed, which Jackson used as ready-made breastworks, were two areas referred to as "dumps." These were areas about one hundred and seventy-five feet long and located where wet weather beds would run through. Had the railroad been completed, trusses suspending rails above the landscape would have been constructed across the grade gap. The construction workers referred to these areas as the "dump" because they would dump shale, rock, and dirt in those areas as fill. One of the two dump sites was about 330 yards to the right of the vortex of Porter's attack (the Deep Cut). It was the same site that Milroy unwittingly meandered into on the morning of the 29th. The second dump site was on Jackson's left flank, occupying the area between the defensive positions of Gregg and Thomas of Hill's command. It is interesting to note that during the construction, workers cleared about 200 feet on both sides of the embankments as a safeguard against fires caused by hot embers thrown from locomotives. Although work had stopped four years prior to the Second Battle of Manassas, allowing time for underbrush and some small trees to have grown, the area around the railroad cut most likely would not have been heavily shrouded.

Jackson's "command occupied the ground and the divisions the same relative position to each other and to the field which they held the day before, forming the left wing of the army...."[101] Poised on the north side of the cut were part of Colonel Leroy A. Stafford's brigade, the regiments of the 9th and 10th Louisiana and Coppen's Louisiana Battalion. Originally, it was Colonel W.E. Starke's brigade, but was later handed down to Stafford after Jackson's division commander William B. Taliaferro was wounded and replaced by Starke. To their left, from west to east, were the regiments of Colonel Bradley T. Johnson's brigade of Virginians. The 48th Virginia of Johnson's brigade took up their position in a copse of woods, in front and south of the railroad cut on Johnson's far right flank. Back on the north side of the cut, from west to east, Johnson's 21st Virginia merged with the 1st Virginia Battalion. On their left was his 42nd Virginia. Next to Johnson's Brigade, Stafford's three remaining Louisiana regiments stood, from west to east, the 15th, 1st, and 2nd. The left flank of the 2nd Louisiana rested on the western edge of the dump. The 15th Alabama rested on the eastern edge of the dump, and next to them, the 21st Georgia. Both were originally a part of Brigadier General Isaac Trimble's brigade, now commanded by Captain W. Brown after Trimble was wounded on the 29th. The beleaguered, battle-weary regiments of Baylor's Stonewall brigade, the 2nd, 4th, 5th, 27th, and 33rd Virginia, took their position about 200 feet to the rear of the cut and some 300 feet behind the 48th Virginia. Jackson's total strength in this sector was about 8,000.

Throughout the morning and early afternoon, Porter was gathering his troops in the Groveton Woods, and by 3 P.M., that number was nearly 10,000. His plan was to make his attack in 2 waves. For his 1st wave, he brought up two divisions: Brigadier General John Hatch's (King) division from McDowell's Corps and two brigades from Major General George W. Morell's division from his own corps. During this time, Morell was in Centreville, having missed a turn on Porter's march to the battlefield during the late evening hours of the 29th, and his command fell upon Brigadier General Dan Butterfield. One of Butterfield's brigades was his own brigade before he replaced Morell as division commander. Colonel H.S. Lansing took command of Butterfield's brigade, but Lansing became ill while placing his units into position, and Colonel Henry A. Weeks took over as commander. Colonel Charles Roberts commanded Butterfield's second brigade.

Porter's line of battle placed Weeks's brigade on the left, Roberts's brigade in the center, and the brigades of Hatch's division on the right. The combined strength was about 5000. While Hatch was aligning his brigades in the woods, Gibbon failed to receive his orders and his brigade never engaged. Sykes's division of Porter's corps was positioned to the rear in Groveton Woods and held in reserve.[102]

As they broke out of the woods, their ill-formed formation file extended for one-half mile. The brigade commanders had strived to align their regiments in seven lines with each line separated by 50 yards. It didn't work out that way; Hatch was minus Gibbon's brigade and therefore had six lines, while Weeks actually had not attempted to put his regiments into formation file until they had moved out of the woods. This created confusion and delays. The confusion was compounded by the incoming artillery shells from Lee's guns enfilading their assembly. It was about 600 yards from the Union left flank to the Confederate line, of which the final 150 yards was uphill. It was about 300 yards from the Union right flank to the Confederate line.[103]

The huge lines of battle broke out of the woods, crossing over the Groveton-Sudley Road and into the fields of Lucinda Dogan. About 100 yards forward of the front line of battle were the flankers. These were the Berdan Sharpshooters of Roberts's brigade, numbering about 250. Berdan's Sharpshooters were readily identifiable, as their uniforms were a bright forest green. As the sharpshooters deployed forward, and followed by the assaulting regiments, S.D. Lee's cannoneers instantly opened up with all 18 guns. Jackson's infantry opened with musket fire at the same time. Shells burst into ranks upon ranks of the Union soldiers. From Douglas Heights, the Confederate artillery enfiladed the entire area for a quarter of a mile. At the same time, the Confederate infantry was firing volley after volley into the advancing forces, with more than a thousand rounds in each volley. As they pushed forward there was no cover except for a dry wet-weather bed known as the School House Branch that ran north to south through Dogan's fields. It quickly filled with the wounded and dead.[104]

The frontal attack required the Union line of battle to wheel to the right, bringing them square with Jackson's lines. Hatch reported, "The left wing of the first line made a partial wheel to the right executed under the heavy artillery fire from S.D. Lee's guns on the left and musketry in their front. Seeing the great disadvantages under which the first and second lines labored, as the other lines moved up, they were ordered to oblique more to the right, enabling them to get a partial flank fire upon that portion of the embankment which they now faced."[105] About this time, Hatch was wounded and forced to leave the field.

As the determined troops of Butterfield's and Hatch's division attempted to move up the approaches to the railroad cut, the scene became a slaughter. Left of center, Weeks's 17th New York and 18th Massachusetts were able to storm through a small

General Robert E. Lee and His Staff. Lee and his staff overlooking the Battle of Second Manassas from Douglas Heights above the Brawner farmhouse. Painting is part of Theophile Poilpot's famous cyclorama of the Second Battle of Manassas. Figure in bottom right-hand corner is Thomas Leachman (of Folly Castle), who acted as guide for General Lee.

copse of woods to succeed in forcing out the 48th Virginia Infantry. In their retreat, the 48th ran through the defensive positions of the Stonewall Brigade.[106] About this time, Weeks was wounded.

The retreat of the 48th Virginia left a large gap in Jackson's line directly behind the copse of woods at the Deep Cut. The Stonewall Brigade was in the woods to the rear of the Deep Cut and rushed forward to fill the gap. Colonel William Baylor, leading the famous brigade, took up the 33rd Virginia regimental flag to encourage his men forward. In a quick few moments, he was cut down and fell, wrapped in the regimental flag. Capt. Hugh A. White of the 4th Virginia, a devoted admirer of his colonel, picked up the flag from Baylor's body and charged forward. When the clouds of smoke and dust had cleared, his men found his body wrapped in the flag, face down, his hands clasped about his face.[107]

At the pinnacle of the attack, less than half of the regiments engaged were able to make it beyond the slope and onto the plateau along the railroad cut. Only the remnants of 9 Union regiments came within 15 to 40 feet of the railroad cut. The 44th and 12th New York of Weeks's brigade advanced on the left into a copse of trees opposite part of Starke's Brigade, but got no further. To the right of the 12th New York was the 17th New York, also of Weeks's brigade, and the 18th Massachusetts of Roberts's brigade was to their right. These two regiments occupied a small copse of woods after sending the 48th Virginia in retreat. They also advanced no further. The 13th New York of Roberts's brigade was to the right of the 18th, while the 2nd Maine, also of Roberts's brigade, was to the rear and right of the 13th. Forward and to the right of the 2nd Maine were two regiments of Hatch's division, the 30th and 24th New York.[108]

The 24th, receiving heavy enfilading fire from its right, was pinned down. Seeing the 24th receiving the devastating fire, General Patrick made a decision to send his 20th New York Militia off to the right in an attempt to strike at the Confederates at the source of the enfilading fire. Patrick's brigade was about 150 yards to the rear. The 20th Militia, led by Colonel George W. Pratt, moved off into the woods on the right and then advanced until it came into contact with the Confederates at the railroad cut. But Pratt had led them too far to the right, and instead of striking near the dump from where the Confederate deadly enfilading fire came, they struck near Brown's right. While the 15th Alabama and the 21st Georgia continued their galling fire into Hatch's right, the rest of Brown's brigade battled the 20th New York. From the moment the 20th approached the railroad cut, they met heavy musketry from the Confederates on Brown's left flank, so much so that soon they were nearly decimated. Musket fire was exchanged at a distance of twenty-five yards. Colonel Pratt received a mortal wound and after ten to fifteen minutes of the slaughter, the 20th retreated in disorder.[109] The 20th's losses amounted to 32 killed, 165 wounded, and 82 missing or captured, for a total of 279 casualties out of an original strength of 450.[110] Colonel Pratt was taken to a U.S. military hospital in Albany, New York, where he died on September 11.

During Hatch's advance, Major Andrew Barney was leading the 24th New York on the far right flank. Barney was on his horse and shouting, "Forward men, forward, follow me," when, as if moved by an overpowering force, he suddenly broke away and galloped to the top of the railroad embankment. Some of the Confederates were immediately taken aback in seeing the lone rider charging forward in a seemingly suicidal action into their positions and started shouting, "Don't shoot, don't shoot him," but he was shot in the head within moments and fell to the ground.[111] A Confederate soldier of the 15th Louisiana crawled up the railroad embankment and pulled him to cover. The major died later that evening.

The 24th New York continued to rush forward and some of the men took cover against the embankment. Later, a Union soldier of the 24th New York had this to say:

> As I looked back, I saw our lines making a grand rush in our direction. Many of the men holding their arms in before their faces as if to keep off a storm. Bullets were pouring into them from the infantry beyond us. But worst of all Longstreet's batteries, freshly posted on a rise of ground a mile or so to our left were enfilading the approaching troops with solid shot, shell and sections of foot long railroad iron, it was horrible to witness.

The 15th Alabama of Trimble's (Brown) brigade was in position at the high embankment to the left of the dump, where they could lay down deadly musketry fire against Hatch's right. It was the 24th New York that received the deadly fire into their flank from the 15th Alabama. A Confederate soldier of the 15th Alabama later wrote, "What a slaughter. What a slaughter of men that was. They were so thick it was just impossible to miss them. At first, bombshell and shrapnel — as they came closer, canister was poured into them which mowed them down. But still those who lived would close ranks and push forward."

Further down on the Confederates' left, men of Colonel Bradley Johnson's brigade ran low on ammunition and began to search the wounded and the dead for more. When they did run out, an Irishman of Johnson's Irish Battalion yelled down the line, "Boys, give 'em the rocks." The Confederates picked up the rocks from the railroad bed and began throwing them at the enemy. The Union troops were taken aback by such an unorthodox manner of fighting and began to respond in kind. It was indeed a rock fight, but short-lived with the arrival of Confederate reinforcements consisting of Colonel J.M. Brockenbrough's (Field's) brigade from Hill's division.[112]

With his ammunition exhausted and his line strained to the breaking point, Jackson sent an urgent request to Lee and Longstreet for reinforcements. Lee responded, telling

Major General Fitz John Porter, Commander, Fifth Corps, Army of the Potomac. A victim to miscarriage of justice from wrongful charges made by General Pope to cover-up his own poor generalship at Second Battle of Manassas. General Porter was brought up on court martial charges of disobeying lawful orders of his superior that resulted in Porter's being cashiered and dismissed from service. Fifteen years later, a retrial was conducted that exonerated Porter and condemned the earlier court.

Longstreet to send a division to Jackson. Longstreet anticipated the request; but he believed that Jackson needed assistance sooner than he could move reinforcements to his aid. He immediately ordered two batteries forward onto the ridge (Battery Heights) that Campbell's artillery had occupied two days earlier during the battle at Brawner Farm. From the ridge, now occupied by four guns of Captain William H. Chapman's Artillery, spewed a merciless barrage of enfilading fire onto Porter's fraught brigades that were trying to move up to support the struggling regiments nearest the railroad cut. Within ten minutes, Porter's columns were broken and sent reeling back in confusion.[113]

Seeing the demise of his attack, General Porter decided not to send in Sykes's division to reinforce his devastated assault force, and instead ordered a retreat. The Union troops now had to make their way back to the Groveton Woods. The cannonade from Lee's guns shelling the hillside and the musket fire from Jackson's infantry were so intense that many of the Union troops surrendered rather than attempt the flight.[114]

Porter had engaged about 5000 men, of which he lost a third. It was said the fields surrounding the areas from the Groveton Woods to the Deep Cut from whence the attack took place was a sea of blue and red, the blue for the Union uniforms and the red for the blood that was shed.

Late Afternoon

Lee Orders Longstreet to Attack Pope's Left Flank

Watching Porter's attack falter, McDowell ordered Reynolds's division of about 4500 men to move off Chinn Ridge to the north side of the turnpike to support his

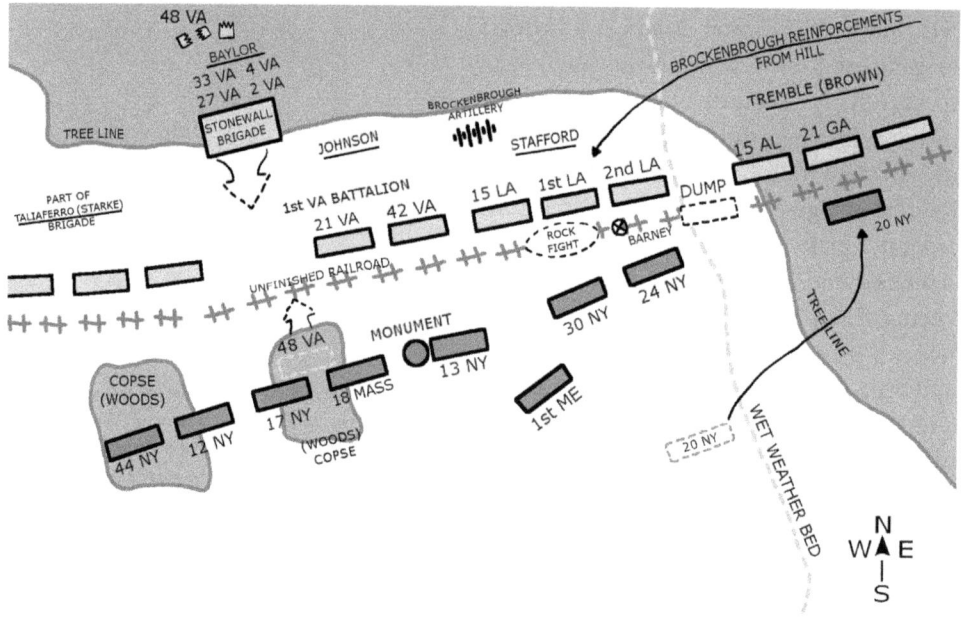

Circa 3:20 P.M.— Pinnacle of Porter's Attack at the Deep Cut (drawing by Rachael R. Johnson).

center.[115] Pope and McDowell continued to allow themselves to remain oblivious to Lee and Longstreet, who were in position on their left flank. The order withdrawing Reynolds' from Chinn Ridge gravely weakened the whole Federal left flank.

The Union forces on Chinn Ridge had been reduced to that of Colonel Nathaniel McLean's brigade of four Ohio regiments from Schenck's Division: the 25th, 55th, 73rd, and 75th. They supported the Wiedrich Artillery battery of four Parrotts commanded by Captain Michael Wiedrich. In addition, the only other Union force south of the Warrenton Turnpike was located approximately one-half mile west of Chinn Ridge deep in the southeast quadrant of the Groveton-Sudley Road and the turnpike. That area was occupied by Colonel Gouverneur K. Warren's small brigade of two New York regiments from Sykes's Division; the 5th New York "Duryee's Zouaves" commanded by Captain Cleveland Winslow; and the 10th New York "National Zouaves" commanded by Colonel John B. Bendix, supporting Battery D, 5th U.S. Artillery of six Parrotts commanded by Lieutenant Charles Hazlett.

Here was the opportunity for which Lee had been waiting: a counterattack all along the line. As he witnessed the repulse of Porter's attack, Lee ordered Longstreet to sweep across Chinn Ridge and onto Henry Hill. He also ordered Jackson to "protect his [Longstreet's] left flank."[116] At about 4:30, Longstreet's long gray lines of infantry, with their battle flags fluttering in the evening sun, now swept forward in a furious assault, anxious for the foray. Hood's brigade of Hood's Division led the advance. The divisions of Richard H. Anderson, James L. Kemper and David R. (Neighbor) Jones moved up in support. Evans's brigade of Kemper's division was to the rear and right of Hood to provide close support. Rushing across the fields and rolling hills, the Confederates pushed forward to cross over Lewis Lane, where skirmishers of Hood's Texas brigade met skirmishers of Warren's 10th New York Zouaves that were moving through the woods in their front. Warren had sent out six companies as skirmishers and held the 10th's other four companies in reserve.

Texas Brigade Quickly Overwhelms Warren's Zouaves

Meanwhile, Warren's other regiment, the 5th New York Zouaves, having stacked their arms, relaxed in a position that had Young's Branch about 150 yards to their back and the 10th New York several hundred yards in their front, moving west through the woods. Hazlett's guns were located about 300 yards west and north of Winslow's Zouaves on a ridge overlooking the Groveton intersection.

Hood's attack came so fast and furious that it caught Warren completely by surprise. The first indication that an attack was coming came from out of the woods in front of the 5th New York as men of the 10th New York came running through their position. Winslow's 5th New York Zouaves excitedly rushed to grab their stacked muskets but could not fire for fear of hitting the onrushing 10th in their retreat. When it was clear to fire, those who had time to shoot were only able to get one shot off at best before Hood's charging brigade were upon them.[117] The shrill cries of the Confederates could be heard above the thunder of the guns and the noise of battle, echoing throughout the valley, the "rebel yell" that had been born across the same battlefields thirteen months earlier.

What happened next was a massacre. As the 10th scrambled through the 5th, many didn't stop until they had reached Henry Hill. Warren had ordered a retreat but he was quickly overwhelmed by the speed of Hood's attacking force. As Winslow's Zouaves raised their muskets to get off that one shot, Hood's brigade was swarming over them no more than forty yards away. Their fire was heavy and rapid, and many of the Zouaves were riddled. Some made it to Young's Branch only to be cut down in the stream. The effective strength of the 10th New York was about 510, of which they had lost 133 in casualties.[118] Remnants of the 5th New York retreated to Henry Hill, where they regrouped around their saved colors. Prior to its devastation, the strength of the 5th New York had been about 490 effectives, but now those who had regrouped around their colors numbered no more than 60. Within ten minutes, they had sustained 290 casualties, 120 killed and nearly 170 wounded.[119] The 5th New York Zouaves suffered the "largest regimental loss of life in any single engagement of the entire Civil War."

Meanwhile, unaware that his supporting infantry regiments were being decimated, Hazlett's artillery was busily firing upon Longstreet's massive attacking forces. During the 5th New York's retreat, 22-year-old Private James Webb of Company F crossed over Young's Branch and happened to look back. From his vantage point, he saw Hazlett's battery still engaged. Realizing that Hazlett's guns were in imminent danger of being captured, Webb made a decision on his own, to reach Hazlett to inform him that he had no support. While dashing the 300 yards across the fields to reach Hazlett, he was spotted by the Confederates, who immediately threw down a hail of musket fire. Despite taking a Minié ball in his side, Webb was able to reach Hazlett and inform him of his situation. Hazlett quickly limbered his artillery, moving his pieces onto Dogan Ridge.[120]

Thirty-five years later, on September 17, 1897, Webb was awarded the nation's highest award, the Medal of Honor. The award stated, "On August 30, 1862, at Bull Run, Virginia, Private Webb, though severely wounded, voluntarily carried information to a battery commander that enabled him to save his guns from capture."[121]

Hardin Sent to Stall Advance and Retreats as Kerns's Guns are Captured

As soon as McDowell learned of the calamity that befell Warren, it didn't take him long to realize the precarious predicament that confronted the Army of Virginia. He knew he had to get forces back onto Chinn Ridge, and he went looking for Reynolds, but two of Reynolds's three brigades had already crossed over the turnpike and onto Dogan Ridge. McDowell quickly became aware that Colonel Martin Hardin's Pennsylvania Reserve brigade (Brigadier General Conrad Jackson), accompanied by Captain Mark Kerns's artillery battery of four guns, was close by. McDowell caught up to Hardin and ordered his brigade, along with Kerns's battery, onto a knoll located between McLean's position on Chinn Ridge and Young's Branch where part of the Zouave slaughter took place.[122]

When Hardin and Kerns reached the knoll, some of Warren's Zouaves were still fleeing up the eastern steep banks of Young's Branch. Kerns quickly unlimbered his four ten-pounders on the crest of the knoll and Hardin formed his four regiments on Kerns's left, placing two regiments each in the front and back of the artillery. Hood now saw that his brigade was alone, with neither Kemper nor Evans in sight; he had outrun his support.

Colonel J.B. Robertson's 5th Texas was near exhaustion. They had already run one and one-half miles; nevertheless, they charged ahead. Finding that they were in the open and being fired upon by canister from Kerns's artillery and musketry from Hardin's 11th and 12th Pennsylvanians, Robertson ordered his Texans to fall back to the woods. While taking a brief rest to drink from Young's Branch, the 4th Texas arrived on their left and continued forward. There was confusion: some of the 5th Texans, thinking they were to advance, began moving forward. To avoid more confusion, instead of trying to untangle the situation, Robertson ordered the regiment forward also. At this time the 18th Georgia and Hampton's Legion also joined in the assault. Kerns's artillery continued to fire canister as quickly as they could load; however, Hood's brigade continued to move fast upon them. Hardin moved his second line of defense, the 9th and 10th Pennsylvanians, to join the fire of the 11th and 12th, but the attack came rushing in upon them too fast. Hardin was taken down by a Minié ball and seriously wounded.[123]

About this time, the regiments began to break up and fled in rapid retreat. Kerns's remained with the guns alone. He went from gun to gun, loading and firing them all by himself. Once again there was admiration of bravery and sympathy for a foe, similar to the incident a short time earlier when Major Andrew Barney, while leading the 24th New York at the Deep Cut, charged ahead onto the Unfinished Railroad and some of the Confederates yelled down the line not to shoot him. In this later circumstance, the Texans saw this lone captain going from gun to gun, continuously loading and firing, doing the work of a crew of eight men for each artillery piece. They, too, seeing his bravery, yelled down the line not to shoot him, but Kerns, who had his hand on a lanyard about to fire his last shot ever, was taken down by a musket ball and killed. As Hardin's Pennsylvanians retreated, Kerns's guns became a prize of the Texas brigade.[124]

Having rolled over the brigades of Warren and Hardin without any "perceivable delay," the Confederate attack continued to press forward unabated, and shortly they were on the approaches of Chinn Ridge.[125] Reynolds was ordered off Chinn Ridge, but no orders or instructions had been given to McLean. McLean was left in a quandary: should he leave with Reynolds or stay? McLean elected to stay, and in making that decision, he played a role much like the one Evans had fulfilled thirteen months earlier on Matthews Hill at the 1st Battle of Manassas: he created a holding action that gained time for reinforcements to be brought up and deployed.

McLean Prepares for Assaults

From on top of Chinn Ridge, McLean and his brigade of 1200 Ohioans watched the destruction of Warren's and Hardin's brigades unfold before them. Upon witnessing the slaughter, regardless of whatever may have been going through McLean's mind at this time, he became committed to hold Chinn Ridge as long as he could. McLean had aligned his four regiments in a straight line next to each other with Wiedrich's four guns in the middle, all facing near west. From left to right, the 73rd and 75th supported Wiedrich's left flank, while the 25th and 55th stood to Wiedrich's right flank. About

150 yards west of the 73rd was the tree line of the woods running up from Young's Branch. North of McLean's position were scrub pines. In addition, there was a ravine in the terrain between McLean's position and the position held by Kerns's guns. The left flank of the 73rd Ohio was about two hundred yards north-northwest of the Chinn house.

As Longstreet's Wing swept across the fields and hills south of the turnpike, a total of some 40 artillery pieces from Union batteries of Sigel's First Corps, McDowell's Third Corps, Reynolds' Pennsylvania Reserves, and all of Porter's Fifth Corps, had been unlimbered on the high ground west of John Dogan's house on Dogan Ridge. In an attempt to counter the Union's artillery barrages, which were causing havoc for Longstreet's infantry, some 20 Confederate artillery pieces unlimbered at three different locations near Groveton. Captains Bachman's and Garden's batteries of Major B.W. Frobel's Artillery from Hood's Division, plus Chapman's Dixie battery from Featherston's brigade of Wilcox Division, moved into battery north of the turnpike, about 400 yards east of Lucinda Dogan's home.[126] Frobel's third battery, commanded by Captain Reilly, unlimbered and moved into the position previously occupied by Kerns's guns, south of the turnpike above Young's Branch. Captain Boyce's battery of Evans's Brigade was sent to the position previously occupied by Hazlett, southeast of the Groveton intersection.

McLean Repulses Assaults and Buys Time for McDowell

After Hood's brigade sent Hardin's brigade into retreat and captured Kerns's guns, the 5th Texas, 18th Georgia, and Hampton's Legion halted in the ravine that ran between Kerns's abandoned guns and McLean's position. The 1st Texas had moved back to the cover of Young's Branch after coming under heavy artillery fire from Union guns on Dogan Ridge and were joined shortly after by the 4th Texas. The two regiments advanced no more the rest of the evening. Hood's three remaining regiments moved off to the right and up the ravine into the cover of the woods west of the Chinn House. The 18th Georgia and Hampton's Legion advanced quickly upon McLean's positions. During this time, Evans's Brigade was beginning to come up on Hood's left, and a part of Holcombe's Legion had entangled confusingly with the 18th Georgia. Described more or less as a mob, their assault took them to within 40 yards of Wiedrich's guns before the heavy musketry fire from McLean's infantry and canister fire from Wiedrich's guns forced them into withdrawal. Their withdrawal took them through the woods to the cover of Young's Branch. From the time of the Texas brigade's first encounter with Warden's brigade through their assaults upon McLean, Hood's total casualties were 628: in killed, wounded and missing, there were "5 officers and 70 enlisted men killed, 33 officers and 507 enlisted men wounded, 1 officer and 12 enlisted men missing."[127] McLean had succeeded in his first repulse and bought some time for McDowell.

The second assault upon McLean came from the 2000-strong brigade of Brigadier General Nathaniel Evans, commanded by Col. P.F. Stevens of Holcombe's Legion and comprised of five regiments: a legion; an artillery battery all from South Carolina, the 17th, 18th, 22nd, 23rd; the Holcombe Legion; and Boyce's battery of Macbeth Artillery.

As Evans moved up the western sloops of Chinn Ridge, heading for McLean's position 150 yards in their front, he instantly came under heavy enfilading cannon fire from Union artillery on Dogan Ridge. The combined fire from the artillerists on Dogan Ridge and Wiedrich's guns forced Evans's brigade into the woods on his right. The 5th Texas had been lying in the woods and became intermingled with Evans's brigade. By the time the brigade came out of the woods, the confusion had been somewhat sorted out: the 5th Texas was on Evans's right flank, joining in the assault, and McLean's left flank was in the brigade's front. After some fierce fighting, the brigade came within 30 yards of the 73rd and 75th, but the Ohioans' heavy concentrated musketry fire, in addition to Wiedrich's battery firing into their flanks, forced Evans to withdraw. However, before his withdrawal, Evans's Carolinians forced Wiedrich's artillery to limber and dash away. Evans suffered serious losses, including several of his commanders, among them former Governor John H. Means, commander of the 17th South Carolina, and Colonel J.M. Gadberry, commander of the 18th South Carolina, who both fell mortally wounded. His total casualties were 631: in killed, wounded and missing, there were "14 officers and 98 enlisted men killed, 48 officers and 463 enlisted men wounded, and 8 enlisted men missing."[128] McLean had succeeded in his second repulse, and it would be up to McDowell to make use of the time McLean was buying him.

Meanwhile, while the lone brigade of McLean struggled against Longstreet's advance across Chinn Ridge, McDowell was frantically trying to do two things: get reinforcements onto Chinn Ridge, and form a high concentration of men on Henry Hill, enough to fend off all of Lee's army for the purpose of saving Pope's army from destruction. It was critical that reinforcements get onto Chinn Ridge to stall for time. Without sufficient defensive measures on Henry Hill, the holding of the turnpike intersection would be lost, and Pope's army would be trapped with no chance of retreat. To his credit, McDowell knew the Second Battle of Manassas was lost and quick action had to be taken if the army was to be saved.

After the repulse of Evans's brigade, there was no rest for McLean and his Ohioans. To the south beyond the Chinn house, three brigades of Kemper's division (Brigadier General Micah Jenkins, and Colonels Eppa Hunton and Montgomery D. Corse) had been moving into the fore. After Longstreet had given his division commanders their orders that their target was Henry Hill, from then on, it was the division and brigade commanders that would be making the tactical decisions. While making their way to Chinn Ridge, Hood and Evans became engaged with Union forces on Chinn Ridge (McLean). Subsequently, Kemper's brigade commanders took the opportunity to swing left and attack from the south. But more time was lost as confusion ensued in Hunton's brigade involving a couple of the regimental commanders, and by the time it was sorted out, the brigade had marched to Chinn Branch. Compounding the mixup, Jenkins's brigade had been closely following Hunton and inadvertently followed him all the way to Chinn Branch. Corse had been following Jenkins, but seeing the plight of the other two brigades, he ordered his own brigade up the slope toward the Chinn house and McLean's location.[129]

Meanwhile, seeing the Confederates on the slopes to his left, McLean changed his front to face the oncoming assault. The 55th Ohio, joined by remnants of the 75th, 25th, and 73rd, was lying in wait behind the fence line to the front of the Chinn House. As Corse's Virginians closed to within 50 yards, the Ohioans rose up from behind the split-rail fence and fired a murderous volley into the ranks of the 17th Virginia. Although stunned, the Virginians pushed forward. Within moments, Richardson's battery of the Washington Artillery plus remnants of Hood's and Evan's brigade arrived, enfilading McLean's right flank with musketry and canister The 55th Ohio held on for almost 10 minutes, at which time Corse ordered an all-out push. The 55th Ohio and the rest of McLean's battered Ohioans were forced into a heated retreat, quickly pursued by the 7th Virginia. McLean's casualties of about 400 were low when compared to the number sustained by his opponents. Another casualty was McLean's division commander, Brigadier General Robert C. Schenck. Soon after McLean changed fronts, Schenck arrived to give his personal aid to McLean and took a Minié ball to his arm while brandishing his sword. McLean made this report regarding Schenck's wounding: "He greatly aided me by his gallant conduct in rallying and cheering on the men until he received the wound which drove him from the field."[130] Schenck's wound led to the amputation of his arm.

McDowell Sends More Brigades to Chinn Ridge

In the meantime, McDowell was making use of the time that McLean had bought him. From Ricketts's division, McDowell got the brigades of Brigadier General Zealous B. Tower and Colonel Robert W. Stiles and sent them in quick-time to Chinn Ridge. In addition, Sigel sent the 41st New York regiment of Brigadier General Julius Stahel's brigade and then followed up by sending Colonel John A. Koltes's brigade of Brigadier General A. Von Steinwehr's division. During his frantic movements, McDowell conferred with Pope. Pope was apprehensive of what McDowell was doing and believed he "had taken too much from the right." McDowell hurriedly explained the peril that faced them. They departed with a mutual understanding that Pope would order up units to Henry Hill and McDowell would look to the delaying actions on Chinn Ridge.[131]

For some unexplained reason, Stiles held his brigade back near the turnpike intersection at the approach to Chinn Ridge and did not accompany Tower onto the crest of the ridge. Crossing over the turnpike and on up the northern slopes to the crest of Chinn Ridge, the four regiments of Tower's brigade, accompanied by Leppien's 5th Main Light Artillery battery, deployed into lines of battle facing the Chinn House 300 yards in their front.[132] Immediately upon ascending, Tower's 88th Pennsylvania and his three New York regiments of the 26th, 90th, and 94th were targets of Richardson's heavy shelling. Corse's front, which included remnants of Hood's and Evans's brigades, extended beyond Tower's left to Chinn Branch. In a very short time, Tower's Pennsylvanians and New Yorkers were being overwhelmed by the Confederates coming from three sides and moving in on Leppien's guns. The 88th Pennsylvania and 90th New York were positioned in direct support of Leppien's guns and began falling back, leaving Leppien's guns exposed to the wrath of Corse's Virginians. Leading the 1st Virginia, Lieutenant Colonel Frederick Skinner was spurred on with excitement as he charged

Eight. August 28, 29, 30— Second Battle of Manassas

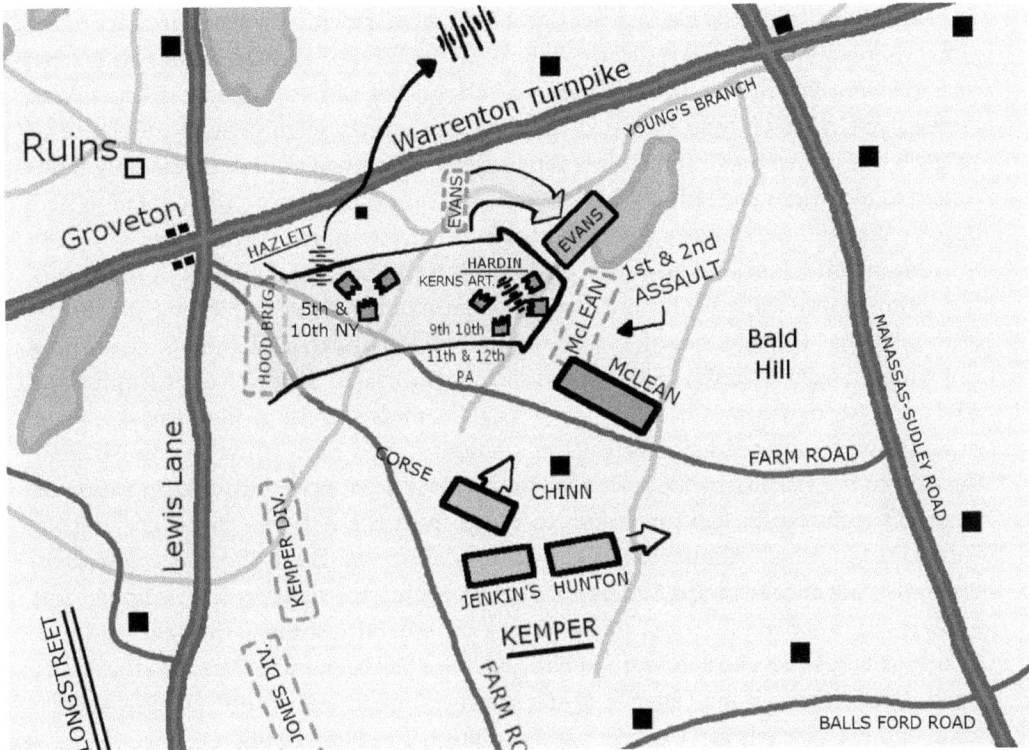

4:30–5 P.M. Longstreet Begins Sweep and McLean Fights to Buy Time (drawing by Rachael R. Johnson)

forward on his horse into the cannoneers. Described as a hulking man carrying an exceptionally large saber, he slashed at artillerymen in his path, nearly severing one's head and slashing down others. The artillerymen quickly fled from their guns, but not before one had shot Skinner at close range with his pistol, wounding him in the arm and side.[133]

While Tower was intensely battling the Virginians, McDowell found Stiles "on the hill slope in column ready to deploy" and using disparaging words, led Stiles's brigade onto Chinn Ridge. Stiles's brigade consisted of four regiments: the 11th Pennsylvania, 83rd New York, and two Massachusetts regiments, the 12th and 13th. McDowell sent the 83rd New York to Chinn Branch to support Tower's left, and the remaining three regiments were sent forward in support of Tower's center and right. The 11th Pennsylvania advanced to the center, the 13th Massachusetts moved to support the left of the line. The 12th Massachusetts, led by Colonel Fletcher Webster, the elder son of the renowned statesman Daniel Webster, moved his 12th in support of the line on the right.

As dusk approached, Jenkins's brigade and Hunton's brigade had reassembled and were now hotly engaged along with Corse. Kemper's division was now carrying the brunt of the fighting on Chinn Ridge. At the time Skinner did his daring saber-slashing dash into Leppien's guns, the 7th and 24th Virginians followed and captured the guns.

During this action, while leading the 12th Massachusetts within a short distance of the guns, Colonel Webster fell mortally wounded.[134] A memorial monument was erected near the spot where Fletcher Webster fell, about 300 yards northeast of the Chinn House. Until as recently as August 2012, when a monument commemorating the Texas Brigade was placed on Chinn Ridge, the Fletcher monument had been the only monument to have been erected on Chinn Ridge. It is now one of only a total of ten to have been erected on the Manassas battlefields representative of the two battles.

Meanwhile, Jones's division arrived on Chinn Ridge and deployed in the area of the Chinn House while Anderson's division continued en route to Henry Hill. Shortly after 5:30 P.M., the brigades of Tower and Stiles were driven off Chinn Ridge. About this time, Longstreet ordered Wilcox to move his division south of the turnpike and advance toward Henry Hill, while Law was also ordered south of the turnpike. Some of Sigel's units engaged Law's brigade in a hot encounter as he moved eastward along the pike to the vicinity of the J. Dogan House. As Wilcox moved from his position off Jackson's right flank, Jackson began to move from the defenses he held along the Unfinished Railroad. About 6 o'clock, with only about one hour of daylight left, Jackson's right advanced toward Sudley road while resting his right on the turnpike. A.P. Hill's division moved forward, pushing back all Federal resistance they encountered. By 6:30, all the Federals in the path of Hill's advance had been pushed back to the Sudley Road. In addition, all the Federals in the southwest quadrant of the Sudley-Manassas Road and the Warrenton Turnpike had been pushed to Henry Hill.

Evening to Night

Pope's Last Stand

Starting about 5 P.M., Pope became conscious of the peril to his left and desperately began building up a new defensive position on Henry Hill, the key to his line of retreat by the Stone Bridge. By 6:30, Lieutenant Colonel William Chapman's brigade of Sykes's Regulars had already taken position to engage the right flank of D.R. Jones's command. Reynolds moved up to reinforce Chapman with the rest of Sykes's Regulars plus Piatt's brigade, Milroy's brigade, and Nagle's brigade of Reno's command. Almost all of Longstreet's Wing was aligned along the Sudley Road from near the turnpike intersection for more than one mile south. D.H. Anderson's division advanced and became heavily engaged in a struggle to turn the Federals' left flank.[135]

While the battle raged for Henry Hill, north of the turnpike, elements of A.P. Hill's division and Starke's division, supported by units of Longstreet's command, swarmed into the open ground to press the broken Federal divisions to the east of Sudley Road. As Kearny's and other Federal commands massed around Pittsylvania" Sigel took a strong position on Buck Hill back of the Stone House.[136]

As the fighting continued north of the turnpike and for Henry Hill, Pope's only hope for preventing annihilation of his army would be to hold out until darkness fell upon the field and the fighting would cease. The battle for Henry Hill raged for another 30 minutes as darkness set in and Longstreet was denied the occupancy of Pope's last stronghold. Since 6 o'clock, Pope had been making plans for his retreat, and about 8 o'clock he issued the formal retreat orders.

Emergence of Cavalry — The First Major Cavalry Battle of the Civil War

At the same time that the battle for Henry Hill was beginning, the first major cavalry battle of the Civil War, and the largest cavalry battle fought on the North American continent up to that time, was starting to unfold.

Earlier, while Longstreet was giving orders to his division commanders to initiate the sweep across Chinn Ridge, Jeb Stuart, anticipating that Pope's army would soon be retreating, ordered Robertson's Brigade of Cavalry to "advance along the extreme right of Longstreet's advancing columns and if possible intercept Pope's retreat in the direction of Centreville by way of the Stone Bridge."[137] Knowing that Lee wanted not just to defeat Pope, but to entrap and destroy his army, it is possible that when Stuart gave his orders to Robertson, it was in his mind that a cavalry force, moving fast and furious, creating pandemonium while hitting and punching away at infantry columns, could disjoint a retreating army and bring about its destruction. Moving at a much quicker pace than the infantry, Brigadier General Beverly H. Robertson and four of his Virginia Cavalry regiments, the 2nd, 6th, 7th, and 12th, had moved far beyond Longstreet's infantry columns and were soon approaching Lewis Ford on the Bull Run, northeast of Portici.[138]

Meanwhile, a Union cavalry brigade under the command of Brigadier General John Buford from Pope's Second Corps had been sent to the fords on the Union left to stop stragglers from leaving the front and protect the Union's rear from a Confederate assault. Buford had led his four cavalry regiments, the 1st Vermont, 5th New York, 1st West Virginia, and 1st Michigan, to an area east of Portici, having just come from reconnoitering Lewis Ford. Buford was shortly joined by Lt. Colonel Ferries Nazer's 4th New York Cavalry from Brigadier General John Beardsley's cavalry brigade of Pope's First Corps. Nazer had been reconnoitering northeastward along Ball's Ford Road, and after proceeding a short distance, "came upon and passed two regiments of rebel cavalry...." Nazer said in his official report, "I informed General Buford of the enemy's whereabouts and intention and at his request quickly formed my command into line behind the 1st Michigan Cavalry...."[139] Buford's brigade was then in a column of regiments with the 1st Michigan in front, followed by the 4th New York, the 1st West Virginia, and the 1st Vermont. While partially shielded behind a small hill, they waited for the Confederates to appear.

As Robertson's Cavalry was making their way past Portici, they observed a small company of Union cavalry off to their right. Colonel Thomas T. Munford, commander of the 2nd Virginia Cavalry, ordered Lieutenant Colonel J.W. Watts to take a squadron and charge them. While pursuing them to a small ridge, they were startled to come upon Buford's four columns of cavalry in their front and quickly halted. Watts sent a rider to Munford, and before long, Munford was dashing forward with the rest of his 2nd Virginians.

Charging forward in a hard gallop, sabers drawn, Munford's cavalry troopers made their way quickly over the small ridge and came upon Buford's 1st Michigan and 4th New York. As soon as the Confederates appeared over the hill, Buford yelled for the two regiments to "draw sabers" and the bugles sounded from both sides. Munford's and Buford's regiments collided and instantly the slashing began. Cavalry battle action involved some pistol and carbine shooting, but for the most part, it was hand-to-hand fighting with sabers. For many, if not for most of Buford's cavalrymen, this was the first time they had ever been in a cavalry fight. The men of Munford's 2nd Cavalry were impressed, as this was "the first time their cavalry [Union] had ever made any show of resistance and the sight of the charges and sabre fighting in the clear, open fields was very fine."[140] Shortly, the Virginians were overwhelmed, and Munford ordered a retreat, at which time they broke off and galloped back to their brigade.

As the 2nd Virginia retreated, Robertson moved the rest of his brigade to their support. The 12th Virginia, led by Colonel Asher W. Harman, was the first in column to move out and make the charge, followed by the 7th Virginia led by Major Samuel Myers. As the two regiments crested the small ridge, they were quickly able to discern that their first attack would be against the 1st Michigan led by Colonel Thornton F. Brodhead and Nazer's 4th New York. Harman moved out with his 12th Virginia and charged hard into the 1st Michigan, slashing, emptying their pistols, and throwing the Wolverines into disorder. At the same time, Myers and his 7th Virginia charged into the 4th New York and sent them reeling. One of Hennessy's sources had this to say about the fighting; "The shooting, and running, cursing and cutting that followed cannot be understood except by an eyewitness."[141] Another of Hennessey's sources provided a brief description in the after action of the cavalry fight: "A terrible sight ... men and horses lying scattered about where they fell, horses were running wildly about, and in the deep, washed gully on the hillside were struggling men and horses...."[142]

In short order, it was all over; the 1st Michigan broke and retreated toward Lewis Ford, followed by the 4th New York. Buford's attempt to reform his brigade proved futile, and very quickly, his other two regiments, the 1st West Virginia and 1st Vermont, joined in the retreat without ever having brandished their sabers or fired a shot. Robertson pursued Buford about three-quarters of a mile beyond Lewis Ford, taking many prisoners.[143]

Although the cavalry battle was of short duration, there was a surprising number of casualties. Nazer's 4th New York's effective strength was 130; of these, 64 were casualties. Fifty-one were missing (captured by Robertson's Cavalry), 12 wounded, and 1 officer killed. Brodhead's 1st Michigan suffered a total of 118 casualties; 8 were killed, including Brodhead, mortally wounded in hand-to-hand encounter with Lieutenant Louis Harman, adjutant 12th Cavalry, 13 wounded, and 97 missing (captured by Robertson's Cavalry). Although Buford's 1st Vermont and 1st West Virginia were not engaged in the battle, they too suffered casualties, likely as they were being pursed during Buford's retreat. The 1st Vermont had 1 killed and 8 missing (captured), while the 1st West Virginia had 5 killed, 22 wounded and 41 missing (captured).

Robertson's Brigade suffered considerably fewer casualties than Buford. The 2nd

Virginia had 3 killed and 39 wounded (Munford himself was slashed across the back). The 12th Virginia had 6 wounded. Robertson's Brigade captured some 300 prisoners (including the wounded of Buford's brigade left on the field), plus large numbers of horses, arms and accouterments.[144]

Buford's retreat to the Warrenton Turnpike almost coincided with the retreat of the rest of Pope's army. That withdrawal started at about 8 o'clock with the issuing of Pope's retreat orders as darkness fell upon the battlefield.

NINE

The Aftermath of the Second Battle of Manassas and an Analysis

The Aftermath

POPE STRUGGLES TO REACH WASHINGTON

Longstreet succeeded in taking Chinn Ridge, but darkness set in before he could occupy Henry Hill. The stiff resistance from Union forces on Chinn Ridge and Henry Hill allowed Pope enough time to organize what could be described as an orderly retreat. At nightfall, Pope's army began their retreat toward Washington.

All during the night, the turnpike and the neighboring fords were jammed with Pope's retreating columns. Gibbon's brigade and units of Sigel's command covered the retreat. By midnight, the major portion of the army had crossed the Bull Run. Sometime after 1 A.M., the Stone Bridge was destroyed by Lt. Colonel Thomas L. Kane's Pennsylvania Bucktails, with the assistance of Captain A. Mitzel's two companies of the Seventy-fourth Pennsylvania.[1]

During the early morning hours of August 31, as drizzly rains fell across northern Virginia, Pope entrenched on the heights of Centreville. Lee recognized the strength of Pope's position and made a decision to go around Centreville, sending Jackson by way of Sudley Ford and the Little River Turnpike to intercept Pope before he could reach Washington. In Lee's official report, he said:

> Jackson proceeded by Sudley Ford to the Little River turnpike to turn the enemy's right and intercept his retreat to Washington. Jackson's progress was retarded by the inclemency of the weather and the fatigue of his troops, who, in addition to their arduous marches, had fought three severe engagements in as many days. He reached Little River turnpike in the evening, and the next day, September 1, advanced by that road toward Fairfax Court-House. The enemy in the mean time was falling back rapidly toward Washington, and had thrown out a strong force to Germantown, on the Little River turnpike, to cover his line of retreat from Centreville. The advance of Jackson's column encountered the enemy at Ox Hill, near Germantown, about 5 P.M. Line of battle was at once formed and two brigades of A.P. Hill's division (those of Branch and Field, under Colonel Brockenbrough) were thrown forward to attack the enemy and ascertain his strength and position. A cold and drenching rain-storm drove in the faces of our troops as they advanced and gallantly engaged the enemy. They were subsequently supported by the brigade of Gregg, Thomas,

and Pender, also of Hill's division, which, with part of Ewell's, became engaged. The conflict was obstinately maintained by the enemy until dark, when he retreated, having lost two general officers, one of whom, Major-General Kearny, was left dead on the field.[2]

The other Union general officer that Lee made reference to as being killed was General Isaac Ingalls Stevens, commander of the Federal army 9th Corps. The next day, September 2, General Lee had the body of General Kearny sent into the Federal lines under a flag of truce with a note to Pope, which read: "The body of Gen. Phillip Kearny was brought from the field last night, and he was reported dead. I send it forward under a flag of truce, thinking the possession of his remains may be a consolation to his family."[3]

Pope's army did make it into Washington. General George B. McClellan met General Pope on the outskirts of Washington and Pope was immediately removed from his command.

THE CASUALTIES

The initial aftermath of the Second Battle of Manassas was very similar to that of the first battle thirteen months earlier, except on a much larger scale. The disposition of the casualties was a priority left to the victors, so, as was the case thirteen months earlier, the enormous task of burying the dead and gathering the wounded for medical attention fell to the Confederates. It began on August 31, shortly after the battle, when Lee gave authorization to Washington for the Federals to send medical personnel and ambulances under a flag of truce to pick up their paroled wounded. In addition, Federal burial details were sent to bury their dead.

Casualty Numbers[4]

	Casualties	Killed	Wounded	Captured/Missing
Union	13,824	1,716	8,215	3,893
Confederate	8,353	1,305	7,048	---
Total	22,177	3,021	15,263	3,893

BURIALS OF THE FALLEN

On August 31, as Jackson proceeded to intercept Pope, "Longstreet remained on the battlefield to engage the attention of the enemy (distract Pope in front of Centreville) and cover the burial of the dead and the removal of the wounded."[5] Details of the burials are sketchy at best. Burials took place on all the fields of battle, including Manassas Plains (Chinn Ridge), Brawner Farm, Lucinda Dogan's property (Deep Cut), John Dogan's property, and other places where men fell. Single graves as well as mass graves estimated to contain anywhere from five or six bodies to as many as eighty and more bodies were made. Very few of the dead were actually identified. Many years later, in an interview given to a writer, Susan Monroe described what she, as a young woman of 20, witnessed of some of the burials, and she had some very disparaging things to say[6]:

> A great many men were killed in that battle, and there were places where the ground was so soaked with blood that not one thing would grow on those spots for years. You'd be surprised how careless the Yankees were about burying their dead. The Confederates did their

part all right. Our men were buried so deep no ploughshare or anything will ever touch 'em. There they'll stay till the Day of Judgment. Some soldiers were sent hyar [sic] from Washington to bury the Union dead.... Of co'se [sic] they made some pretense at doin' their work, but often they'd leave a corpse right on top the ground and throw on a little dirt, or turn half a log over it. One man had rocks piled on him, and another they put in a little narrow ravine and laid some rails on top. A detachment of artillery drove across the rails afterward, but a day or two later the man was removed ... I reckon by soldiers who knew him. They buried him near an oak tree and cut his initials on the tree-trunk.

Susan said regarding a mass burial she witnessed: "Our men buried some of the Yankees. A railroad had been begun hyar [sic] and abandoned, and they gathered up six hundred and eighty-three Yankees and piled 'em up good at the end of this railroad embankment and then threw dirt down on top of 'em and covered 'em deep."[7]

Recovery of the Wounded

The recovery and disposition of the wounded after the battle was much déjà vu for any who had lived through the aftermath of First Battle of Manassas. Most of the standing structures in the area served as field hospitals for the thousands of wounded. A Confederate cavalry soldier observing the battlefield on September 1 wrote the following: "White flags were flying all over the field today and the Citizens Relief Commission of Washington, with two hundred ambulances, were on the field burying the dead and gathering the wounded. I saw at one place where they were burying eighty men in one trench."[8]

In the early morning of September 1, the Confederates setup a parole station at the Stone House. For the next several days, thousands of wounded Union soldiers were processed for parole and released to be carried back to Washington hospitals.

Lee Prepares for Invasion of the North

Meanwhile, while his army was returning from Chantilly, Lee was planning his next campaign: an invasion northward into Maryland. Lee's army was in terrible shape; since the beginning of his Manassas campaign, he had sustained 9,000 casualties. His men were tired and needed rest, hungry from living on sparse rations, and dressed in tatters while many were shoeless and walking on bleeding feet. Lee was very much aware of this, but he strongly believed that with the victory of Second Manassas and Pope's defeated army sent reeling back to Washington, the Confederate army could not afford to remain idle. "In a letter to President Davis, on Sept. 2, Lee gave as reasons for the invasion of Maryland, that it would relieve the Confederacy from the presence of hostile armies on her soil; and that the position of the army would be favorable for reaping the fruits of a victory, if one could be gained."[9] It is possible that Lee also reasoned that if the South could gain European diplomatic recognition by achieving a victory on Northern soil, then the North's resolve to continue the war would weaken and the Confederacy would surely achieve independence.

After a rest of one day, on September 4, with Jackson in the lead, the Army of Northern Virginia was put in motion for the fords of the Potomac, near Leesburg.[10]

Suffering Continues for the Civilians of Sudley and Groveton Communities

The families of the communities of Sudley and Groveton underwent insurmountable hardships beginning in May 1861, the start of hostilities, as the geographical setting of Manassas Junction became a known strategic location by both North and South. In the area from Pageland Lane east to Centreville and from Sudley south to Manassas Junction, the communities, the farmlands and families suffered deprivations. First, these difficulties were brought on by the influx of Confederate troops over the area prior to the First Battle of Manassas, and then as the two armies came together for that battle. Following the battle, there was the thirteen-month interval when the area was occupied by troops of both sides; first the Confederates for six months, and then Union troops for seven months. Farmlands became void of almost all timber; the farm fields were stripped of fencing rails, most of the farm animals had been stolen, and the fields were stripped of staple crops like wheat, corn, oats, and hay. In addition, the locals' personal store houses for the most part were emptied.

Thirteen months after the first battle, the aftermath of the second battle meant the families were once again unable to go back to their homes for another two to three weeks, as most all structures were being used as hospitals or aid stations for the wounded. After the wounded had been taken away and the families occupied their homes once again, it was not uncommon for them to find most of their personal belongings gone or destroyed. A particularly gruesome report came from the Benjamin Chinn family; when they returned to their home, they found they no longer could use the well, as it had been filled with amputated arms and legs.[11]

Years later, in an exclusive article written for a newspaper by Marianne E. Compton, Marianne described what took place where she lived on the battlefield at the conclusion of the battle and after. Marianne Compton was 17 years of age in 1862. Her father Alexander Compton had been the minister of the Sudley Methodist Church until his death in the spring following the First Battle of Manassas. The Comptons were the owner of the servant girl Lucy Griffith, who had been wounded while caring for Mrs. Judith Henry, the first civilian killed on a Civil War battlefield. On August 30, the Comptons had been ordered away from their home of Greenville, located along the old Warrenton–Washington Turnpike (modern-day Ball's Ford Road). Marianne, her mother, and her siblings spent the day on a hillside before going to the house of a colored woman about a quarter of a mile away, where they spent the night.

> Next morning, the rain, which seems always to follow a battle, was falling. My young brother, now the Rev. William Compton, of Oregon, went home and got a cart to carry us back. When we reached there what a scene of desolation presented itself to our eyes! The yard paling was gone — used to make fires. Soldiers, our own Southern groops [sic], were everywhere, in stable, barn, and smaller outhouses. All the lower part of the house was filled with wounded. We walked through a lane of ghastly horrors on our way upstairs. Amputated legs and arms seemed everywhere. We saw a foot that had just been cut off lying on one of our dinner plates. We were lucky in having a place to go. Our old friend, Mr. Henry [Hugh Fauntleroy Henry, son of Mrs. Judith Henry], had stood all night at the

foot of the steps and kept the second floor from being occupied. There we now took refuge, and there we stayed for three long weeks. We were much crowded; the rooms were cramped, and filled up with all our belongings that could be spared from below. As someone remarked: "Everything had to be taken there to save anything." We sat, ate and slept there; a prey to illness and many anxieties; but all was cheerfully borne, for were not the poor sufferers below our own Southern men? Before the end of the time many wounded had died, others had been carried away.[12]

Several families found they had nothing to go back to. Besides plundering homes, some retreating soldiers willfully destroyed three homes by fire: the John Dogan family home, Rosefield; the Edwin Carter family home, Pittsylvania; and the Frank Lewis family home, Portici. Units of Sigel's command were covering Pope's retreat, and it is believed that it was troops of Sigel's command that torched Rosefield and Pittsylvania. Portici was destroyed during this same period of time, and it is possible that it was torched by some of the Pennsylvania Bucktails (suggested in the manuscript *Virginia Lineages, Letters & Memories*.)[13] The Bucktails are a likely candidate as they were in the area during the retreat, having been given the task sometime after 1 A.M. August 31 to destroy the Stone Bridge.

Analysis of the Second Battle of Manassas

THE DEFEATED

The Second Battle of Manassas was a catastrophe of the first order for Pope's Army of Virginia. Lee's Confederates were outmanned, outgunned, and vastly under-equipped compared to Pope's army, so why did Pope fail? Although many factors came into play that brought on the Union's defeat, the most significant factor was Pope himself; he was his own worst enemy. He made bad, inexcusable tactical decisions that were based on illogical assumptions driven by his inflated ego. In simple terms, he really didn't know what he was doing.

Highlights of Pope's Major Blunders

Blunder 1 On August 26, Pope moved his entire command from in front of Longstreet to go after Jackson at Manassas Junction. He departed without leaving any safeguards against Longstreet's joining Jackson, such as an adequate force to block Longstreet at Thoroughfare Gap. When he reached Manassas and found no Jackson, he sent out orders to his other corps to march on Centreville. He believed Jackson would be found at Centreville, a false assumption he reached after talking to two Confederate prisoners.

Blunder 2. After the Battle of Brawner Farm, for most of the next two days, Pope falsely assumed that Jackson was retreating to Thoroughfare Gap, a conclusion he held to as he ignorantly gave orders to pursue the "retreating" Jackson, who was, in actuality, entrenched along the Unfinished Railroad.

Blunder 3. In the morning hours of August 29, Porter and McDowell came within sight of Longstreet south of the turnpike. McDowell also had a message from Buford giving details of Longstreet's infantry and artillery moving through Thoroughfare Gap. Throughout the day and evening of August 29 until 10 A.M. of August 30, Pope ignored reports from his commanders pertaining to Longstreet's presence.

Blunder 4. During the day of August 29, Longstreet was in position no more than two miles away from Pope himself. Pope continued to proceed on his false assumption that Lee and Longstreet would not arrive for another day or two, and he would not listen otherwise. Also, in keeping with his false assumptions, he failed to properly use his cavalry to reconnoiter, while there are indications that he ignored their reports too.

Blunder 5. Throughout the day of August 29, Pope expected to hear of Porter attacking Jackson's right flank and rear. Why he would have expected that is a mystery, as he never sent out any orders to that effect. It was not until late in the evening of August 29 that Pope did send orders to Porter to attack Jackson, but Porter did not receive them until nearly nightfall. In addition, Porter and McDowell knew that had he moved forward, it would not have been Jackson he would be confronting, but Longstreet.

Blunder 6. Another telltale factor that should have tipped off Pope about his situation was that, on the evening of August 29, he had McDowell send King's division (Hatch) west along the turnpike, presumably to pursue Jackson in retreat, but instead he clashed with Hood's division of Longstreet's command. That should have awakened him to Longstreet's presence and the fact that Jackson was there and wasn't going anywhere.

The Bad and the Good

Not many good things can be said of McDowell's conduct, either. He was aware of Porter's situation and knew of the Confederate forces on Pope's left flank on August 29. Later, in the afternoon of August 30, he made a major blunder by ordering Reynolds off Chinn Ridge, leaving only two brigades protecting their left flank.

As Longstreet's Wing swept across Chinn Ridge, rolling up Pope's left flank, only then did McDowell show any semblance of leadership. A light must have dawned in McDowell's head, for he understood their situation and knew what he had to do to save Pope's army. In addition, he spoke out forcefully to Pope in a manner that finally gave Pope an understanding of their precarious situation.

The brave actions of McLean and his brigade of Ohioans, as well as those of Tower and Stiles, did much to provide McDowell and Pope with the precious time needed to set up defensive measures on Henry Hill, enabling Pope's army to retreat intact.

A Despicable Man

After leading an army of embarrassed men to the outskirts of Washington, not once did Pope take any responsibility for his defeat, but instead he embarked on a crusade to place the blame on Major General Fitz John Porter. On November 27, 1862, Porter went before a general court-martial and was subsequently found guilty on two charges of disobeying lawful orders of his superior. These findings were sent to President Abraham Lincoln, who signed them.[14] The following are the orders of the president:

> The following proceedings, findings, and sentence in the foregoing case of Maj. Gen. Fitz John Porter are approved and confirmed; and it is ordered that the said Fitz John Porter be, and he hereby is, cashiered and dismissed from the service of the United States as a major-general of volunteers, and as colonel and brevet brigadier-general in the regular service of the United States, and forever disqualified from holding any office of trust or profit under the Government of the United States.
>
> Abraham Lincoln
January 21, 1863

Porter was a ruined man; a terrible injustice had been cast upon him. Those who could have spoken out to tell what really transpired, like McDowell and others, did not.

For the next fifteen years, Porter worked diligently for a rehearing. Finally, in 1878, through President Rutherford B. Hayes, a board was convened to examine the record of the initial trial by court-martial of Major General Porter. As a result, nothing was held back. The Chief of the Army Engineers scanned the battlefield, detailed maps were drawn, sketches and notes of the area and terrain were made, interviews with locals took place, and more. Much of the information the Park Service has today of the battlefield can be attributed to the information gathered for Porter's retrial. The comprehensive retrial brought out all facets of Pope's campaign. It is interesting to note that Confederate generals Longstreet and Jubal Early gave testimony at the retrial.

The Retrial Court's Findings

The court brought out the fact that Longstreet's arrival on August 29 had been reported to Pope on several occasions. The Court had this to say:

> Porter had repeatedly reported to McDowell the presences of the enemy in large force in his front. Presumably these reports had gone to Pope, as one of them had in fact. Porter had also sent an aide-de-camp with a written message to Pope about 4 P.M., and had sent a written reply to the 4:30 P.M. order after 6:30 P.M. These last two dispatches have not been preserved by General Pope, and hence their contents are not known to us; but we are bound to presume that they reported the situation as Porter then knew it, and as he had frequently reported it to McDowell, and the last of these dispatches, in reply to the 4:40 P.M. order, was later than the latest of those in which Porter had spoken of any intention to fall back. Hence Porter had already given to his superior all the information which it was possible for him to give, and nothing remained for him but to obey the order. This movement of Porter's corps on the morning of the 30th was the beginning of the unfortunate operation of that day. This corps, which had been protecting the left flank of Pope's army, was withdrawn from its important position, leaving the left wing and flank exposed to attack by greatly superior force of the enemy, brought to the center of the field and then ordered 'in pursuit of the enemy....'[15]
>
> General Pope appears from his orders and from his testimony to have been at that time wholly ignorant of the true situation. He had disapproved of the sending of Ricketts to Thoroughfare Gap to meet Longstreet on the 28th, believing that the main body of Lee's army could not reach the field of Manassas before the night of the 30th. Hence he sent the order to Porter dated 4:30 P.M., to attack Jackson's right flank or rear. Fortunately that order did not reach Porter until about sunset — too late for any attack to be made. Any attack which Porter could have made at any time that afternoon must necessarily have been fruitless of any good result. Porter's faithful, subordinate, and intelligent conduct that afternoon saved the Union army from the defeat which would otherwise have resulted that day

from the enemy's more speedy concentration. The only seriously critical period of that campaign, viz, between 11 A.M. and sunset of August 29, was thus safely passed. Porter had understood and appreciated the military situation, and, so far as he had acted upon his own judgment, his action had been wise and judicious. For the disaster of the succeeding day he was in no degree responsible. Whoever else may have been responsible, it did not flow from any action or inaction of ßis.[16]

The Report of the Board of Army Officers, written by Major General J.M. Schofield, dated March 19, 1879, also stated: "These charges and specifications certainly bear no discernible resemblance to the facts of the case as now established."[17]

The retrial completely exonerated Porter and condemned the earlier court. The fact remains that Pope was responsible for destroying an otherwise most distinguished military career of a general officer and taking sixteen years or more out of Porter's life. Pope's actions went beyond disingenuous; they were despicable.

THE VICTORS

Pope shouldn't be held fully responsible for his defeat at Manassas. After all, Lee had been there, a general who seemed to have an uncanny ability to read his opponents, which Pope only made easier for him. However, the victory was not all sweet for Lee and the Confederacy, for it gained nothing toward ending the war. Lee's goal was to annihilate Pope's Army of Virginia, and he might have succeeded had not darkness prohibited the taking of Henry Hill and the turnpike intersection.

The campaign and the Battle of Second Manassas sent a message, both to the Lincoln administration and throughout the North and South, that Lee was a most formidable foe, without equal. The new organization of the Army of Northern Virginia put into play by Lee worked extremely well, thanks to his Wing commanders, Longstreet and Jackson. Lee's biographer Douglas Southall Freeman wrote, "The special satisfaction of Lee was in the evidence that the Army at last had what every Army requires, capable corps commanders. Both Longstreet and Jackson, he felt, now were qualified to handle large numbers of men and to throw the entire force simultaneously into action."[18]

Lee also knew the value of cavalry and how to use them. Lee's cavalry commander, Jeb Stuart, was a great asset to him and is considered by many to be the best cavalry officer ever.

Lee's Wing commanders were also fortunate to have some good division and brigade commanders. It would be too tedious to go through the exploits of the different individuals, but some should be given proper recognition. Ewell showed exceptional leadership in the manner of his disengagement at Broad Run. Gregg, of Hill's command, held off the many attacks over a period of nine hours on the 29th, his valor showing through. General Early came to Gregg's rescue in an exemplary manner on the afternoon of the 29th. John Bell Hood superbly selected the gun placements for S.D. Lee's guns which played the dominant role in the repulse of Porter's attack at the Deep Cut on the 30th. In addition, Hood daringly led his Texans across Chinn Ridge, decimating two brigades in his path while setting the pace of Longstreet's sweep across Chinn Ridge.

One of the most daring actions taken by an army commander during the Civil

War took place on August 25, when Lee split his forces in an effort to get around to the rear of Pope's army. This was the action that would get Pope to move off the Rappahannock. In his book, *History of the Civil War*, John Ropes wrote the following of Lee's strategy[19]:

> The disparity between Pope's force and that of Jackson is so enormous that it is impossible not to be amazed at the audacity of the confederate general, in thus risking an encounter in which the very existence of Jackson's command would be imperiled, and to ask what was the object Gen. Lee considered as warranting such an extremely dangerous maneuver. The answer is not an easy one.... We shall ... only remark here that this move of Gen. Lee's in dividing his army, was an illustration of the daring, not to say hazardous, policy which he pursued in this summer of 1862.

In a later published discussion of this maneuver, Lee is reported to have answered for it himself[20]: "Such criticism is obvious, but the disparity of force between the contending forces rendered the risks unavoidable."

Some years after the war, Longstreet wrote in his book, *Manassas to Appomattox*, that Jackson had been sent orders to advance soon after his advance began. This brought on controversies that still linger today that Jackson did not give proper support to Longstreet in the late afternoon of August 30, when Lee's target was Henry Hill and the turnpike intersection. There is no record of an order for Jackson to do so at that time.

Very little is known about why Jackson did not advance until about 6 P.M., but it can be conjectured. To gain a destructive defeat of Pope, it would have been necessary that Lee obtain control of Henry Hill and the turnpike intersection before nightfall. Jackson didn't move out of his positions along the Unfinished Railroad until about 6:00 P.M. At the time Longstreet began his advance, Lee's orders to Jackson were to "look out for and protect his [Longstreet's] left flank."[21] Wilcox was on Jackson's front (Longstreet's left flank), and didn't move out until about 6 P.M. What is known is that about 4 to 4:30 P.M., at the conclusion of Porter's attack against Jackson's right flank, the condition of Jackson's divisions on his right flank was not good. Jackson had reported near the conclusion of Porter's attack that he was out of ammunition. His supply wagons were some distance in the rear of his positions. The regiments would have to make their way to the wagons to pick up their ammunition and also rations. In addition, their losses had been heavy, brigades had been reduced to the size of regiments and regiments to the size of companies, and the men were tired and weary. Given their condition, they probably did well to have moved out in that time span of an hour to an hour and a half. In addition, it's speculative that Longstreet may have misspoken about Jackson in his book.

Calamities of War Resume

The next day after the battle, Lee's army was on the march to Chantilly. On September 4, his tattered and bruised army was on the march again, embarked on a new campaign that took them across the Potomac into Northern territory.

Chapter Notes

Chapter One

1. R. Jackson Radcliff, *This Was Prince William*, p.78.
2. *Richmond Dispatch*, September 16, 1861.
3. J. Davis and A. Stephens, *Robert E. Lee*, p. 16. Letter to the editor from Kenneth W. Rapp, Archivist, United States Military Academy, dated December 7, 1965: "[H]e [Lee] was designated a 'Distinguished Cadet' at the end of each academic year and at his graduation July 1, 1829. [The term "Distinguished Cadet" was awarded only to the first five cadets in relative class academic standing.] As a third classman (sophomore) he served as a staff sergeant, a cadet rank usually reserved for second classmen (juniors). During both his third and second class years, Lee was appointed an acting assistant professor of mathematics. Acting assistant professorships were normally filled by first classmen (seniors). The most coveted and important cadet rank at West Point was that of corps adjutant. The corps adjutant was selected by the superintendent of the Academy from among the first classmen who had the best record on the drill grounds. Robert E. Lee was selected to fill this key position. Other fine achievements attained by Lee during his four years at the United States Military Academy included perfect scores in his final exams (as a first classman) in both artillery and tactics."
4. Capt. Robert E. Lee (son of Gen. R.E. Lee), *The Recollection and Letters of Robert E. Lee*, p. 25.
5. Ibid., pp. 24, 25; Jefferson Davis, *Robert E. Lee*, p. 43.
6. *War of the Rebellion: A Compilation of the Official Records of the Union and Confederate Armies*, O.R. Series I, Vol. II, pp. 775–776 (hereafter referred to as O.R.).
7. Ibid., p. 806.
8. Ibid., p. 817.
9. Ibid., p. 821–822.
10. Ibid., p. 824.
11. Ibid., pp. 841, 845.
12. Ibid., p. 847.
13. *Battles and Leaders of the Civil War*, vol. 1, pp. 240–241 (hereafter referred to as BL).
14. Jefferson Davis, *The Rise and Fall of the Confederate Government* (Abridged), p. 175.
15. William J. Cooper Jr., *Jefferson Davis, American*, pp. 389–391. Davis quickly put an official end to Johnston's protest; he showed the letter to his cabinet and some members of Congress, including his sharp reply to Johnston that stated: "I have just received and read your letter of the 12th instant. Its language is, as you say, unusual; its arguments and statements utterly one-sided; and its insinuations as unfounded as they are unbecoming."
16. BL, vol. 1, pp. 111–117.
17. O.R. Series I, Vol. II, pp. 5, 6.
18. O.R. Series I, Vol. II, pp. 784–785.
19. Ibid., p. 607.
20. Ibid., p. 877; BL, vol. 1, p. 124.
21. *Richmond Dispatch*, July 19, 1891. Interview with Dr. Hunter Holmes McGuire, Jackson's doctor.
22. O.R. Series I, Vol. II, p. 472.
23. Ibid., pp. 469, 470.
24. Ibid., pp. 472, 473.

Chapter Two

1. Ishbel Ross, *Rebel Rose*, pp. 4, 92.
2. Ibid., pp. 6–10, 17, 18.
3. Nash K. Burger, *Confederate Spy: Rose O'Neale Greenhow*, p. 64; Ishbel Ross, *Rebel Rose*, pp. 42, 91.
4. O.R. Series I, Vol. II, pp. 40–44.
5. William B. Styple, *Writing and Fighting the Confederate War*, pp. 16, 17; BL, vol. 1, p. 179 (footnote).
6. R.P. Broadwater, *Civil War Medal of Honor Recipients*, pp. 33, 34.
7. O.R. Series I, Vol. II, p. 865.
8. Ibid., p. 891. After Governor Letcher issued the proclamation on June 8, 1861, that transferred all Virginia forces to the National Army of the Confederacy, Brigadier Gen. Robert Selden Garnett was ordered to Staunton to assume a command in northwestern Virginia. On July 13, Garnett was directing the disposition of a skirmish line in rear guard action near Corrick's Ford on Cleat River when he was mortally wounded while being pursued by troops of Union Generals McClelland and Rosecrans. He was the first general officer on either side to fall on field of battle in the Civil War.
9. Ibid., p. 896.
10. Ibid., pp. 901–902.
11. Virginia Writers Project, *Prince William: The Story of Its People and Its Places*, pp. 143, 144.
12. O.R. Series I, Vol. II, p. 911.
13. Ibid., pp. 947, 943–944.
14. An English Combatant, *Battlefields of the South*, pp. 21–23.
15. E.P. Alexander, *Military Memoirs of a Confederate*, p. 16.

Chapter Three

1. Marianne E. Compton, "A Woman's Recollection of Two Famous Battles," *Manassas Journal* (newspaper), July 4, 1913.
2. Testimonial Letter, Laura Thornberry Fletcher (daughter of John Thornberry), November 18, 1936, MNB Library Files.
3. William Smith, "Reminiscences of the First Battle," *Southern Historical Society Papers* 10, p. 437.
4. R.J. Ratcliffe, *This Was Prince William*, p. 120.
5. Southern Claims Commission, National Archives, Elizabeth A. Van Pelt Claim No. 36,994.
6. Edmund J Raus, *Banners South*, p. 177.
7. Ibid.; J.J. Hennessy, *Return to Bull Run*," p. 300.
8. MNB Archives, Lucinda Dogan File, letters and newspaper articles.
9. Ibid.
10. Ibid.
11. Ibid.
12 Ibid.
13. W.W. Blackford, *War Years With Jeb Stuart*, p. 119, 120.
14. Ibid.
15. MNB Archive Files, Brownville (Folly Castle).
16. Ibid.
17. MNB Archive Files, "Cultural Resource Survey and Inventory of War Torn Landscape: The Stuart's Hill Tract, Manassas National Battlefield Park, Virginia," 1992.
18. Clifton Johnson, *Battleground Adventures*, pp. 30–60.

Chapter Four

1. W.C. Davis, *Battle at Bull Run*, p. 77.
2. O.R. Series I, Vol. II, pp, 719–721.
3. Ibid., p. 969.
4. Ishbel Ross, *Rebel Rose*, p. 100.
5. Ibid.
6. Ibid.
7. Alexander, *Military Memoirs of a Confederate*, p. 17.
8. Ibid., p. 18; O.R. Series I, Vol. II, p. 478.
9. O.R. Series I, Vol. II, pp. 980–981.
10. Ibid., p. 168.
11. Ibid., p. 168.
12. Ibid., p. 447.
13. BL, vol. 1, p. 178; O.R. Series I, Vol. II, p. 312.
14. Ibid., pp. 178, 179.
15. O.R. Series I, Vol. II, p. 442.
16. Ibid., p. 443.
17. Ibid., p. 329, 330; BL, Vol. I, pp. 178–180.
18. Ibid., p. 178. In the months following the First Battle of Manassas, Major General Patterson's reputation had come under attack because of his failure to prevent or delay Johnston from joining Beauregard. Patterson wrote several letters to Secretary of War Simon Cameron, seeking a court of inquiry charging the General-in-Chief Lieutenant General Winfield Scott with keeping Patterson's command in a crippled condition, and with demanding his advance upon Johnston after having withdrawn from him all his available artillery. On March 31, 1862, Scott provided a written ten-item statement to the House of Representatives, Joint Committee on the Conduct of the War. Item 5 of his statement reads: "But although General Patterson was never specifically ordered to attack the enemy, he was certainly told and expected, even if with inferior numbers, to hold the rebel army in his front on the alert, and to prevent it from re-enforcing Manassas Junction by means of threatening maneuvers and demonstrations— results often obtained in war with half numbers."
19. Alexander, *Military Memoirs of a Confederate*, p. 19; O.R. Series I, Vol. II, p. 473.
20. Ibid.; BL, vol. 1, pp. 178–180.
21. O.R. Series I, Vol. II, p. 473.
22. Ibid., p. 985.
23. Ibid., p. 474.

Chapter Five

1. A narrative compiled from multiple sources: BL, vol. 1, p. 203; Dabney, *Life and Campaigns of Lt. Gen. Thomas J. Jackson*; George Wilkes, *The Great Battle Fought at Manassas*, pp. 17–18.
2. O.R. Series I, Vol. II, pp. 362, 364, 365.
3. Ibid., pp. 318, 319.
4. Ibid., 362.
5. Ibid., pp. 318, 319.
6. Alexander, *Military Memoirs of a Confederate*, pp. 28, 29.
7. O.R. Series I, Vol. II, p. 491; Alexander, *Military Memoirs of a Confederate*, p. 31; T.H. Williams, *P.G.T. Beauregard*, p. 83.
8. Ibid.; BL, vol. 1, p. 259. Per accounts provided to BL, contradictions pertaining to Ewell's actions vs. inactions to Beauregard's orders for his flanking attack plan on the Federal left were reconciled four days after the battle when the subjoined correspondence of the principle participants, namely D.R. Jones, Ewell, and Beauregard were examined. However, the controversy was reignited after Ewell's death some 20 years later, when Beauregard wrote an article in 1884 for *The Century* criticizing Ewell and rehashing the issue. Major Campbell Brown, aide-de-camp and assistant adjutant general to General Ewell, responded harshly to Beauregard's article on behalf of the late General Ewell. Brown wrote General Fitzhugh Lee, who was Ewell's assistant adjutant general at Manassas. Fitzhugh Lee provided a detailed account which refutes Beauregard's claims.
9. O.R. Series I, Vol. II, pt. 2, pp. 491, 492.
10. Alexander, *Military Memoirs of a Confederate*, p. 30; E.P. Alexander, *Fighting for the Confederacy*, p. 50; *National Tribune*, "The First Signal Message," January 8, 1903.
11. O.R. Series I, Vol. II, pp. 559–561.
12. Ibid., p. 346.
13. Ibid., pp. 346, 395, 988; Augustus Woodbury, *The Second Rhode Island Regiment*, pp. 34–36.
14. BL, vol. 1, pp. 232, 233.
15. O.R. Series I, Vol. II, pp. 489, 490; BL, vol. 1, p. 207.
16. MNBF Archive Files, 7th Georgia. Historians can be indebted to Park Ranger Jim Burgess for uncovering factual accounts that the 7th Georgia Infantry Regiment of Bartow's brigade was held in reserve during the engagement on Matthews Hill. Some statements in O.R. accounts reported that the 7th Georgia accompanied the 8th Georgia along with the 2nd Mississippi and two companies of the 11th Mississippi into

the fight on Matthews Hill. Over the years, major details have come to light disputing those reports. In 2005, Jim summed up an in-depth investigation that clarified six positions the 7th Georgia occupied during the First Battle of Manassas on July 21, 1861, and one that identified their position late on August 30, 1862, in the Second battle of Manassas (7th Georgia Regiment Position Markers at Manassas National Battlefield Park, dated June 8, 2005). In 1905, during their annual reunion, 7th Georgia veterans placed seven small monument markers that identified each of the seven positions. Of the seven monuments, only two remain today, plus a few fragments of two others. While the 7th Georgia was held in reserve, it appears they occupied three and possibly four different positions. The positions they held near the turnpike would have been subjected to artillery fire from Matthews Hill. There were other Confederate units in the area such as Hampton's Legion for which they most likely gave way, possibly accounting for those changes of position.

17. O.R. Series I, Vol. II, p. 490.
18. Ibid., p. 346; BL, vol. 1, p. 233.
19. Charles L. Dufour, *The Gentle Tiger*, p. 142; *Confederate Veteran* 19, p. 427.
20. O.R. Series I, Vol. II, pp. 358, 359.
21. William Todd, *The Seventy-ninth Highlanders New York Volunteers in the War of the Rebellion*, p. 34: J.J. Hennessy, *The First Battle of Manassas — An End to Innocence*, p. 62.
22. O.R. Series I, Vol. II, p. 396.
23. Ibid., p. 563.
24. Ibid., p. 369.
25. BL, vol. 1, p. 187.
26. O.R. Series I, Vol. II, pp. 353, 566, 567.
27. Ibid., pp. 566, 567.
28. Ibid., p. 481; *Charleston Mercury*, July 26, 1861.
29. Ibid., p. 481.
30. BL, vol. 1, p. 234.
31. O.R., Series I, Vol. II, p. 394.
32. Ibid., p. 396.
33. BL, vol. 1, p. 234.
34. Ibid., p. 234.
35. O.R., Series I, Vol. II, p. 491, 492.
36. Ibid., p. 481.
37. BL, vol. 1, p. 210.
38. Susan P. Lee, *Memoir of William Nelson Pendleton, D.D.*, p. 149.
39. O.R. Series I, Vol. II, pp. 492, 494; "Sketch of the Rockville Artillery," *SHSP* 23, 1895, p. 113; BL, vol. 1, p. 235.
40. BL, vol. 1, p. 236.
41. Committee on the Conduct of the War (CCW), pp. 168, 169, Griffin Testimony.
42. CCW, p. 243, Ricketts's Testimony.
43. CCW, p. 219, Hazlett's Testimony; O.R. Series I, Vol. II, p. 394.
44. Letter dated August 2, 1861: Thomas J. Goree to Dr. H.W. Kittrell, Headquarters, 4th Brigade, Centreville, VA, Dept. of Archives, Louisiana State University. The fourth brigade comprised three regiments, the 10th Virginia, 1st Maryland, and 3rd Tennessee, plus Lt. R.F. Beckham's Battery of 4 guns (Culpeper Artillery). Brigadier General E.K. Smith was the initial commander, and Colonel Arnold Elzey took command on July 21 after Smith was wounded. More than likely, Goree was a member of one of those units.
45. CCW, p. 216, Averill's Testimony; O.R. Series I, Vol. II, p. 385.
46. J.J. Hennessy, "The First Hour's Fight on Henry Hill," pp. 6, 7; CCW, pp. 30, 31, Heinzelman's Testimony.
47. O.R. Series I, Vol. II, p. 392. Major John G. Reynolds's Report (U.S. Marines) mistakenly identified the Zouave unit as the Fourteenth New York vice the Eleventh New York. The Fourteenth New York had been ordered into the woods to the right of Ricketts's position and east of the Sudley Road after the arrival of the 11th New York, Hennessy, "The First Hour's Fight on Henry Hill," pp. 4, 8, 14.
48. BL, vol. 1, p. 236.
49. O.R. Series I, Vol. II, p. 483.
50. Blackford, *War Years with Jeb Stuart*, pp. 28–31.
51. Ibid., p. 31.
52. O.R. Series I, Vol. II, p. 403; CCW, pp. 30, 31, Heintzelman's Testimony.
53. Hennessy, *An End To Innocence*, p. 84.
54. William Smith, "Reminiscences of the First Manassas," *Southern Historical Society Papers* 10, p. 437.
55. CCW, Griffin Testimony, p.169; CCW, Barry's Testimony, pp. 145, 146; Barton Casler, *Four Years in the Stonewall Brigade*, p. 41.
56. CCW, Griffin Testimony, p. 169.
57. Hennessy, "The First Hour's Fight on Henry Hill," p. 32.
58. John Hennessy, "Stonewall Jackson's Nickname," *Civil War* 22, pp. 10–17.
59. Ibid.
60. O.R. Series I, Vol. II, p. 406.
61. O.R. Series I, Vol. II, p. 403.
62. Ibid., p. 496.
63. Ibid., p. 369.
64. Ibid., p. 370; J.M. Hanson, *Bull Run Remembers*, pp. 90, 91. Wade Hampton was slightly wounded, having received a bullet gash to his head. Hanson writes an account about Cameron's mortal wounding after Hampton's wounding and the New York Highlanders' charge after having been repulsed. The Highlanders "surged partway up the slope from the Sudley road and the Legion was forced eastward out of the yard, leaving Hampton lying between the lines accompanied only by his orderly. The Federals, however, were driven back to the road by the intense Confederate musketry and artillery fire; reformed and came on again, and were again repulsed. Nothing daunted their commander, Colonel James Cameron, who started up the hill a third time, waving his sword and crying to his men to follow. But they had taken about all they could stand and few of them obeyed. Colonel Hampton, lying where he would certainly be captured, and probably killed, should the New Yorkers complete their charge, was watching Cameron intently, completely oblivious to his own danger. Suddenly he exclaimed to his lone companion: 'Isn't it terrible to see that brave officer trying to lead his men forward, and they won't follow him?' (A few seconds later, Hampton witnessed Cameron fall, mortally wounded)." Initially, Cameron was buried in the yard of the John Dugan home. After the Confederate army moved out in March of 1862, Cameron's body was exhumed for reburial in Lewisburg, Pennsylvania. Dr. Richard Sauers provided the following interesting information as to what took place in the aftermath of Cameron's death: "Once he was

dead and buried, [Cameron's] brother Simon bought James' two farms out from under his widow and sent her packing back to Lancaster, where she died in 1890. James' one farm is now home to the Milton Historical Society."
65. O.R. Series I, Vol. II, p. 370.
66. Ibid.
67. Ibid., p. 495.
68. Ibid., pp. 496, 497.
69. Ibid., p. 476.
70. Ibid., p. 409.
71. Ibid.
72. BL, vol. 1, p. 249.
73. O.R. Series I, Vol. II, pp. 320, 370.
74. Edmond Ruffin, *Ruffin Diary*, manuscript at Library of Congress, p. 169; OR Series I, Vol. II, p. 397.

Chapter Six

1. O.R., Ser. 1, Vol. II, pp. 351, 387, 405, 426, 570.
2. O.R., Ser. 1, Vol. II, p. 571.
3. Ibid.
4. *Richmond Dispatch*, July 19, 1891, Interview with Dr. Hunter Holmes McGuire, Jackson's doctor.
5. Ibid.
6. Ibid.
7. BL, vol. 1, pp. 219–229, Beauregard speaks of his differences with Davis and Johnston; pp. 240–245, Johnston speaks of his differences with Davis and Beauregard.
8. Joseph Johnston, *Narration of Military Operations During the Civil War*, pp. 59–61.
9. Surgeon General, Medical and Surgical History, Part 1, Vol. 1, p. 510.
10. O.R., Vol. II, Part 1, pp. 482–484.
11. Andrews to Charles P. McIlvaine letter, Cincinnati, Ohio, Aug. 1, 1861, Duke University (MNB Library).
12. *New York Times*, Tuesday, August 6, 1861.
13. Testimonial Letter, Laura Thornberry Fletcher (daughter of John Thornberry), Nov. 18, 1936, MNB Library.
14. Architectural Changes In the Stone House—Established by Historical Research, MNB Files. In an interview documented by National Park Service personnel on November 4, 1958, with Mrs. Mary Ayres, widow of George H. Ayres, the son of Henry J. Ayres, who bought the Stone House and property in 1902. Mrs. Ayres had lived in the Stone House with her husband and family from 1912 until it was acquired by the National Park Service on June 17, 1949. The following are excerpts from that interview as pertains to the well located in front of the Stone House:
Question: Did you folks ever use the well out front?
Answer: Yes, indeed, that old well was used.
Question: When did you cease to use it?
Answer: I would say about 1928 when we built the Inn. We then dug a well on the hill back of the house. The old well was a dug well 25 feet deep and stones lined its side. Water came up nearly to the top. We were told may times that on the hot July day in the First Battle of Manassas the soldiers drank the well completely dry.
15. O.R. Vol. I, p. 551. Note: Although the medical personnel found at the Stone House as reported by Preston were a surgeon and assistant surgeon, no record of actual surgery being performed at the Stone House has been found.
16. *The Republican* (newspaper), Springfield, Massachusetts, 1886; Walbrook D. Swank, Col. USAF Ret., *Confederate War Stories, 1861–1865*, MNB Library.
17. Ibid.
18. Testimonial Letter, Elenea H. Henry (widow of Arthur Lee Henry, son of John Henry), MNB Library.
19. Clarence Cannon, *The Wigginton Book*. Mr. Cannon served in the U.S. House of Representatives for 12 years and served as congressman from Missouri in the 68th and 69th Congress. Cannon was married to Ida Wigginton in 1906, a direct descendant of the Wigginton sisters. I am greatly indebted to Mr. Dave Wigginton of Sterling, Illinois, a direct descendant of Lucy and Susan Wigginton, for supplying me with this material relating to the Wigginton sisters.
20. Ibid.
21. BL, vol. 1, p. 237.
22. Ibid., p. 238.
23. *Richmond Dispatch*, July 19, 1891, Interview with Dr. Hunter Holmes McGuire, Jackson's doctor.
24. *Boston Daily Journal*, July 23, 1861.
25. Lenoir Chambers, *Stonewall Jackson*, vol. 1, pp. 402, 403.
26. Ibid., p. 403.
27. T.H. Williams, *P.G.T. Beauregard: Napoleon In Gray*, pp. 109, 110; BL, vol. 1, pp. 165, 166.
28. Ibid., pp. 113–115.
29. Virgil C. Jones, *First Manassas (Bull Run) and the War Around It*, pp. 34–37, 59. This book was adapted from excerpts from Jones's book *Gray Ghosts and Rebel Raiders* (Holt, Rinehart and Winston).
30. Testimonial Letter, Laura Thornberry Fletcher (daughter of John Thornberry), Nov. 18, 1936, MNB Library.

Chapter Seven

1. BL, vol. 2, p. 168.
2. O.R. Series I, Vol. XII, pt. 2, pp. 10, 11; Bruce Catton, *The Civil War*, p. 116, 117.
3. BL, vol. 2, p. 172, 173.
4. O.R. Series I, Vol. XII, II, p. 20.
5. Douglas Southall Freeman, *Lee's Lieutenants*, vol. 1, p. 485.
6. Douglas Southall Freeman, *R.E. Lee*, vol. 2, pp. 102–104, 108, 109.
7. O.R. XII, II, pp. 12, 13.
8. Freeman, *Lee's Lieutenants*, vol. 2, p. 238.
9. Ibid.
10. Ibid., pp. 238, 239.
11. Ibid.; O.R. XII, II, p. 198.
12. O.R. XII, II, p. 5.
13. Ibid., pp. 181–185.
14. Ibid., p. 6.
15. Blackford, *War Years With Jeb Stuart*, pp. 102–107; O.R. XII, II, p. 732.
16. O.R. XII, II, pp. 553, 554.
17. Blackford, *War Years With Jeb Stuart*, pp. 112–115; O.R. XII, II, pp. 554, 747–748.
18. O.R. XII, II, p. 643.
19. Ibid., pp. 722–724.
20. Ibid., p. 406.
21. Freeman, *R.E. Lee*, p. 320, source note 9.

22. BL, vol. 2, p. 529; O.R. XII, II, p. 406, 409; ibid., pp. 260, 262.
23. Hennessy, *Return to Bull Run*, p. 130.
24. O.R. XII, II, p. 644.
25. Campbell Brown, *Military Reminiscences of Major Campbell Brown*, pp. 94, 95.
26. O.R. XII, II, pp. 709–710; T.T. Munford, *History of the Second Virginia Cavalry* (unpublished ms).
27. O.R. XII, II, pp. 546–551.

Chapter Eight

1. O.R. XII, pt. II, p. 72.
2. Blackford, *War Years with Jeb Stuart*, p. 116.
3. James Longstreet, *Our March Against Pope*, p. 517.
4. John C. Ropes, *The Army Under Pope*, pp. 69, 70.
5. O.R. XII, pt. II, pp. 393, 336; XII, pt. I, p. 195.
6. Ibid., pt. I, p. 198; pt. II, p. 336.
7. John Gibbon, *Personal Recollections of the Civil War*, p. 50.
8. O.R. XII, pt. II, pp. 337, 360, 361; O.R. XII, pt. I, pp. 213, 214; Ropes, *The Army Under Pope*, pp. 69, 70.
9. *National Tribune*, July 14, 1892, p. 4 (refer to Alan D. Gaff, *Brave Men's Tears*, p. 67).
10. Blackford, *War Years with Jeb Stuart*, p. 120.
11. O.R. XII, pt. II, p. 242.
12. Remnants of the original apple orchard existed until sometime in early 2010, when the Park Service at Manassas had the orchard cut down.
13. O.R. XII, pt. I, p. 121.
14. Gibbon, *Personal Recollections of the Civil War*, p. 51; O.R. XII, II, p. 381.
15. Ibid., pp. 51, 52; R. Dawes, *Sixth Wisconsin*, p. 60, note 9 of Chapter VIII.
16. Hennessey, *Return to Bull Run*, p. 179, note 9.
17. Gibbon, *Recollections*, pp. 51, 52; O.R. XII, pt. II, pp. 378, 381.
18. O.R. XII, pt. II, pp. 651, 652, 656.
19. Alan D. Gaff, *Brave Men's Tears*, p. 65, note 20; Blackford, *War Years with Jeb Stuart*, pp. 120–121.
20. Abner Doubleday, Manuscript Manual, August 28, 1862; *National Tribune*, January 7, 1862, March 31, 1892.
21. O.R. XII, pt. II, pp. 377, 378.
22. Gibbon, *Personal Recollections of the Civil War*, p. 52; Charles King, *Gainesville, 1862*, p. 272; Gaff, *Brave Men's Tears*, p. 69.
23. Ibid., p. 52.
24. O.R. XII, pt. II, pp. 661–664.
25. Ibid., pp. 378, 381, 657.
26. Gaff, *Brave Men's Tears*, pp. 80, 81,103.
27. Ibid., 378, 381, 661; Gibbon, *Personal Recollections of the Civil War*, p. 52.
28. O.R. XII, II, pp. 378, 381.
29. Ibid.; R.R. Dawes, *Service With the Sixth Wisconsin Volunteers*, pp. 60, 61.
30. O.R. XII, II, pp. 656, 657, 661; Isaac Trimble, "Report of Operations of his Brigade from 14th to 29th of August 1862," *SHSP* 8 (1880), pp. 307, 308.
31. O.R. XII, II, p. 381; Porter Retrial, pt. II, pp. 225–227.
32. O.R. XII, II, pp. 369, 371, 378, 381.
33. Ibid., p. 369.
34. *Civil War Times Illustrated*, from an unpublished journal by Ewell's aide and stepson, Major Campbell H. Brown, "How Ewell Lost His Leg," June 1964; Krick, *R.E. Lee*, untitled research article, summer 1989, MNB Archives.
35. O.R. XII, II, p. 657.
36. Ibid., p. 754.
37. Ibid., p. 657; Gaff, *Brave Men's Tears*, p. 82.
38. Hennessy, *Return to Bull Run*, pp. 183, 184.
39. O.R. XII, II, p. 754.
40. Ibid., p. 378.
41. Rufus Dawes, *Service With the Sixth Wisconsin*, p. 62.
42. Blackford, *War Years with Jeb Stuart*, pp. 123, 124.
43. Ibid.
44. Kevin Leahy, *King Council of War*, unpublished manuscript, 1993.
45. Freeman, *Lee's Lieutenants*, vol. 2, pp. 107–109.
46. Ibid; O.R. XII, pt. 1, pp. 212, 213; BL, vol. 2, p. 500; O.R. XII, II, p. 645.
47. O.R. XII, pt. II, p. 670.
48. BL, vol. 2, p. 495.
49. Gibbon, *Personal Recollections of the Civil War*, pp. 58, 59.
50. Ibid.
51. Ibid.
52. O.R. XII, II, Supplement, pp. 903, 904.
53. Ibid.
54. Blackford, *War Years with Jeb Stuart*, p. 125.
55. Ibid., p. 127.
56. O.R. XII, pt. II, pp. 607, 626.
57. James Longstreet, *Manassas to Appomattox*, p. 182.
58. O.R. XII, II, p. 299.
59. Ibid., pp. 311, 312.
60. O.R. XII, pt. II, p. 685.
61. Ibid., p. 680.
62. Ibid., p. 685.
63. Ibid., p. 680.
64. Ibid., pp. 297, 298.
65. Ibid., p. 298.
66. Ibid., p. 680.
67. Ibid., p. 298.
68. Ibid., p. 298.
69. O.R. XII, pt. II, p. 297.
70. Ibid., pp. 319, 320.
71. Oates, *Union and Confederacy*, p. 143; Hennessy, *Return to Bull Run*, note 5 of Chapter 12, p. 509.
72. O.R. XII, pt. II, pp. 319, 320, 251.
73. O.R. XII, pt. II, p. 712, Early's Official Report.
74. Freeman, *Lee's Lieutenants*, vol. 2, p. 118, note 105.
75. O.R. XII, II, p. 39; O.R. XII, II, Supplement, pp. 1044, 1046.
76. John Hennessey, *Second Manassas Battlefield Map Study*, pp. 148, 149.
77. O.R. XII, pt. II, p. 439, Grover's Report.
78. Martin Hayes, *Second New Hampshire*, p. 132.
79. O.R. XII, pt. II, p. 441.
80. Hayes, *Second New Hampshire*, p. 132.
81. O.R. XII, pt. II, pp. 687, 698.
82. Ibid., p. 439.
83. Hennessey, *Return to Bull Run*, pp. 258–267; Hennessey, *Second Manassas Map Study*, pp. 188–190, 200, 201.
84. O.R. XII, pt. II, pp. 41, 42.

85. Ibid., p. 18.
86. O.R. XII, pt. II, pp. 513–535, Report of the Board of Army Officers in the case of Fitz John Porter (Retrial of Fitz John Porter, 1879).
87. O.R. XII, pt. II, p. 671.
88. O.R. XII, pt. II, pp. 416, 671, 700, 712.
89. BL, vol. 2, p. 519, 520; Longstreet, *Manassas to Appomattox*, p. 183.
90. O.R. XII, pt. II, p. 317; Hennessey, *Return to Bull Run*, p. 295.
91. Ibid.
92. O.R. XII, pt. II, p. 369, 370.
93. Ibid., p. 605.
94. O.R. XII, pt. II, pp. 513–535, Report of the Board of Army Officers in the case of Fitz John Porter (Retrial of Fitz John Porter, 1879). The court-martial retrial board determined that Pope had been informed by more than one officer at different times.
95. O.R. XII, pt. II, p. 41.
96. Ibid.
97. O.R. XII, pt. II, Supplement, p. 973; O.R. XII, pt. II, p. 472.
98. Royall W. Figg, *Where Men Only Dare to Go*, pp. 27, 28.
99. O.R. XII, pt. II, pp. 340, 341.
100. Ibid., p. 530.
101. Ibid., p. 646.
102. Ibid., p. 479.
103. Ibid., p. 368.
104. Ibid., p. 476.
105. Ibid., p. 368.
106. Ibid., p. 479.
107. *Confederate Veteran* 22 (1914): p. 231.
108. O.R. XII, II, reports of Roberts, 13th and 12th New York, pp. 471–473, 474, 476, 477.
109. Hennessy, *Return to Bull Run*, p. 354.
110. O.R. XII, pt. II, p. 254.
111. G.F.R. Henderson, *Stonewall Jackson and the American Civil War*, vol. 2, p. 174; Hennessy, *Return to Bull Run*, p. 343, note 12.
112. O.R. XII, II, p. 666.
113. SHSP 6; J. Longstreet, "The Artillery at Second Manassas—General Longstreet's Reply to General S.D. Lee," pp. 216, 217.
114. T.W. Haight, *Gainesville, Groveton, and Bull Run*, War Papers Read Before the Commandery of the State of Wisconsin, Military Order of the Loyal Legion of the United States, vol. 2, p. 370, Milwaukee, 1876.
115. O.R. XII, pt. II, p. 394.
116. Ibid., p. 563.
117. Ibid., pp. 609, 610, 615, 617.
118. Ibid., pp. 502, 504, 505, 609, 610.
119. Ibid., p. 502.
120. Ibid., p. 469, 470, 503.
121. Robert P. Broadwater, *Civil War Medal of Honor Recipients*, p. 213.
122. O.R. XII, II, pp. 340, 394, 395.
123. Ibid., pp. 618, 619, 395.
124. Ibid., pp. 606, 609; J.B. Polley, *Hood's Texas Brigade: Its Marches, Its Battles, Its Achievements*, pp. 87, 88, 90–93.
125. O.R. XII, II, pp. 618–620.
126. Ibid., pp. 286, 290, 291, 600, 602, 603, 607, 609, 610, 624, 640.
127. Ibid., pp. 606.
128. Ibid., pp. 304, 628–631, 633.
129. Ibid., pp. 626, 628, 633.
130. Ibid., pp. 286, 287, 290–293, 295.
131. Ibid., pp. 269, 285, 307, 341, 501.
132. Ibid., pp. 390–392.
133 *Confederate Veteran* 2 (1894): p. 184; O.R. XII, II, p. 626.
134. B.F. Cook, *History of the Twelfth Massachusetts Volunteers*, p. 159; "McDowell At Bull Run," *National Tribune*, January 1908.
135. O.R. XII, II, pp. 269, 398, 482, 595.
136. Ibid., p. 269.
137. Ibid., pp. 745, 746.
138. Ibid., pp. 746, 798.
139. O.R. XII, II, pp. 274, 746.
140. Blackford, *War Years With Jeb Stuart*, p .134; O.R. XII, II, pp. 274, 746, 748.
141. O.R. XII, II, p. 752.
142. J.B. Fay, "Cavalry Fight At Second Manassas," *Confederate Veteran* 23 (1916): pp. 263, 264; Letter, John B. Fay to Munford, August 15, 1906, Munford-Ellis Family Papers, Duke University.
143. O.R. XII, II, pp. 748, 752.
144. O.R. XII, II, pp. 147, 737.

Chapter Nine

1. O.R. XII, II, p. 311, 74th Pennsylvania Report.
2. Ibid., p. 558, Lee's Report.
3. Alexander, *Military Memoirs of a Confederate*, p. 218.
4. Union Casualties, O.R. XII, II, pp. 249–262; Confederate Casualties, Ibid., pp. 560–562, 568, 716, 717, 810–814.
5. Ibid., pp. 557, 558, Lee's Report.
6. Johnson, *Battleground Adventures*, p. 44.
7. Ibid., p. 45. Park Ranger Jim Burgess, curator at Manassas, provided this information pertaining to documentation records of mass burial locations: "If such a record exits, we haven't found it yet. I suspect, and there is some documentation supporting the possibility, that the unfinished railroad cut on the Brawner Farm was used as a convenient mass grave. Today the railroad grade just seems to end on the north side of Brawner Farm as if it was never graded there."
8. George M. Neese, *Three Years in the Confederate Horse Artillery*, p. 108.
9. Alexander, *Military Memoirs of a Confederate*, p. 222.
10. Ibid., p. 223.
11. Alice Jean Nelson, *Virginia Lineages, Letters & Memories*, published by author, Sarasota, Florida, 1984
12. *Manassas Journal*, July 4, 1913, excerpts from article "Woman's Recollection of Two Famous Battles," reprinted in the *Manassas City Museum News* 6, No. 2 (February 1988).
13. Nelson, *Virginia Lineages, Letters & Memories*.
14. O.R. XII, II, p. 512.
15. Ibid., p. 530.
16. Ibid., p. 532.
17. Ibid., p. 533.
18. Freeman, *Lee's Lieutenants*, vol. 2, p. 137.
19. Alexander, *Military Memoirs of a Confederate*, p. 191.
20. Ibid.
21. O.R. XII, II, p. 563.

Bibliography

Books

Alexander, Edward Porter. *Fighting for the Confederacy.* Chapel Hill: University of North Carolina Press, 1993.

_____. *Military Memoirs of a Confederate.* New York: Da Capo Press, 1993.

Bates, Samuel P. *History of Pennsylvania Volunteers, 1861–1865.* 5 vols. Harrisburg: B. Singerly, State Printer, 1869.

Bearss, Edwin C. *First Manassas Battlefield Map Study.* Lynchburg, VA: H.E. Howard, 1981.

Blackford, Susan Leigh, comp. *Letters from Lee's Army.* New York: Scribner, 1947.

Blackford, William W. *War Years with Jeb Stuart.* New York: Scribner, 1945.

Bond, Christiana. *Memories of General Robert E. Lee.* Baltimore: Norman Remington, 1926.

Bradford, Gamaliel. *Lee the American.* Cambridge, MA: Cambridge Press, 1927; reprint, New York, 1967.

Broadwater, Robert P. *Civil War Medal of Honor Recipients.* Jefferson, NC: McFarland, 2007.

Burger, Nash K. *Confederate Spy: Rose O'Neale Greenhow.* New York: K.S. Ginger, 1967.

Caldwell, J.F.J. *The History of a Brigade of South Carolinians Known First as "Gregg's" and Subsequently as "McGowan's Brigade."* Philadelphia: King and Baird Printers, 1866.

Cannon, Clarence. *The Wigginton Book.* Elsberry, MO: Elsberry, 1958.

Casler, James Overton, Jedediah Hotchkiss, and James I. Robertson, ed. *Four Years in the Stonewall Brigade.* 4th ed. Dayton, OH: Morningside Bookshop, 1971.

Catton, Bruce. *The Civil War.* New York: McGraw-Hill, 1971.

Chamberlayne, John Hampton, and C.G. Chamberlayne, ed. *Ham Chamberlayne—Virginian: Letters and Papers of an Artillery Officer.* Richmond: Dietz, 1932.

Chambers, Lenoir. *Stonewall Jackson.* 2 vols. New York: William Morrow, 1959.

Cook, B.F. *History of the Twelfth Massachusetts Volunteers.* Boston: Twelfth (Webster) Regiment Association, 1882.

Cooper, William J. Jr. *Jefferson Davis, American.* New York: Random House, 2001.

Dabney, Robert Lewis. *Life and Campaigns of Lt. Gen. Thomas J. Jackson.* New York: Bielock, 1866.

Davis, Jefferson. *The Rise and Fall of the Confederate Government.* New York: T. Yoseloff, 1958.

Davis, Jefferson, Alexander Stephens, and Col. Harold B. Simpson, ed. *Robert E. Lee.* Waco, TX: Davis Bros., 1983.

Davis, William C. *Battle of Bull Run.* Garden City, NY: Doubleday, 1946.

Dawes, Rufus. *Service with the Sixth Wisconsin Volunteers.* Madison: State Historical Society of Wisconsin for Wisconsin Civil War Centennial Commission, 1962.

Douglas, Henry Kyd. *I Rode with Stonewall.* Chapel Hill: University of North Carolina Press, 1940.

Dowdey, Clifford. *The War Time Papers of R.E. Lee.* Boston: Little, Brown, 1961.

Dufour, Charles L. *Gentle Tiger: The Gallant Life of Roberdeau Wheat.* Baton Rouge: Louisiana State University Press, 1957.

Durkin, Joseph T., ed. *John Dooley, Confederate Soldier: His War Journal.* Tuscaloosa: University of Alabama Press, 2005.

Early, Jubal Anderson. *Autobiographical Sketch and Narrative of the War Between the States.* Philadelphia: J.B. Lippincott, 1912.

_____. *Jackson's Campaign Against Pope in August, 1862: An Address—Before the First Annual Meeting of the Association of the Maryland Line.* Baltimore: Foley Bros. Printers, 1883.

English Combatant, An. *Battlefields of the South.* Whitefish, MT: Kessinger Publishing, 2008.

Ewell, Alice M. *A Virginia Scene or Life in Old Prince William.* Lynchburg, VA: J.P. Bell, 1931.

Figg, Royall W. *Where Men Only Dare to Go.* Richmond: Whittet & Shepperson, 1885; reprint, Louisiana State Press, 2008.

Freeman, Douglas Southall. *Lee's Dispatches to Davis*. New York: G.P. Putnam's Sons, 1915.
_____. *Lee's Lieutenants*. 3 vols. New York: Charles Scribner's Sons, 1942–44.
_____. *R.E. Lee*. 4 vols. New York: Charles Scribner's Sons, 1934–35.
Gaff, Alan D. *Brave Men's Tears: The Iron Brigade at Brawner Farm*. Dayton: Morningside House, 1988.
Gallagher, Gary W. ed. *Fighting for the Confederacy: The Personal Recollections of General Edward Porter Alexander*. Chapel Hill: University of North Carolina Press, 1989.
Gibbon, John. *Personal Recollections of the Civil War*. New York: G.P. Putnam's Sons, 1928.
Gottfried, Bradley M. *The Maps of First Bull Run*. New York: Savas Beatie, 2009.
Hanson, Joseph Mills. *Bull Run Remembers*. Chelsea, MI: Prince William County Historical Commission by BookCrafters, 1951, 1991.
Hayes, Martin. *A History of the Second Regiment, New Hampshire Volunteers, Its Camps, Marches and Battles*. Manchester, N.H: C.F. Livingston, 1865.
Henderson, G.F.R., Lt. Col. *Stonewall Jackson and the American Civil War*. 2 vols. Secaucus, NJ: Blue and Grey Press, 1989.
Hennessy, John J. *First Battle of Manassas: End of Innocence, July 18–21, 1861*. Lynchburg: H.E. Howard, 1989.
_____. *Return to Bull Run: The Campaign and Battle of Second Manassas*. New York: Simon & Schuster, 1993.
_____. *Second Manassas Battlefield Map Study*. Lynchburg: H.E. Howard, 1990.
Hood, John Bell. *Advance and Retreat*. Lincoln: University of Nebraska Press, 1996.
Hotchkiss, Jedediah, and Archie McDonald, ed. *Make Me a Map of the Valley*. Dallas: Southern Methodist University Press, 1973.
Hunter, Alexandria. *Johnny Reb and Billy Yank*. New York: Neale, 1905.
Hunton, Eppa. *Autobiography of Eppa Hunton*. Richmond: William Byrd, 1933.
Johnson, Clifton. *Battleground Adventures: The Stories of Dwellers on the Scenes of Conflict in Some of the Most Notable Battles of the Civil War*. New York: Houghton Mifflin, 1915.
Johnson, Robert U., and Clarence C. Buel. *Battles and Leaders of the Civil War*. 4 vols. New York: Century, 1887–1888.
Johnston, Joseph Eggleston. *Narrative of Military Operations During the Civil War*. New York: D. Appleton, 1874.
Johnston, Robert Matteson. *Bull Run: Its Strategy & Tactics*. Boston: 1913, reprint, Carlisle, PA: Kallman, 1996.
Jones, Virgil C. *First Manassas (Bull Run) and the War Around It*. Manassas, VA: First Manassas Corp., 1961.
Krick, Robert K. *Stonewall Jackson at Cedar Mountain*. Chapel Hill: University of North Carolina Press, 1990.
Lee, Susan Pendleton. *Memoirs of William Nelson Pendleton*. Philadelphia: J.B. Lippincott, 1893.
Long, Armistead L. *Memoirs of Robert E. Lee*. Philadelphia: J.M. Stoddart, 1886.
Longstreet, James. *From Manassas to Appomattox*. Philadelphia: J.B. Lippincott, 1896.
McCabe, James D. *Life and Campaigns of General Robert E. Lee*. Atlanta: National, 1866.
McGuire, Hunter H. *Stonewall Jackson: An Address by Hunter McGuire at the Dedication of Jackson Memorial Hall, Virginia Military Institute*. Lynchburg: J.P. Bell, 1897.
Neese, George M. *Three Years in the Confederate Horse Artillery*. New York: Neale, 1911.
Nelson, Alice Jean. *Virginia Lineages, Letters & Memories*. Sarasota, FL: published by the author, 1984.
Oates, William C. *The War Between the Union and the Confederacy*. Dayton, OH: Morningside Bookshop, 1974.
Polley, J.B. *Hood's Texas Brigade: Its Marches, Its Battles, Its Achievements*. New York: Neale, 1910.
Porter, Fitz John. *Narrative of the Services of the Fifth Army Corps in 1862 in Northern Virginia*. Morristown, NJ: Banner Steam, 1878.
Proceedings and Report of the Board of Officers—In Fitz-John Porter Case. Washington, D.C.: Government Printing Office, 1879.
Rafuse, Ethan S. *The Papers of the Blue and Gray, Fitz John Porter—The Campaign of Second Manassas and the Problem of Command and Control in the 19th Century*. Blue and Gray Education Society, Number 7, Summer 1998.
Ratcliffe, R. Jackson. *This Was Prince William*. Leesburg, VA: Potomac Press, 1978.
Raus, Edmond J. Jr. *Banners South*. Kent, OH: Kent State University Press, 2005.
Robertson, James J. *General A.P. Hill: The Story of a Confederate Warrior*. New York: Random House, 1987.
_____. *The Stonewall Brigade*. Baton Rouge: Louisiana State University Press, 1963.
_____. *Stonewall Jackson*. New York: Simon & Schuster Macmillan, 1997.
Ropes, John C. *The Army Under Pope*. New York: C. Scribner's Sons, 1881.
Ross, Ishbel. *Rebel Rose*. St. Simmons Island, GA: Mockingbird Books, 1973.
Silverman, Jason H., Samuel N. Thomas., and Beverly D. Evans IV. *Shanks: The Life and Wars of General Nathan G. Evans, CSA*. New York: Da Capo Press, 2002.
Sorrel, Gilbert Mozleg, and Bell Wilex, ed. *Rec-

ollections of a Confederate Staff Officer. Jackson, TN: McCourt–Mercer, 1958.

Southern Historical Society Papers (SHSP).

Sparks, David S. ed. *Inside Lincoln's Army: The Diary of General Marsena Rudolph Patrick*. New York: T. Yoseloff, 1964.

Stevens, C.A. *Berdan's United States Sharpshooters in the Army of the Potomac, 1861–1865*. St. Paul: Price-McGill, 1972.

Styple, William B. *Writing and Fighting the Confederate War*. Kearny: Belle Grove, 2002.

Summer, George C. *Battery D, First Rhode Island Light Artillery in the Civil War, 1861–1865*. Providence: Rhode Island Printing, 1897.

Taylor, Walter H. *General Lee: His Campaigns in Virginia, 1861–1865*. Brooklyn: Baunworth, 1906.

Thomson, Osmund R.H. *History of the Bucktails*. Philadelphia: Electric, 1906.

Todd, William. *The Seventy-ninth Highlanders New York Volunteers in the War of the Rebellion*. Albany, NY: Brandow Barton, 1886.

U.S. Surgeon General's Office. *The Medical and Surgical History of the War of the Rebellion (1861–1865)*. Washington, D.C.: U.S. Government Printing Office, 1870–88.

Vautier, John D. *History of the Eighty-eighth Pennsylvania Volunteers in the War for the Union*. Philadelphia: J.B. Lippincott, 1894.

Virginia Writers Project. *Prince William: The Story of Its People and Its Places*. W.P.A. Guide. Richmond: Whittet and Shepperson, 1941.

Warder, T.B., and J.M. Catlett. *Battle of Young's Branch or Manassas Plain*. Richmond: Enquire Book and Job Press, 1862; reprint by Prince William County Historical Commission, 1991.

Wellman, Manly Wade. *Giant in Gray*. New York: Charles Scribner's Sons, 1999.

White, William S. *Sketches of the Life of Captain Hugh A. White of the Stonewall Brigade*. Columbia: South Carolina Steam Press, 1864.

Wilkes, George. *The Great Battle Fought at Manassas, between the Federal Forces, under General McDowell, and the Rebels, under Gen. Beauregard, Sunday, July 21, 1861*. New York: Brown & Ryan, 1861.

William, Harry T. *P.G.T. Beauregard: Napoleon in Gray*. Baton Rouge: Louisiana State University Press, 1955.

Wise, Jennings. *The Long Arm of Lee*. New York: Oxford University Press, 1959.

Woodbury, Augustus. *The Second Rhode Island Regiment: A Narrative of Military Operations in Which the Regiment Was Engaged from the Beginning to the End of the War for the Union*. Providence, RI: Valpey, Angell and Company, 1875.

Worsham, John H. *One of Jackson's Foot Cavalry*. New York: Neale, 1912.

Records

U.S. Census, Virginia 1860.

Committee on the Conduct of the War (CCW), 1861.

Unpublished

Munford, T.T. *History of the Second Virginia Cavalry*, manuscript. Duke University, Durham, NC.

Newspapers

Boston Daily Journal.
Charleston Mercury.
Manassas Journal.
New York Times.
The Republican (Springfield, MA).
Richmond Daily Dispatch.

Magazines

Civil War 22.
Civil War Times Illustrated, June 1964.
Confederate Veteran.

Index

Adams and Company Express 7
Alabama Regiments (CSA): 4th 15, 59, 66, 68, 81–83, 152; 15th 132, 156, 158–159
Alburtis, E.G., Captain (Wise Artillery, CSA) 15, 82
Aldie 54
Alexander, Captain (Union) 57
Alexander, Edward P., Captain (CSA) 62–63, 89
Alexandria 8–9, 18–21, 28–29, 32–33, 50–51, 85, 102, 108, 113
Alexandria (Kemper) Light Artillery 85
Alexandria Turnpike 22, 23, 27–28, 31, 34, 37–38, 45–46, 50, 60–61, 100
Allen, J.W., Captain (CSA) 71
Alston (ex-governor, South Carolina) 97
Amissville 8, 112
Anderson, R.H., Major General (CSA) 127, 154, 161, 168
Anderson's Division 121
Andrews, Charles Wesley (minister) 93
Appomattox 55–56
Archer, J.J., Brig. General (CSA) 138, 151
Arkansas Regiments (CSA): 1st 53
Arlington Heights, Virginia 18, 51
Army of Mississippi (Union) 108
Army of Northeastern Virginia (Union) 48–50, 109–110, 121
Army of Shenandoah (CSA) 10, 14, 73
Army of the Confederate States of America (A.C.S.A.) (Provisional) 8
Army of the Potomac (CSA) 11, 59, 89, 103, 108, 114, 143, 146, 148; Artillery of the Third Corps 119, Artillery of the Fifth Corps 120, Artillery of the Ninth Corps 121
Army of Virginia: Artillery of the First Corps 115, Artillery of the Second Corps 116, Artillery of the Third Corps 118; 1st Michigan Cavalry (Buford's Brigade) 169–170; 1st Vermont Cavalry (Buford's Brigade) 169–170; 1st West Virginia Cavalry (Buford's Brigade) 169–170; 4th New York Cavalry (Beardsley Brigade) 169–170; 5th New York Cavalry (Buford's Brigade) 169
Army of Virginia (Union) 10, 46, 106, 109, 111, 115, 139, 162, 176, 179
Artillery see Confederate Artillery; Union Artillery
Ashby, Richard, Captain (CSA) 11
Ashby, Turner, Captain (CSA) 11, 13
Ashby Gap 58
Averell, Colonel (Union) 76

Bachelor Hall (Brawner Farm) 44
Ball, Alfred 35
Ball, Elizabeth (Carter) 35
Ball, Spencer 35
Ball's Ford 54
Ball's Ford Road 25, 169
Balou, Sullivan, Major (Union) 65, 103, 106
Baltimore and Ohio Railroad 11
Banks, Nathaniel P., Major General (Union) 101, 108–109, 111
Barbour, Alfred M. 11
Barnard, John G., Major (Union) 56
Barnes, Dixon, Colonel (CSA) 143–144
Barney, Andrew, Major (Union) 158–159, 163
Barry William, Major (Union) 74–76, 80
Bartow, Francis, Colonel (CSA) 15, 58, 61, 63, 66, 68–69, 72, 83, 99–100
Battery Heights 129–130, 132–133, 160
Baylor, W.S.H., Colonel (CSA) 132, 137; killed 158
Beardsley, John, Brig. General (Union) 169
Beauregard, Pierre G.T., General (CSA) 5, 11, 17, 1–21, 36, 38, 48, 50–55, 58–59, 61–63, 72–73, 77–81, 83–85, 89–91, 94; Battle Flag 102; transferred Western Theater 102–103
Beckham, R.F., Lieutenant (CSA) 15, 85
Bee, Barnard E., Brig. General (CSA) 15, 61, 63, 66, 68, 70–72, 80–82; mortally wounded 83, 97
Bendix, John, B., Colonel 161
Benjamin, Judah, Acting Secretary of War (CSA) 101
Benson, Amos 27, 94–95, 105
Benson, Margaret 27, 94–95, 105
Berdan Sharpshooters 156
Bethlehem Church 139
Bidwell, A.F., Major (Union) 83
Birney, David B., Brig. General (Union) 144–145, 151
Black Hat Brigade, Iron brigade 131
Blackburn's Ford 27, 35; Battle at Bull Run 54–56, 60–61, 69
Blackford, William W., Captain (CSA) 42–43, 77–78, 127, 129, 136, 140
Blair, Francis Preston, Sr. 8
Blaisdell, William, Colonel (Union) 147
Blenker, Lewis, Colonel (Union) 49
Blue Ridge Mountains 7, 58, 100–101
Bonham, Milledge L., Brig. General (CSA) 19, 21, 50–51, 54, 61–62, 71, 78
Boteler, A.R. (Congressman, Colonel, CSA) 109–110
Botts, Lawson, Colonel (CSA) 135
Bouvier, John V., Lieutenant (Union) 34
Branch, L. O'B., Brig. General (CSA) 138, 172
Brawner, Charles 44–45
Brawner, James 44–45
Brawner, John 43–44
Brawner Farm 43–45; Battle of 43; Brawner Woods 129–131; Douglas family 129
Brawner Lane 133
Brentsville 100
Bridges see Chain Bridge; Cub

Index

Run Bridge; Long Bridge; Stone Bridge
Bristol Station: Raid 112
Broad Run 50, 179
Brockenbrough, J.M., Colonel (CSA) 150, 159, 172
Brodhead, Thornton F., Colonel (Union) 170
Brown, Campbell (aide to Ewell) 114
Brown, John 13
Brown, W.F., Captain (CSA) 146, 149, 156, 158–159
Brownell, Francis, Private (Zouaves, Union): Medal of Honor 19
Brownsville (Folly Castle) 43
Buchanan, James 16
Buck Hill 63, 65–66, 72, 146, 168
Buckner House: Ewell leg amputated 134
Buford, John, Brig. General (Union) 139, 153, 169–171, 176
Bull Run 20–22, 25, 27, 35–36, 43, 50, 52, 54–56, 60–4, 67–70, 78, 95, 97, 100, 104, 111, 113, 127, 139, 162, 169, 172
Bull Run Mountains 111
Bunker Hill 15, 58
Burgess, Tristan, Private (Union) 104
Burnside, Ambrose E., Colonel (Union) 49, 64–65, 67, 69, 95, 111
Butterfield, Dan, Brig. General (Union) 156–157

Calhoun, John C. 16
Cameron, James, Colonel (Union): 84
Cameron, Simon, Secretary of War (Union) 8, 13, 84
Camp Bradley 100
Camp Pickens 21, 100
Camp Prior 100
Camp Walker 100
Camp Wigfall 100
Campbell, Joseph, Captain (Union) 130–133, 160
Cantwell, James, Colonel (Union) 145
Capitol prison 107
Carlisle, J. Howard, Captain (Union) 60
Carter, Betsy 31
Carter, Edwin 28, 176
Carter, George 35
Carter, John 22
Carter, Landon, Jr. 31; father of James Robinson 33
Carter, Landon, Sr. 22–25, 28, 32
Carter, Robert ("King") 21, 28, 35
Carter, Thomas Otway 28
Carter, Welby (Union) 77
Carter, Wormely 28
Cary, Constance, Jennie, and Hettie 102

Cash, E.G.B., Colonel (CSA) 85, 87
Catharpin Run 22–25, 64, 92
Catlett Station 111
Cedar Mountain 111, 131
Centreville 21, 42, 50–52, 54, 56, 60–62, 97, 100, 103, 106, 108, 127–128, 130, 138–139, 153, 156, 169, 172–173, 175–176
Chain Bridge 50
Chantilly 174, 180
Chapman, William, Lt. Colonel (Union) 168
Chapman, William H., Captain (Dixie Artillery, CSA) 160, 164
Charlottesville, Virginia 110
Chase, Salmon P., Treasury Secretary (Union) 48
Chesapeake and Ohio Canal 11
Chinn, Benjamin T. 37–38, 175
Chinn Branch 38, 165–167
Chinn Plantation (Hazel Plain) 37–38
Chinn Ridge 23, 37–38, 74, 83, 85, 155, 160–163, 165–169, 172–173, 177, 179
Christian Hill 27
Cipher 17
Citizen's Relief Commission of Washington 174
Clark, John, Private (Union) 104, 106
Clark Mountain 111
Cocke, Philip Saint George, Brig. General (CSA) 8–9, 19, 21, 27, 54, 61–63, 67, 71, 78
Cockpit Point 100
Comet 78
Compton, Alexander H. (Reverend) 25, 31, 175
Compton, Marianne E. 25, 175
Compton, William 175
Conestoga wagons 29
Confederate Artillery: Alexandria (Kemper) Light Artillery 85; Anderson's Division 121; Culpeper (Beckham) 15, 85; Danville (Wooding) 130; Ewell's Division 125; Hill's Division 138, 147, 150; Hood's Division 122; Jones' Division 121; Kemper's Division 122; Lee (Stephen D. Lee) Artillery Battalion 127, 154; Loudoun (Heaton) 68, 73; Lynchburg (Latham) 68; Rockbridge (Pendleton) 14, 73, 76; Shumaker Artillery 139, 154; Staunton (Asher Barber) 130; Staunton (Imboden) 11, 15, 66–67, 70–74, 77, Stuart Horse Artillery (Pelham) 134; Stuart's Cavalry 77; Taliaferro/Starke 123; Thomas Artillery (Stanard) 71–73, 76; Washington (Walton) 73, 80, 141; Wilcox's Division 122; Wise (Alburtis) 15, 82
Confederate Battle Flag 101; St. Andrew's Cross 102

Confederate Congress 5, 9, 18, 92, 103, 110
Connecticut Regiments (Union): 1st 70; 2nd 70; 3rd 70
Conner, James, Captain (CSA) 184
Constellation (frigate) 32
Contagious diseases (typhoid, measles) 100
Cooper, Samuel, General (CSA) 9–10, 51
Corcoran, M., Colonel (Union) 84
Corse, M.D., Colonel (CSA) 141, 165–167
Council of War 91, 110, 136
Court of Inquiry 133, 137
Covert operations 16–17
Cox, Jacob D., Brig. General (Union) 113
Craig, Samuel, Captain (Union) 113
Cross Keys 110
Cub Run Bridge 61, 87
Culpeper, Virginia 8, 9, 27, 111
Culpeper Artillery (Beckham) 15, 85
Cummings, A.C., Colonel (CSA) 71, 78, 80
Cundiff, John 45–46

Danville Artillery (Wooding) 130
Davidson, George S., Lieutenant (CSA) 63, 69
Davies, Thomas A., Colonel (Union) 49
Davis, Jefferson, President of Confederacy 5, 10–11, 14, 19, 21, 50–53, 58–59, 91, 98, 101, 103, 174
Dawes, Rufus, Colonel (Union) 131–133, 136
Dawkin's Branch (creek) 138, 140
Deep Cut 145, 155, 158, 160, 163, 173, 179
Department of Northern Virginia (CSA): General Order No. 15 101
Dogan, John D. 34, 67, 146, 164, 168, 173, 176
Dogan, Lucinda (Lewis) 34, 38–40, 42–43, 152, 156, 164, 173
Dogan, Mary Jane 34, 39–40
Dogan, Medora 39
Dogan, William Henry 39–41
Dogan (Rosefield) home 34, 176
Dogan's Ridge 65–67, 70–71, 74, 162, 164, 165
Doherty, Edward P. (Union) 93
Donellan, G. (Confederate spy courier) 51
Doubleday, Abner, Brig. General (Union) 130–133, 135, 141, 152
Douglas, M., Colonel (CSA) 137
Douglas Heights (ridge) 129, 141, 154, 157
Dumfries 100
Dump (area) 145, 147, 155–156, 158–159
Duval, Betty (Confederate spy courier) 50–51

Index

Early, Jubal, Colonel (CSA) 21, 56, 62, 85, 87, 138, 140, 146, 151, 178–179
Echols, J., Lt. Colonel (CSA) 71
Edmond 58
Edwards, D.E., Colonel (Union) 143
8th New York 67
Ellsworth, Elmer E., Colonel (Union) 18–19
Ely, Alfred, Congressman (Union) 55
Elzey, Arnold, Colonel (CSA) 15, 85
Evans, Nathan G. (Shanks), Colonel (CSA) 30, 54, 57, 60–63, 66–68, 70–72, 79–81, 152–153, 161, 163–166
Evansport 100
Ewell, Richard S., Colonel (CSA) 21, 42–43, 54–55, 61–62, 112–113; 130, 132–135, 135, 137, 146, 172, 179; Battle of Kelly Run 114
Ewell's Division 125

Fair Oaks, Battle of 109
Fairchild, Lucius, Lt. Colonel (Union) 132–133
Fairfax County 22
Fairfax Court-House 19, 21, 50–52, 172
Farnham, W.C., Colonel (Union) 76–77
Fauquier and Alexandria Turnpike 22, 23, 28, 31, 34, 37–39, 44–46, 60–61
Featherbed Lane 26–27, 138
Field, C.W., Brig. General (CSA) 138, 150, 159, 172
5th U.S. Artillery (Rickets) 65, 137, 161
First Battle of Manassas 1, 20, 38, 45, 47, 55–56, 60, 93, 101, 112, 174–175
First Civil War Monument 99
1st New Jersey 49
1st New York (Reynolds) Light Artillery 130
1st U.S. Artillery (Griffin) 65–67, 69–71, 74–75, 78, 80, 83, 85
Fisher, W.C., Colonel (CSA) 83–84
Fletcher, Laura (Thornberry) 93, 106
Floyd, John B., Brig. General (CSA) 101
Folly Castle (Brownsville) 41, 43
Foot Cavalry 112
Forno, Henry, Colonel (CSA) 138, 140, 151
Fort Sumter 5, 11
Fortress Monroe 108
4th New Jersey 49
4th U.S. Artillery (Campbell, Co. B) 130–133, 160
Franklin, William B., Colonel (Union) 49, 76, 82–83
Fredericksburg, Virginia 53, 108, 111

Freeman, Douglas Southhall 109–110, 179
Frémont, John C., Major General (Union) 49, 108–110
Frobel, B.W., Major (Union) 164
Front Royal, Virginia 7
Fry, James, Major General (Union) 69
Funsten, Oliver R. 11
Gadberry, J.M., Colonel (USA) 165
Gainesville, Virginia 28–29, 44–46, 112, 128–129, 137–139, 142
Gainesville, Battle of 129
Garnet, Robert, Adjutant General (CSA) 8, 19
Gartrell, Lucius J., Colonel (CSA) 66, 72
Gaskins, Susan (Robinson) 33
Georgia Regiments (CSA): 7th 66, 72, 83; 8th 15, 58, 66, 99, 152, 163–164; 12th 132–133; 13th 151; 14th 147; 18th 152, 163–164; 21st 112, 132, 134–135, 156, 158; 26th 132, 134–135; 31st 132, 134; 35th 148; 38th 132; 45th 147–148; 49th 147–148; 61st 132
Germantown 21, 28, 172
Gerrish, George A., Captain (Union) 152
Gettysburg, Battle of 134, 146
Gibbon, John, Brig. General (Union) 130–131, 132–133, 135–136, 138, 141, 156, 172
Goose Creek 58
Gordonsville 7, 110, 111
Grant, Ulysses S., General (Union) 56
Greeley, James G., Doctor 104–105
Green, J.S., Captain (CSA) 8
Greenhow, Robert 16
Greenhow, Rose O'Neale (CSA spy) 16–17, 50
Greenville (Compton Farm) 25, 175
Gregg, Maxey, Brig. General (CSA) 138, 144–145, 147–148, 150–151, 153, 155, 172, 179
Griffin, Charles, Captain, Brig. General (Union) 65–67, 69–71, 74–76, 78, 80–81, 83, 85; division commander 153
Griffith, Lucy 25, 31, 75, 175
Grigsby, A.S. 55
Grover, Cuvier, Brig. General (Union) 146–148
Groveton 22, 23, 38, 40–43, 96, 106, 129–130, 137–138, 146, 152, 161
Groveton, Battle of 129–130
Groveton House (L. Dogan Home) 38, 41
Groveton Sudley Road (Featherbed Lane) 27, 38, 43, 137–138, 145, 148–149, 151–152, 156, 161
Groveton Woods 142, 145, 149, 154, 156, 160

Hagerstown, Maryland 14
Hains, Peter C., Lieutenant (Union) 60–61, 63
Haislip, Samuel 38
Halleck, Henry W., Major General, General-in-Chief (Union) 111, 113
Hampton, Wade, Colonel (CSA) 53, 70–72, 84
Hampton Legion 53, 70, 72, 74, 80, 84, 152, 163–164
Hardin, Martin, Colonel (Union) 162–164
Harman, John A., Captain (CSA) 11
Harman, Lewis, Lieutenant (CSA) 170
Harper, Kenton, Major General (CSA) 11–12
Harpers Ferry 10–15, 19, 21, 57
Harrisonburg 21
Harrison's Landing 110
Hatch, John P., Brig. General (Union) 43, 129–130, 133, 138, 151–153, 156, 157–159, 177
Haupt, Herman, Colonel (Union) 113
Hayes, Rutherford B. 178
Haymarket 23
Hazel Plain Plantation 37
Hazlet, Charles, Lieutenant (Union) 74, 76, 80–81, 161–162, 164
Hazlet's Battery 74, 76, 80–81, 161–162, 164
Heaton, Lieutenant, (Loudoun Artillery, CSA) 68, 73
Heintzelman, Samuel P., Colonel (Union) 49–50, 60, 63–65, 67, 69, 76–77, 82–83, 87, 111, 128, 139, 143, 145–146, 150, 153, 155
Henry, Ellen Phoebe Morris 31–32, 75, 96
Henry, Hugh Fauntleroy 32–33, 175
Henry, Isaac 32
Henry, John 32–33, 75, 96
Henry, Judith 25, 31–32, 74, 96, 175
Henry, Landon 32
Henry Hill 22, 36, 45, 66, 69–72, 74–76, 78, 80–84, 86, 91, 94, 96, 106, 161–162, 165–166, 168–169, 172, 177–180
Henry House 32, 66, 71–75, 80–82, 84, 96
Henry Spring Hill 25
Hill, Ambrose P., Major General (CSA) 137–138, 143, 147, 150–151, 155, 159, 168, 172, 179
Hill, D.H., General (CSA) 110
Hill, Mrs. H.V. 16
Hill's Division 138, 147, 150
Hogue, J.B., Captain (CSA) 77
Holcombe's Legion (Evans Brigade, CSA) 164
Holmes, Theophilus, Brig. General (CSA) 52–53, 62, 101

Index

Hood, John Bell, Brig. General (CSA) 34, 140–141, 151–154, 161–166, 177, 179
Hood's Division 122
Hooker, Joseph, Major General (Union) 114, 145–146
Hopewell Gap 137
Hospital 26, 29–30, 36, 38, 46, 55, 65, 90–95, 103, 106, 136, 158, 174–175
Howard, Major (Bee Staff Officer, CSA) 71, 97
Howard, Oliver O., Brig. General (Union) 49, 83, 85
Hunter, David, Colonel (Union) 49–50, 52, 60, 63–64; wounded 65, 67, 69, 76, 83, 87
Hunton, Eppa, Colonel (CSA) 27, 45, 80, 84, 152, 165, 167
Hydropathic treatment 98

Imboden, John D., Captain (CSA) 11, 15, 66–67, 70–74, 77, 97–98
Indiana Regiments (Union): 12th 151; 19th 131–136
Interlude (occupancy of Manassas) 21, 47, 102

Jackson, Andrew 27
Jackson, Conrad, Brig. General (Union) 162
Jackson, James 19
Jackson, Thomas Jonathan, General (CSA) 12–15, 21, 41–43, 58, 61, 63, 71–76, 77–78, 80–81, 83, 90–91, 97–101, 108–109, 110–114, 127–132, 134–135, 137–161, 168, 172–174, 176–180
Jackson's Valley Campaign 109, 131
James River 110
Jeffersonton 112
Jenkins, Micah, Brig. General (CSA) 165, 167
Johnson, Bradley, Colonel (CSA) 137, 149, 156; rock fight 159
Johnston, Albert Sidney, General (CSA) 10, 102
Johnston, Joseph Eggleston, General (CSA) 13–15, 21, 36, 48, 50–52, 54, 58–59, 61–62, 72–73, 85, 91–92, 101–103, 108, 109
Joint Congressional Committee on the Conduct of the War (JCCCW) 74
Jones, Colonel (4th Alabama, CSA) 66
Jones, D.R., Brig. General (CSA) 21, 54, 61–62, 141, 161, 168
Jones, Roger, Lieutenant (Union) 12
Jones' Division 121
Jordan, Thomas, Colonel (CSA) 16–17, 21, 51, 91
Judson, J.A., Captain (Union) 152

Kane, Thomas L., Lt. Colonel (Union) 172
Kearny, Philip, Major General (Union) 128, 143–144, 148, 150–151, 153, 168, 175
Kelly Run, Battle of 114
Kelly's Ford 134
Kemper, D., Captain (CSA) 8, 85, 87
Kemper, James L., Brig. General (CSA) 142, 152, 161, 163, 165, 167
Kemper's Division 122
Kennedy, Jacqueline Lee (Bouvier) 34
Kennedy, John F. 34
Kerns, Mark, Captain (Union) 162–163, 164
Kerns' Battery 162–164
Kershaw, J.B., Colonel (CSA) 85, 87
Keyes, Erasmus D., Colonel (Union) 48, 61, 69–71, 85, 87
King, Charles 137
King, Rufus, Brig. General (Union) 42–43, 46, 128–132, 136–139, 151, 155–156, 177
Krzyzanowski, Wladimir, Colonel (Union) 142–145, 147

Lackland, Lt. Colonel (CSA) 81
Lansing, H.S., Colonel (Union) 156
Latham, H.G., Captain (Lynchburg Artillery, CSA) 63, 67
Law, E.M., Colonel (CSA) 152, 168
Lawler, John, Private (Union) 147
Lawton, A.R., Brig. General (CSA) 132–135, 137–138, 145–146, 149, 151
Leachman, Bettie (Lewis) 41, 43
Leachman, John Thomas 41, 43
Leasure, Daniel, Colonel (Union) 151
Lee, Fitzhugh, Brig. General (CSA) 45
Lee, Robert E., General (CSA) 7–10, 12–14, 17, 19, 21, 42–43, 47, 56, 109, 110, 110–112, 114, 127, 134, 138, 140–142, 146, 151–152, 154, 159–161, 165, 169, 172–174, 176–180
Lee, Stephen D., Colonel (CSA) 154, 156–157, 160, 179
Lee's (Stephen D. Lee) Artillery Battalion 127, 154
Leesburg 25, 27, 99, 174
Leftwich, Clark, Lieutenant (Lynchburg Artillery, CSA) 63
Leppien's 5th Main Light Artillery Battery 166–167
Letcher, John 8, 11–13, 21
Lewis, Benjamin Franklin (Frank) 41
Lewis, Fannie Tasker (Ball) 35–36
Lewis, Frank 35, 176
Lewis, Mary 41
Lewis Ford (Bull Run Crossing) 35, 54, 67, 78, 169–170
Lewis House (Portici) 22, 27, 36–37, 67, 69–70, 73–74, 77, 83, 85, 91, 97, 169, 176

Lewis Lane (road) 43, 146, 154, 161
Libby Prison 55, 95
Liberia (Weir Plantation) 20–21, 51, 55, 91
Lincoln, Abraham 5, 7–8, 17–18, 48–51, 84, 98, 108–109, 177
Little River Turnpike 49, 172
Little Sorrel 75
Long Bridge 18
Longstreet, James, General (CSA) 38, 42, 54, 56, 61–62, 101, 110–111, 114, 127–128, 136–137, 139–142, 144, 146, 150–154, 159–162, 164–165, 167–169, 172–173, 176–180
Loudoun (Heaton) Artillery 68, 73
Louisiana Regiments (CSA): 1st (Tigers) 57, 63, 65, 67, 156; 2nd 149, 156; 8th 151; 9th 155; 10th 155; 15th 156, 159; Coppen's Battalion 155
Lynchburg (Latham) Artillery 68

Madison, Dolly 16
Magruder, D.L., Assistant Surgeon (Union) 92–93
Maine Regiments (Union): 2nd 70, 158; 3rd 85, 119; 4th 85, 151; 5th 85
Manassas Gap Railroad 27, 41, 47, 100, 114
Manassas Junction 7–9, 11, 17–21, 27, 33, 53, 58–59, 62, 70, 91, 95, 99–100, 108, 127–128, 136–138, 175–176; Pope's Supply Depot 112–114
Manassas Plains 38, 173
Mansfield, Joseph K.F., Colonel (Union) 49
Marshall, Foster J., Colonel (CSA) 143–144
Marshall House 18–19
Martinsburg, Maryland 15
Maryland Regiments (CSA): 1st Battalion 15, 85
Maryland Regiments (Union): 2nd 149–150
Mason, Ocie 55
Massachusetts Regiments (Union): 1st 147; 5th 83; 11th 83, 146–147; 12th 167–168; 13th 167; 16th 147; 18th 157–158
Matthews, Carson, and Jane 29
Matthews, Henry, and Jane 28
Matthews, Martin, and Edgar 29, 65
Matthews Hill 29, 62–73, 76, 81, 92, 94–95, 103, 163
McClellan, George C., General (Union) 21, 101, 103, 106, 108–111, 114, 143, 148, 173
McCrady, Edward, Lt. Colonel (CSA) 143
McDowell, Irving, General (Union) 21, 27, 34, 36, 38, 46, 48–51, 54, 56–64, 67, 69–70, 72, 74–76, 83, 85–86, 90–94, 103,

Index

108–109, 128, 133, 136–139, 151–153, 155–156, 160–162, 164–167, 176–178
McGowan, Samuel, Colonel (CSA) 143–144, 148
McGuire, Hunter Holmes (Doctor, CSA) 13–14, 91, 97–98, 146
McLean, Nathaniel C., Colonel (Union) 161–166, 177
McLean, Virginia Beverley Hooe (Mason) 55
McLean house (Yorkshire Plantation) 55
McLean's Ford 54, 61–62, 100
Means, John H., Colonel 165
Medal of Honor 19, 162
Medical aid station 29
Meigs, Montgomery C., Brig. General (Union) 49
Meredith, Solomon, Colonel (Union) 131–132
Mexican War 8, 10–11, 12, 16, 19, 48–49, 54, 109
Michigan Regiments (Union): 1st 83, 85, 169–170; 3rd (Marksmen) 151
Miles, Dixon S., Colonel (Union) 49, 60
Militia see Union Militia
Milledgeville, Georgia 27
Milroy, Robert H., Brig. General (Union) 142, 145–147, 149, 155, 168
Minnesota Regiments (Union): 1st 68, 76–78
Mississippi Regiments (CSA): 2nd 59, 66, 152; 11th 15, 59, 66, 152
Mitchell, Mathias C. 56
Mitchell's Ford 52, 54, 61
Mitzel, A., Captain (Union) 172
Monroe, Susan 47, 173
Monroe, William W. 46
Monroe Hill 47, 128, 141
Morell, George W., Major General (Union) 139, 150, 153, 156
Mosby, John, Colonel (CSA) 31
Munford, Thomas T., Colonel (CSA) 112, 169–170

Nagle, James, Colonel (Union) 148–150, 168
Nazer, Ferries, Lt. Colonel (Union) 169–170
Neff, John, Colonel (CSA) 135
New Hampshire Regiments (Union): 2nd 64–65, 95, 146–147; 6th 149
New Jersey Militia: 1st New Jersey 49; 2nd New Jersey 49; 3rd New Jersey 49; 4th New Jersey 49
New Jersey Regiments (Union): 1st 49; 2nd 49; 3rd 49
New York Militia: 8th New York 67; 20th New York 158
New York Regiments (Union): 1st 130, 144–145, 151; 2nd 67–68, 113; 5th Duryee's Zouaves 161–162, 169; 8th (Militia) 67, 93; 10th, National Zouaves 161–162; 11th, Fire Zouaves 18, 74, 76–78; 12th 56, 158; 13th 84, 158; 14th Brooklyn, Zouaves 67, 76, 80, 83, 130, 143; 17th 157–158; 20th (Militia) 158; 24th 158–159, 163; 27th 67; 29th 144; 30th 158; 38th 82–83; 40th 157; 41st 49, 166; 54th 143–144; 58th 143; 69th 84; 71st 64–65; 72nd 114; 76th 133–134; 79th, Highlanders 84; 83rd 167; 95th 133; 101st 151
Newman, Burkett 105
Norris, Charles, Captain (CSA) 81, 89
Norris, Joseph L. 99
North Carolina Regiments (CSA): 6th 15, 83–84, 152; 21st 112, 132, 134

Occoquan 19, 54, 100
Occoquan Run 20
O'Connor, Edgar, Colonel (Union) 131, 132, 136
Official Records 38; Beauregard Report 83, 129
Ohio Regiments (Union): 1st 67–68; 2nd 67–68; 25th 161, 163, 166; 55th 161, 163, 166; 61st 143–144; 73rd 161, 163–164, 166; 75th 161, 163, 166; 82nd 145–146
Orange (hamlet) 106
Orange and Alexandria Railroad 7, 27, 50, 100
Ordinance of Secession 17–18
"ordinary" 28
Ordnance Department, Army of the Potomac (CSA) 89
Orlean 112
Ox Hill 172

Pageland Lane 43–44, 46, 129, 154, 175
Paris (hamlet) 58
Parole-station 94, 174
Parrott (cannon/rifle) 60–61, 65, 74–75, 80–81, 89, 154, 161
Patrick, Marsena, Brig. General (Union) 31, 34, 129–130, 133, 152–153, 158
Patterson, Robert, Major General (Union) 13–15, 21, 48, 50, 53–54, 58
Pawnee 18
Peach Grove Estate 39–41
Pelham, John, Lieutenant (CSA) 73, 134
Pender, William D., Brig. General (CSA) 138, 148, 172
Pendleton, William N., Colonel (CSA) 14, 73, 76
Peninsular Campaign 131
Pennsylvania Bucktails 172, 176
Pennsylvania Regiments (Union): 9th 163; 10th 163; 11th 163, 167; 12th 163; 13th, Kane's Pennsylvania Bucktails 172, 176; 26th 146–147; 48th 149; 56th 133–134; 63rd 151; 74th 143–144; 75th 143; 100th 151; 105th 151
Philadelphia 13, 32
Piatt, A. Sanders, Brig. General (Union) 153, 168
Piedmont Station 58
Pittsylvania (Plantation) 22, 28, 30–33, 63, 96, 168, 176
Pope, John, General (Union) 34, 37, 95, 106, 109–114, 127–128, 130, 135, 137–139, 142, 146, 148, 150–155, 159–161, 165–166, 168–169, 171–174, 176–180
Pope's Supply Depot 112–114
Port Republic 110
Porter, Andrew, Colonel (Union) 64–65, 67, 76, 80
Porter, David, Colonel (Union) 49
Porter, Fitz John, Major General (Union) 111, 138–140, 142, 148, 150–151, 153–156, 160–161, 164, 176–180
Portici (Plantation) 22, 35–37, 67, 69–70, 73–74, 77, 83, 85, 91, 97, 169, 176
Potomac River 11, 18, 50–51, 92, 100, 174, 180
Pratt, George W., Colonel (Union) 158
Preston, R.T., Colonel (CSA) 85, 84
Prince William County 20, 22, 34
Provisional Army of South Carolina 19
Purcell Artillery (CSA) 53

Quaker Guns 100
Quinby, Isaac, Colonel (Union) 84

Raccoon Ford 111
Ramey, Douglas, Lieutenant (Union) 82
Rapidan (river) 110–111
Rappahannock River 50–51, 103, 108, 111–113, 1128, 154, 180
Rebel Yell: birth of 81, 151, 161
Recovery of the wounded 92, 174
Redman, Andrew 38
Regiments see Individual States Regiments
Reno, J.L., Brig. General (Union) 111, 128, 139, 146, 148, 150–151, 168
Report of the Board of Army Officers 179
Reynolds, J.G., Major (Marine Battalion, Union) 76–77
Reynolds, John A., Captain (Union) 130
Reynolds, John F., Brig. General (Union) 111, 128, 142, 150, 154–155, 160–164, 168, 177
Reynolds, William H., Captain (2nd Rhode Island Artillery) 65–67, 72
Rhode Island Regiments (Union): 1st 64–65; 2nd 64–65, 103–104

Rice, John L., Private, Colonel (Union) 95–96
Richardson, Isaac B., Colonel (Union) 49, 56, 60–61, 67, 166
Richardson, Josiah W., Private (Union) 104
Richmond, Virginia 5, 7, 10–12, 14, 18, 20–21, 50, 52, 55, 70, 85, 90, 95, 100–101, 103, 108–111
Richmond Armory 12
Richmond Enquirer 11
Ricketts, Fanny 36–37
Ricketts, James B., Captain, Brig. General (Union) 36, 65, 67, 69–77, 80–81, 82–85, 96, 99, 128, 136–138, 153, 155, 166, 178
Roberts, Charles, Colonel (Union) 156, 158
Robertson, Beverly H., Brig. General (CSA) 169–171
Robertson, J.B., Colonel (CSA) 163
Robinson, James 33–34
Robinson, John C., Brig. General (Union) 151
Robinson, William, Colonel (Union) 131–132, 136
Robinson house 33–34, 66, 69–70, 72–73, 80, 83–85
Robinson River 111
Rockbridge (Pendleton) Artillery 14, 73, 76
Ropes, John 180
Rosefield (John Dogan's farm) 34, 176
Ruffin, Edmund 87

Salem (hamlet) 112
Sangster's Cross-roads 21
Scammon, E. Parker, Brig. General (Union) 113
Schenck, Robert C., Brig. General (Union) 48, 67–68, 142, 146, 161, 166
Schimmelpfennig, A., Colonel (Union) 142–145, 147
Schofield, J.M., General (U.S. Federal Army) 179
Schurz, Carl, Brig. General (Union) 138, 142–147
Scott, Winfield, Bvt. Lt. General (Union) 8, 11, 14, 48–51, 53–54, 58
Secession 5, 11, 16–18, 30, 53, 62
Second Battle of Manassas 22, 31, 34, 36–38, 42–47, 127, 137, 155, 165, 172–173, 176
2nd New Jersey 49
2nd Rhode Island Artillery (Reynolds) 65–67, 72
2nd U.S. Sharpshooters 152
"Secretary," No. 6 Engine 112
Seven Days Battle 110
Seven Pines, Battle of 109
Shenandoah River 11, 58
Shenandoah Valley 7, 14, 21, 48, 59
Sherman, William T. (Union) 16, 49, 69–70, 76, 83–84, 87

Shumaker, L.M., Major (CSA) 134, 154
Shumaker Artillery 139, 154
Sigel, Franz, Major General (Union) 34, 109, 128, 138–140, 142–144, 146, 150, 164, 166, 168, 172, 176
Signal Hill 61–62
Skinner, Frederick, Lt. Colonel (CSA) 166–167
"Slackers" (stragglers, miscreants) 145
Slocum, John, Colonel (Union) 64–65, 103–106
Smith, E. Kirby, Brig. General (CSA) 15, 85
Smith, Samuel James, Captain (Union) 104
Smith, William, "Extra Billy," Colonel (CSA) 27, 78–80, 82
Snow Hill 36
Somerville Ford 111
South Carolina Regiments (CSA): 1st 19, 143, 147–148; 1st South Carolina, Orr's Rifles 144; 2nd 19, 85; 4th 63, 65, 79; 8th 85; 12th 143, 148; 13th 143, 147–148; 14th 143, 148; 17th 164–165; 18th 164–165; 22nd 164; 23rd 164
Southern Claims Commission 30
Sprague, William 65, 103–105
Spring Hill 22, 25; Spring Hill Farm 31–32, 34
Spy 16, 50
Stafford, Leroy A., Colonel (CSA) 137, 149, 155–156
Stanard, P.B., Captain (CSA) 71–73, 76
Stanton, Secretary of State (Union) 109
Starke, W.E., Brig. General (CSA) 137, 145, 155, 158, 168
Stars and Bars 18, 101
Stars and Stripes 78, 101
Staunton Artillery (Asher Barber) 130
Staunton Artillery (Imboden) 11, 15, 66–67, 70–74, 77
Stevens, Isaac, Brig. General (Union) 173
Stiles, Robert W., Colonel (Union) 166–168, 177
Stone Bridge 34, 42, 54, 56–57, 60–63, 67, 69–71, 79, 85, 87, 104, 168–169, 172, 176
Stone House 23, 28–30, 40, 72, 83, 85, 87, 94, 146, 152, 168, 174
"Stonewall": birth of Jackson sobriquet 15
Stonewall Brigade 15, 101, 131–132, 135, 137, 156, 158
Stony Ridge 114, 127, 134
Stovall, George T. (CSA) 99
Stuart, James Ewell Brown (J.E.B.) (CSA) 13–14, 31, 34, 42, 58, 77–78, 85, 87, 93, 95, 111, 113, 127, 131, 134, 140, 142, 169, 179
Stuart Hill 47, 128

Stuart Horse Artillery (Pelham) 134
Stuart's Cavalry 77
Sturgis, Samuel D., Brig. General (Union) 153
Sudley (community) 22, 24–28, 31, 34, 36–38, 41, 54, 60, 64, 93, 105, 175
Sudley Ford (Bull Run) 60–64, 87, 104, 172
Sudley Mansion (Plantation) 22
Sudley Methodist Episcopal Church 23–28, 64–65, 92–96, 103–105, 114, 134, 136, 154, 168, 175
Sudley Mills 23, 27–28
Sudley Road 26–28, 31, 34, 37–38, 63–67, 71–72, 74–78, 80, 82–85, 87, 104, 127–128, 139, 142, 144, 146, 151–153
Sudley Spring Ford (Catharpin Run) 26, 64
Sullivan, T., Colonel (Union) 152
Swan, Major (CSA) 77
Sykes, George, Major (Union) 65, 68–69, 85, 87, 156, 160–161, 168

Taliaferro, Alexander G., Colonel (CSA) 134, 137
Taliaferro, William B., Brig. General (CSA) 132, 134–135, 137, 155
Taliaferro/Starke Artillery 123
Taylor, George W., Brig. General (Union) 113–114
Terrett, George H., Colonel (CSA) 18, 21
Tennessee Regiments (CSA): 2nd 53; 3rd 15, 85
Texas Brigade 152, 161, 163–164, 168
Texas Regiments (CSA): 1st 152, 164; 4th 152, 163–164; 5th 152, 163–165
3rd New Jersey 49
Thomas, E.L., Brig. General (CSA) 138, 147–148, 151, 155
Thomas Artillery (Stanard) 71–73, 76
Thornberry, John 26–27, 105–107
Thornberry, Samuel 26, 105, 107
Thoroughfare Gap 42, 111–112, 128, 136–137, 139, 151, 153, 176–178
Tiger Rifles 57
Tower, Levi, Captain (Union) 104–106
Tower, Zealous B., Brig. General (Union) 166–168, 177
Trimble, Isaac, Brig. General (CSA) 112–113, 132–135, 137, 146, 149, 156, 159
Tudor Hall 7
20th New York 158
Tyler, Daniel, Brig. General (Union) 48–50, 56, 60–61, 63, 67, 69–70, 83, 87
Tyler, "Nat" 11

Unfinished Railroad 27, 41, 114, 129, 134, 137, 142–143, 145, 151, 154–155, 163, 168, 176, 180
Union Artillery: Army of the Potomac Artillery of the Third Corps 119, Artillery of the Fifth Corps 120, Artillery of the Ninth Corps 121; Army of Virginia Artillery of the First Corps 115, Artillery of the Second Corps 116, Artillery of the Third Corps 118; 5th U.S. Artillery (Rickets) 65, 137, 161; 1st New York (Reynolds) Light Artillery 130; 1st U.S. Artillery (Griffin) 65–67, 69–71, 74–75, 78, 80, 83, 85; 4th U.S. Artillery (Campbell, Co. B) 130–133, 160; Hazlet's Battery 74, 76, 80–81, 161–162, 164; Kerns' Battery 162–164; 2nd Rhode Island Artillery (Reynolds) 65–67, 72; Wiedrich Battery 161, 163–165
Union Militia: 1st New Jersey 49; 2nd New Jersey 49; 3rd New Jersey 49; 4th New Jersey 49; 8th New York 67; 20th New York 158
Union Mills Ford 54, 56, 100
Union Occupation 103
Urbanna 103, 108
U.S. Cavalry Regiments: 2nd 67
U.S. Marine Corp Battalion 67, 76, 90
U.S. Regulars 13, 65–66, 68–69, 85, 87; 21st New York 69

Valley Campaign 109, 112, 131
Valley of Young's Branch 66, 72, 94
Van Dorn, Earl, General (CSA) 102
Van Pelt, Abraham 30–31
Van Pelt, Elizabeth 30
Van Pelt House 57, 71
Vermont Regiments (Union): 2nd 85
Virginia Central Railroad 7
Virginia Military Institute (VMI) 12; VMI Artillery 73, 81
Virginia Provisional Army 7, 8
Virginia Regiments (CSA): 1st Virginia Battalion 156, 166; 1st Virginia Cavalry 85, 87; 2nd 14, 71–72, 80–82, 112, 132, 135, 156, 169–170; 2nd Virginia (Robertson's Brigade) 169–170; 2nd Virginia Cavalry 112, 169; 4th 14, 45, 71–72, 81, 132, 156, 158; 4th Virginia Cavalry 45; 5th 14, 70–73, 132, 156; 6th Virginia (Robertson's Brigade) 169; 7th Virginia (Robertson's Brigade) 169; 7th 166, 170; 8th 25, 27, 45, 80; 10th 15, 85, 134; 12th Virginia (Robertson's Brigade) 169–171; 17th 166; 21st 156; 23rd 134; 24th 167; 27th 14, 71–72, 81, 99, 132, 156; 28th 85, 94; 33rd 14, 71–72, 77–78, 80, 83, 132, 135, 156, 158; 37th 134; 42nd 156; 48th 156, 158; 49th 20, 27, 78, 80, 82–83, 106
Virginia Secession Convention 11
Visitor Center and Museum 75, 83

Wainwright, William, Colonel (CSA) 133
Walker, L.P., Secretary of War (CSA) 21
Walton, J.B., Colonel (CSA) 73, 80, 141, 154
Warren, Gouverneur K., Colonel (Union) 161–163
Warrenton Junction 114
Warrenton Springs Hotel 33
Warrenton-Washington Turnpike 25, 43, 128–129, 138–140, 142, 146, 152–153, 155–156, 161, 168, 171, 175
Washington, D.C. 5, 8, 11, 16–18, 21, 27, 34, 37, 42, 51–52, 58–59, 61, 88, 90–92, 94–95, 100–101, 103, 107–109, 111, 127, 172–174, 177
Washington Artillery (CSA) 62, 67, 73, 80, 141, 166
Washington Globe 8
Watts, J.W., Lt. Colonel (CSA) 169
Webb, James, Private (Union) 162
Webster, Daniel 16
Webster, Fletcher, Colonel (Union) 167–168
Weeks, Henry A., Colonel (Union) 156–158
Weir, William James 20
Wellington Road 128
West Point (U.S. Military Academy) 5, 7–13, 15–16, 48–49, 54, 57, 109
West Virginia Regiments (Union): 2nd 145–146; 3rd 145; 5th 145; 8th 143–144
Wet-weather bed (s) 157
Wheat, Roberdeau, Major (CSA) 57, 63–65, 67
Wheeler, Addie (Lewis) 41
Wheeler, William L.B. 40–41
White, Alexander, Captain (CSA) 57
White, Hugh A., Captain (CSA) 158
White House on the Pamunkey 108
Wiedrich, Michael, Captain (Union) 161, 163–165
Wiedrich's Battery 161, 163–165
Wig-wag (signaling system) 62–63
Wigginton, Ann E. 39
Wigginton, Lucy 39, 96
Wigginton, Susan 39, 96
Wigginton House 39
Wilcox, C.M., Brig. General (CSA) 141, 152, 154, 164, 168, 180
Wilcox's Division 122
Wilkins, William 27
Willcox, Orlando B., Colonel (Union) 49, 76, 82–83, 85
Williamsburg 108
Willow Green 41
Winchester, Virginia 9, 14–15, 21, 58, 112
Wings (vice-corps) 110
Winslow, Cleveland, Captain (Union) 161–162
Wisconsin Regiments (Union): 2nd 84, 131–134, 136; 6th 131–133, 136; 7th 131–134
Wise, Henry A. 11
Wise Artillery (Alburtis) 15, 82
Wood, A.M., Colonel (Union) 76, 80
Wooding, George, Captain (CSA) 130

Young's Branch 38–39, 66–67, 71–72, 74, 86, 94, 97, 161–164

Zeigler, John L., Colonel (Union) 145
Zouaves 18–19, 57, 74, 76–78, 80, 83, 101, 161–162

www.ingramcontent.com/pod-product-compliance
Ingram Content Group UK Ltd.
Pitfield, Milton Keynes, MK11 3LW, UK
UKHW050525150426
5217IPUK00026B/1808